A STUDIED MADNESS

A STUDIED MADNESS

Heywood Hale Broun

"Actors are the only honest hyprocrites.
Their life is a voluntary dream;
a studied madness."

William Hazlitt

1965

DOUBLEDAY & COMPANY, INC.   GARDEN CITY, NEW YORK

On Monday (Dec. 8, 1823) a person was brought before the mayor of Windsor for having the preceding day committed an act of vagrancy by begging in the streets. The mayor demanded what he had to say to the charge. He replied that such were the calls of Nature, that he begged from absolute necessity. The Magistrate said, What are you? He answered, I am the son of a general in the army; and I *unfortunately* received a liberal education, which led me to associate with those who like myself were infatuated with theatricals; the result of which was, that I went on the stage, and have latterly been travelling about the country seeking for engagements. At some towns I was retained a short season; at other places, where the manager had no room for me, the company raised a subscription to help me on the road to the next likely station.

"His hopes led him to Windsor; but not finding a company here, he was reduced to the humiliating situation in which he was apprehended. He further stated, that he belonged to London, whither he was going. The Magistrate commiserated his situation; but informed him, if he was again found in the streets of Windsor, under the above circumstances, he should be committed to prison as a vagrant."

RYLEY
The Itinerant

FOR MY WIFE JANE AND MY SON HOB

A STUDIED MADNESS

O<small>NE OF THE FIRST THINGS</small> I did on becoming an actor was to begin planning the movie which was to commemorate my fiftieth year on the stage. I thought of it as a prestige short subject, the kind that is shown in little East Side theaters before the French film. It begins with the title, *Broun*—the name conjures up more than could any elaborate quotation—superimposed on a shot of the famous hands. They are gnarled, of course (I will be eighty-one after fifty years on the stage), but the wonderful expressiveness which has delighted millions rivets our attention as the fingers move with a sort of fragile grace over a rich green velvet surface which will be revealed when the camera pulls back as the smoking jacket I wore in the revival of *Raffles*. While some Beethoven-y music plays (Emperor Concerto?) the hands climb indomitably up from buttonhole to buttonhole until, to the sound of massed horns, the shot widens, and we see, still majestic despite many wrinkles, that wonderful face, the sensitive chin supported by the long fingers. The music respectfully dies on a long cello note, which somehow continues on. We realize that it has become my voice welcoming the audience with the thrilling intimacy that has made massed thousands believe I was performing only for one person, and each one thought it to be himself. An interviewer (who is never seen) asks me to show some of my memorabilia, and we have a guided tour of my perfectly appointed home. Using, with beautifully controlled sensitivity, my silver-mounted ebony stick, I point out a lot of stuff that I have used on stage or which has been given to me—medals, awards, scrolls, and the like—while with winning modesty I pay tribute to the many humble folk —supporting actors, stagehands, directors, and producers— who have helped me. In a stroll through the garden I chat informally about acting secrets and give a lot of valuable tips to those who would follow, however distantly, in my footsteps, and then we withdraw to tea in my library. Here, while the firelight plays marvelously over my face, I display some of the scripts I have revived or helped to make famous. Several times I give the famous grin which is made all the more disarming by the gray, snaggly teeth which I never had capped. (Even in imagination I don't get to the dentist.) As the talk continues the audience sees that the old gentleman is growing drowsy and in the last shot the camera gently draws back and we see me, a scrapbook of favorable notices in my lap, in repose in my thronelike chair beside the fireplace. The music takes up an elegiac strain and the interviewer says, "Goodnight, Sweet Prince, we shall not look upon your like again, for you were a fellow of infinite jest and the noblest Roman of them all." There is a swell of triumphant music and darkness.

I don't know that there is going to be any great demand for this picture, but it is as well to be ready. All of us, like the young man maddened by his liberal education, come into the theater with tremendous aspirations. I don't suppose that everybody who goes to work in a bank dreams of being Secretary of the Treasury, and I know that newspapermen don't dream of becoming editors. Ugh! But the theater is such a difficult and heartbreaking place that there is no point in entering it with the modest dream that you may get to be second character man in a repertory company within walking distance of a good, cheap boardinghouse.

It's hard to keep the dream intact. I haven't given much thought to my movie in recent years and I imagine that I will celebrate fifty years on the stage by going out to try to find a job which will support me through my fifty-first year on the stage, but just typing the words of the précis still gives me a wistful glow. The dream is kept in a sort of psychological strongbox to be taken out and looked over at propitious moments. There aren't, goodness knows, many of these. Work is sometimes more destructive of the actor's dream than unemployment, although better than being arrested in Windsor. Still, a young person nourished on Shaw and Ibsen sometimes finds it a bit depressing to do the available work, which more often than not consists of something like running through a crepe-paper jungle pursued by a TV camera and shouting, "Look out! It's a big white gorilla!"

When you are not working at all you can kid yourself that the big call may be coming at any moment, but when you are fleeing the gorilla, or recovering with unbelievable rapidity from stomach distress in a commercial, or playing a stockroom boy in one of those Broadway satires on advertising designed to please the agency trade, then you do

wonder uneasily sometimes whether the theater is a place
for grown-ups to work, or a big, disorganized nursery school
sandbox which the cats are using too.

Still, there are good plays and good parts in them, and
somebody has to get the good parts, and why not me who
is the best actor—or actress—in the world? And once, we
all believe, we have been seen we will never be forgotten
and part will follow part in quick succession. Sometimes,
of course, they do.

Hazlitt describes us as lovingly and as unsparingly as
anyone. Actors, he says, "are the only honest hypocrites.
Their life is a voluntary dream; a studied madness. The
height of their ambition is to be *beside themselves*. Today
kings, tomorrow beggars, it is only when they are themselves, that they are nothing. Made up of mimic laughter
and tears, passing from the extremes of joy or woe at the
prompter's call, they wear the livery of other men's for-
tunes; their very thoughts are not their own. They are, as
it were, trainbearers in the pageant of life, and hold a glass
up to humanity, frailer than itself. We see ourselves at
second hand in them: They show us all that we are, all
that we wish to be, and all that we dread to be."

It is, of course, as playwrights have found out, dangerous
to lard your work with quotations from your betters. Rice
pudding without raisins is more bearable than gummy
grains hard on the heels of a couple of plump muscats.
Still, the actor who cannot show himself off will try to
show off some agreeable side of his nature, such as his
erudition. There will be more quotations from my betters
as we go along.

If I may quote myself, however, I want to say to the
unbelieving ears of other actors and the unhearing ears of
the world that acting ought to be a pleasure, ought to be, to
use a debased word, fun. If it isn't intensely enjoyable,

more enjoyable than almost anything else in the world, why bother to be a part of the rather nasty world of the theater? An actor, when acting, ought to have such a feeling of joy that he can carry it and taste it through the months of not acting, be able to touch it like a talisman while he is being subject to the casual rudeness of the administrative branch of the theater, a rudeness so pointless and habitual that it does not even give the actor the dignity of martyrdom, a rudeness which can be sharpened to an edge of malevolence if it is questioned or deplored.

When the curtain goes up everything belongs to the actor. It is for the privilege of owning the small world inside a theater that an actor surrenders so much in the way of dignity, security, and structure in his life. What surprises and depresses me is how many actors don't enjoy acting.

"A devotion to truth is incompatible with pleasure. Art is too serious for so frivolous a word as fun. The self-revelation which is a part of a serious actor's equipment cannot give enjoyment to him. After all, how can you enjoy self-revelation? Do you know what you're really like? If you want to kid around you go ahead, but I'm dedicated, and dedication is not enjoyable. It hurts. It ought to. That shows that it is a real dedication and not a self-indulgence."

I've heard all that and lots more. Indeed, since actors desire approval, I have spent some time simulating appropriate gravity so nobody would think I was indulging myself, but why are we all so afraid of indulging ourselves?

It seems to me that our penance, if penance is needed, has been done in producers' waiting rooms, unemployment insurance lines, on park benches, in answering the eternal question, "What are you doing these days?" with the jaunty negative, and in consenting to keep trying to make a shape to life out of such odd and often repellent pieces as we can pick out of the flood that continually threatens to drown us.

When the time of fulfillment comes, and several hundred people are sitting still for us, answering in overflowing measure the basic cry, "Hey, look at meeee!" it's time for all the self-indulgence that the size of the part allows. If that phrase seems disagreeable, try gusto, a word which can cover the solemn zest of a great tragic performance as well as the simple joy of comedy. But all of us might take a lesson from Cavanagh the great English athlete, of whom our friend Hazlitt said, "The noisy shout of the ring happily stood him in stead of the unheard voice of posterity!"

In what follows I may seem sometimes more jaundiced than this opening flourish would justify, but none of the acid has to do with how I feel onstage.

Once, when a producer sacked me from a wonderful part during the out-of-town tryout of a play, I spent the afternoon staring sightlessly at a bad movie and debating whether I shouldn't just stay in the movie house till boredom mercifully carried me off, or try for some simple repetitive work, like sorting nuts and bolts or molding plastic —if that's what they do to it. That evening, when I was returning to New York, I ran into the producer, shuttling home on some errand. Since we could not avoid each other, we murmured inaudible politenesses, and he said he was sorry that things had turned out as they had. Standing in the aisle of the train, I thought of an answer to it all.

"Thank you," I said, "but I feel the theater is such a wonderful place that if things like this didn't happen, everybody would want to be in it."

I was pleased with the answer then, and it will do for now. I don't think the theater is a fabulous invalid which will survive all the ineptitude, greed, and cultural pretensions which hang, like weighted fishhooks, from its heart. We can kill it, all right, and I've been in some of the plays which have driven spears into its side. The parade of peep shows, black masses, spongy satires, and obscurantist finger paintings grows longer, and massed against the future of purposeful theater it makes a terrible army, an army without banners, an army which marches to the beat of an adding machine and the penny-whistle piping of anxious chic.

Every year the invalid is a little feebler, and every year it deserves to be. Still, every year there are plays that every actor wishes he were in, plays which everybody ought to see, and until the last cast puts on the last of those plays, the theater is still a wonderful place.

In my first play I got a break that I've never had since. I got to write my own lines. The occasion was a medieval pageant on the lawn of a progressive school in Croton, New York. It was the climax to a year of doing the Middle Ages in everything from colored paper to plain song on the ocarina.

The actor-writer team consisted of about twenty ten- to twelve-year-olds who drew lots for characteristic thirteenth-century types and then wrote what the child psychologist Piaget calls "a group monologue." Afterward, the teachers pushed and hauled our contributions into something on a par with those plays with which southern towns relieve their present dullness by recalling their lively colonial past.

I drew the Kindly Friar ("Do not be cruel to Little Brother Chicken") and the Irrepressible Jester ("Marry come up, sirrah, how now is it that, that I know not how," etc.).

I suppose the whole thing was a nightmare to the audience, but I loved every minute—every minute I was performing, that is—as I have later loved every minute of a number of things which were nightmares to audiences.

Indeed, our pageant was in one way superior to many professional enterprises I've been with. If the social historians are right, we had a documentary authenticity, since, like real medieval people, we were small, hysterical, and dressed in colorful but ill-fitting clothes (we made them between bouts of writing).

The pageant was the first step on a long, circuitous trip to the professional theater. In the twenty-one years between the pageant and my first paid appearance, there were thirty-one more amateur shows, a couple of abortive careers, and the war, in which I played four and a half years in a walk-on role. My amateur theatricals did bear some small but delicious fruit in these army years as I earned a number of three-day passes by putting on officers-club shows employing stolen night-club material.

As a high-school boy I reached heights which I don't suppose I'll ever manage again. As a bearded, international criminal I brooded over the unconscious form of the hero and then, almost in time to the metronome ticking in the bomb beside his head, spoke my all-time favorite line: "In five minutes, my friend, you will be in Kingdom Come. You, Sir William, the girl, and the papers. And a very pleasant journey to you all!" A sweep of the cloak which almost dislodged my beard, a sinister, gliding walk to the door, and my first exit hand.

Later, veteran actors explained to me that if you delay your exit long enough, audiences are forced to applaud, as they can be forced to it by a tap dancer repeating a step. But this was the real thing. This was catching the pass in the big game, breaking five minutes in the mile (I went to school a long time ago), or winning all the scholarship prizes and the poetry competition too. At least, I imagine it was, since I never actually did any of those other things. I know I can hear that applause still, and sometimes while I am sitting in a producer's waiting room an hour beyond my appointed time, I give a little push on the swell pedal and add a few bravos to the ghostly sound.

Another waiting-room recipe which I commend was that employed by Talleyrand when, after the fall of Napoleon, he was kept kicking his heels for hours in the drafty corridors of the British Foreign Office. "He waited," said his biographer, Duff Cooper, "with a tolerance born of scorn." This is a wonderful formula. Sometimes I get feeling so superior and scornful over my detective story that I am quite sorry when the secretary finally says, "You can go in now, Mr. Brown." Scorn is then struck to earth by the sharp sword of Anxiety.

In a college musical I reached another high point when, for the first—and last—time, I sang with, and to, the Girl. It was a real girl, too, and none of your football players fitted out with grapefruit halves.

It was a catchy number called "Tarzan, King of the Apes," and included the couplet: "I swing from tree to tree, won't you come and swing with me." My only regret is that I never had myself photographed in the leopard-skin outfit.

The direction of college musicals is rather loose and divided, and I found that after appearing in the first act, I was to direct the second. I mention this because the star whom I got to direct in a splendid impersonation of Groucho is now one of America's most distinguished psychiatrists. For the peace of mind of his patients I shall conceal his name, but I must say when I see him on TV talking gravely about the stresses of our times, I keep waiting for the bobbing eyebrows and the flicked cigar.

In my last year of college I got caught in the fantasy of the lovable professor, the fascinating don, the teacher whose lectures are "better than a show." I decided that I would spend a couple of years at Oxford or Cambridge and then return with some beautiful tweed jackets, a fund of stories about Dr. Johnson, and a reputation for learned wit that would get me a teaching job at a small, rich, coeducational college. I saw rows of girls hanging, moist-lipped and adoring, on my polished performances on the lecture platform—pretty much the same girls who were not paying any attention to me as a witty and polished undergraduate. After class, groups of students would come to my rooms to hear my philosophy and drink rather special sherry sent over by the pipe from an old London firm.

Because of the war, Oxford and Cambridge became unavailable before the dream got very far, but I still think teaching is a splendid substitute for the theater, although a number of academic friends tell me that they think the theater is a wonderful substitute for grinding literature into the slack-jawed faces of girls who conceal knitting behind their notebooks and boredom behind their eyes. The boys don't even get any knitting done.

The question of who is better off occurred to me also when I got a job on a newspaper and was writing my first story. Having made this smooth connection with the previous paragraph, I now have to stop for a little exposition, like the modern playwright who, deprived of the maid-butler device, has to scatter his background like sand through the whole custard of his play.

In the early days of the newspaper *PM*, a staff was being hastily assembled, and the managing editor, seeing my name in the papers in connection with records I was making of old-time New Orleans jazz, called me in for a talk.

"I don't know anything about you," he said. "But I liked your father, and if you want to start in the newspaper business, I'll give you a job. For the first six months you can think, if you want to, about how you got a job on your father's name. After that, forget about it, because if I don't like you on your own merits by then, I'll fire you."

I've always thought that was a brisk and competent way to handle a problem that's in the mind of every child of famous parents, but thinking and feeling are two different things, and my feelings were too complicated to tell at anything less than twenty-five dollars an hour—my twenty-five dollars.

I reminded myself that the editor didn't have to call me at all, that I had, in fact, no qualifications except some hard-hitting sports columns in the Swarthmore College *Phoenix*, a paper with an even smaller circulation than *PM*, and that college writers are the bane of newspapers because they arrive with a crust of adjectives as thick as the barnacles on a pearling lugger, and harder to remove.

Still, I felt a little Oedipian, not so much so that I didn't take the job, but in poor shape for my greeting from my immediate boss, the sports editor. He was going to take no guff from dilettante college boys with famous names, and he didn't wait to find out whether guff was in my repertory.

On my arrival at his desk, he asked my name to make sure I was the guff-laden, dilettante college boy with the famous name and then pointed at the clock. "What the hell do you think this is, Old Home Week? You're five minutes late. Here, write me a humorous feature on this," and reaching behind him, he tore off what was drooping from the teletype machine. It proved to be a one-line item which said that the West Side Tennis Club might have to pay income taxes on the take from the Nationals. Timidly I asked if I might use the phone at his elbow, and sensing some veiled insolence in this, he gave me a long lecture on initiative and, at last, the phone. I called the club and asked if they were going to have to pay income tax, and they told me, I think quite properly, that it was none of my business, so I hung up and went to the bathroom and counted how many days were left of my six months.

When I came back, my boss said briskly, "There's a girl out at the World's Fair in one of those knock-me-out-of-bed-by-hitting-a-target-with-a-baseball concessions who says she can tell a potential professional ball player by the way he throws. Go out, find that girl, interview her, and bring me a humorous feature."

In all fairness, I must say he gave me a pass to the Fair, and, anxious to escape the office, I took it and left on my quest.

My investigations at the Fair revealed that there were about fifteen of these booths where one could satisfy obscure, Freudian impulses by hitting a small disk which released a spring and tipped a thinly clad nifty off a divan with a satisfying, to some, thump. I went from one to the other with my unlikely story and was usually turned away with the contemptuous advice that pickups could be made at ten o'clock when the concessions closed. I had started at about three in the afternoon, and about four hours and twelve booths later I found a man who said, "Oh yes, she's here. She wrote a letter to Connie Mack. But I can't let her stop now to talk to you. I tell you what, though. There's a little screen next to the bed, and you crouch behind that and talk to her." So there I was, a real reporter at last, getting my first story while crouching at the foot of a bed like a character in a Feydeau farce and having the questions and answers interrupted by what appeared to be the pitching staff of the Yankees.

Now at last we come to the point where this all started. It appeared that the young lady was an actress and had thought this up as a publicity stunt. She had indeed written the letter to Mr. Mack, and made to me some good-natured, not-intended-to-be-believed, claim to the talent mentioned in the letter. More surprisingly, Mr. Mack had answered, saying he'd be glad to hear of any prospects. But then, the Athletics were in last place that year and probably could have used the bunch that were firing away during my interview.

As we bumped along, verbally and otherwise, through our talk, it occurred to me that the two most glamorous professions in the world, journalism and the stage, seemed at that moment to compare unfavorably with the counting-house, the blacking factory, the treadmill, and all the other jobs that literature had taught me were undesirable.

I would like to end this story by saying that that young actress was Julie Harris. Theater books are full of that kind of thing, except that in American theater books, which are more serious, it usually is: "That kindly man in the shabby dark suit who casually gave me a priceless artistic secret was Constantin Stanislavski," while English theater books, which are livelier and tonier, do: "A quiet lady in dove-grey told me with earnest warmth how much she enjoyed my performance. As she turned unaffectedly away, I asked the stagedoorman if he knew her. 'Lumme, Guv'nor,' he expostulated, 'You 'ain't 'arf pullin' me leg. That there's the Princess Royal.'"

Well, anyway, it wasn't Julie Harris, and although the light wasn't very good, I'm pretty sure it wasn't the Princess Royal.

When I got back to the office everyone was gone, so I

wrote a humorous feature and stumbled away to dreams of my father flunking me out of Oxford.

I turned up early the next day, but my boss was ill and unable to give me credit. The late Tom Meany, with whom I was to have many years of happy association on the paper, kindly went over my story with a barnacle scraper, meeting all my objections with the incontrovertible statement, "Doesn't it still say the same thing?" Aided by his pruning, my story got into the paper and when the boss got back he handsomely admitted that he hadn't expected to see me or the story, told me to come in when I wanted as long as I got the work done, and showed so much appreciation that it took me nine more years to get into the professional theater.

Somebody else's illness got me a promotion a few months later, and I became a baseball writer, that luckiest of men, paid to see every day what others have to pay to see occasionally. Living in the finest hotels, packed with steak and wine, spending the springs in Florida, Arizona, California, Havana, allowed, nay required, to talk continually with the nation's idols, is he not the favorite of the gods?

I am reminded of Max Beerbohm's words about being a theater critic: "I daresay that there are many callings more uncomfortable and dispiriting than that of dramatic critic. To be a porter on the Underground Railway must, I have often thought, be very terrible. Whenever I feel myself sinking under the stress of my labours, I shall say to myself, 'I am not a porter on the Underground Railway.'"

It has been complained that our drama these days is too predictable, but there is a kind of non-Aristotelian inevitability about August doubleheaders that beats them all. When a sixth-place team and a seventh-place team divide by scores of 11–7 and 13–8, and you are being paid to breathe a little interest into an account of the doings, you earn your steak and wine many times over.

Even harder on the writer are those spring stories. Have you ever tried to be lyrical about calisthenics? I've done it, but those eighteenth-century poets who were commissioned to write lengthy birthday odes to nasty little dukes had an easier time of it.

Then there are the inevitable spring flowers, the rookie players, who, like the seed cast upon stony ground in the Bible "sprung up because they had no deepness of earth" —or in baseball terms sufficient seasoning—but "When the sun was up," and the regulars got warm, "They were scorched; and because they had no root, they withered away," and were sent to Waycross in the Georgia-Florida League.

Still, each year, for lack of other things to write, we maddened the hopes of these young men by puffing their deeds in pickup games and predicting a summer in New York on the basis of two scratch singles and the need to file six hundred words a day.

Later in the summer, traveling from Waycross to Valdosta in an old bus driven by whatever player was too injured to get in the game that day, they must have hated us. Or perhaps, more foolishly, they hated the management.

I remember an outfielder from Montreal who was having his last chance to catch on with the parent Brooklyn club. I honestly thought he deserved it and so wrote a number of times. Dimly he regarded me as his friend at court, not knowing how far from the king's ear was this particular courtier.

One day in an exhibition game he dropped the ball in the ninth inning, and thereby two runs scored and the Dodgers lost, a fact that was written by all the reporters present. A day or two later he approached me in the lobby of the hotel, and said in tones of deep reproach, "I thought you were my friend."

"I am," I said. "I want to see you stay with the club."

"Then why did you put it in the paper that I dropped the ball?"

"I just wrote the story of the game. How could I explain how the Dodgers lost?"

"If you were really my friend, you wouldn't have put it in the paper." He didn't speak to me again, and in a few weeks was returned to Montreal, convinced that he had been destroyed by the printing press. As actors are always uneasy with critics, as schoolboys are with teachers, so ballplayers never really believe that writers are human. There are, of course, exceptions but not enough to keep you from being lonely a good deal of the time.

At the end of the game, when players are showering and changing and writers are filing their stories, the crowd leaves the park, and all the gates are closed save one from which writers and players will exit through a circle of fans, most of them kids. As we would approach the gate from within, the kids would surge forward, but if they saw a typewriter, someone would always shout to those behind, "It's nobody." To anyone with the actor's temperament, this was hard to bear.

Once a year the baseball writers of New York take the spotlight, however. The occasion is their annual dinner and show. A hotel ballroom is filled with ballplayers, fans, executives, glove manufacturers, and others connected with the game, all wanting to sit at the same table as Joe DiMaggio or the Commissioner, all wanting a little of that glamour that seems to be around baseball, all hoping to get the right people to autograph the souvenir program—"for my boy. He knows your batting average better than you do."

After some speeches and some awards, the curtains draw back at the end of the ballroom, and the writers get their revenge for all the frustrations of the long season. Nobody says, "It's nobody," now, as the writers satirize the hero, the man who hires him, the man who manages him, and all the apparatus that surrounds the game clubowner Phil Wrigley once said was "too much of a business to be a sport and too much of a sport to be a business."

In sketches and parody lyrics written to popular tunes, the newspapermen commit genial mayhem, and sometimes the operative word is genial and sometimes it is mayhem. All told, it is a colorful mixture of Major Bowes and Jonathan Swift.

I had no sooner got my card in the Baseball Writers' Association than I began dreaming of this chance to take another step toward Broadway.

Before I had even gotten a part in the show I had done a lot of work on a fantasy in which a famous agent called me, bubbling with admiration and remembered mirth.

"Mr. Broun, I'm a great baseball fan, and I happened to catch you the other night at the Writers' Show. Have you ever thought of giving up the newspaper business and trying your hand at the stage? Honestly, that thing you did on the Mexican League, that peon, was priceless. Oscar and Dick were at our table, and I thought they'd split. Say, that's an idea! Do you sing, Mr. Broun?" Etc.

Nobody in my fantasies ever said that they enjoyed the sketch I'd *written* and had I ever thought about writing a play. Now that I've seen what playwrights go through, I am pleased that my fantasies had such good sense.

I did, in fact, perform in several shows, and although no famous agents said anything, my colleagues were warm and generous in their praise, and several of them said: "Have you ever thought of giving up sportswriting and becoming an actor?" Looking back, I suppose that argued for a certain lack of enthusiasm about my writing, but at the time I was pleased no end, and when the New York *Star* followed in the footsteps of *PM*, I announced to my friends that I was now an actor. I had no idea of the difficulties an actor faces, no notion of the terrible over-supply of talent and the wasting effect of long stretches of inactivity. I just thought my daydreams were going to come true, and I must say that in a modified, scaled-down way, they have.

Since this is not one of those *Thirty Years in the Green-room* books, I'm not going to drag you down Memory Lane and read old reviews and programs to you, but just to round this out, I'll get myself as far as Broadway and then we can leave me, drifting slowly and agreeably toward fame, or the Actors' Home, or both.

Phil Silvers gave me my first professional job after shaking his head in disbelief that anyone would want to give up being a baseball writer. During all my years as a news-paperman I had hung about actors and their gathering places, like the small boys around the ball park, and had been delighted to meet Phil, who, in turn, had been pleased to meet someone with whom he could talk about baseball. Both of us spent a lot of time trying to change the subject.

Phil felt that a sportswriter going into the theater made about as much sense as a violinist signing on as a lumber-jack, but being a nice man he said he would give me a job on his television show.

"There are lots of nuts in this business," he said. "And it's a big help if anybody ever hired you. It shows you're not a complete nut. When you go for a job you won't have to say you haven't done anything. Tell them you've been on my TV show many times. If they ask me, I'll back you up."

This was good advice. The actor who is modest about his accomplishments is not admired as a gentleman but dismissed as a mediocrity without the wit for basic embellishment.

When I had a reversion to sixth-form mores a few years later and said to the director Garson Kanin that the parts I had played on Broadway were small and tangential, he was kind enough to stop me and admonish me.

"If you say that kind of thing to people in the theater," he said, "they will assume that you have not been on Broadway at all and are presuming to imaginary parts that they are not expected to remember. Always overstate your credits to twice what they were, remembering that the hearer will discount your statement by half."

Silvers was as good as his word, and I received my first acting fee for appearing on the Arrow Television Theater with Phil and a group of veteran burlesque comics who treated me with the sympathetic amusement of World War I aces greeting the green pilot—"I've had six and a half hours of solo, sir—and I'm not afraid of Von Richthofen or any other Hun!" Gruff with all too familiar emotion, the colonel replied, "I don't doubt your pluck and ability for a moment, my boy, but we're going to have to give you rather an old Spad, and I'd appreciate it if you'd stick close to formation for a couple of days while the motor wallahs check her over."

My Spad in this case was the role of a man who comes to talk to Phil about an acting award, convinces him through inadvertence that he is to be the recipient, then asks him to present it to someone else. Explosion. Pursuit. Blackout. It was, of course, familiar, but Phil gave the worn bit such a high polish that it shone like new, and I provided a kind of pathetic and frightened intensity which happened to fit the part. (This isn't a breach of my modesty rule. It is the overstatement.)

Everyone treated me with the kindness appropriate to a survivor of the first patrol, and I went home with a small check, a large vanity, and the conviction that long, straight, and smooth before me lay the road to my golden-anniversary movie. It did run straight and smooth for a while. Phil used me again to make my claim of "many times" come easier to my lips, and the summer-stock company in Woodstock, New York, where I had a cabin in which I vaguely hoped someday to sit and write a novel—"His vision clarified by wilderness life, this young American writer takes an unsparing look at our society and finds it wanting. A book to stand beside . . ."—accepted me as a home-town boy with some professional experience. Guiltily but firmly I followed Phil's advice and hinted at a relationship with Silvers which made us seem a veteran comedy team, rather than the chela and guru we had been in our brief association.

The stock director soon learned that he had the lesser half of the team, but he accepted this with the good nature that stock directors must acquire if they are to survive in the never-enough-time-or-talent world of summer theater. Thoughtfully he gave me as a starter the role of Mr. Thorkelson, the nervous undertaker in *I Remember Mama*. On opening night my resemblance to a nervous undertaker was almost complete, and once again I had been gifted with perfect flying weather and no problem beyond the limits of my fledgling state.

My Broadway debut of which, I'm afraid, more later, was in a part requiring of the actor only an audible monotone. Indeed any effort to change from robotic behavior spoiled the point of the part which was that of a simple man stunned by the antic behavior of some sophisticated people. At that time I probably could do expressionlessness as well as anybody in the country. It was only acting that I couldn't manage.

The result of my anti-acting was a delighted audience, roars of laughter for my every line and a set of notices which both delighted and frightened me. Vanity purred like a cat, but conscience said that the fates would certainly punish anyone who got all that praise for something a train conductor could have done.

All this raises a tricky question about the acting business. How do you apportion credit? I really do think I did the three parts just mentioned quite well. Perhaps I could do them better now, or perhaps the mixture of fear and delight that I brought to those early jobs will never come out quite so bubbly again.

Certainly the fear and delight would not have been enough to carry me through Hamlet, but I don't want to try that even now. It would be all fear. But granting that I did a good job on those occasions, what kind of business do we have here? You can't just decide that you're going to be a pianist and go out and give a concert—not somebody else's compositions, at least.

Cries from the rear of "False analogy! An actor is his own instrument. He's been learning to play it all his life!"

Well, of course, that's true, but he isn't learning to use it in an organized way if, like Sherlock Holmes, he scrapes random notes on the Strad until Watson almost screams. Better the Holmes who would then "catch it up and play a whole series of my favorite airs," something which takes a little practice.

Maybe we can't bring with us to the arts the "worthiness" values which the nineteenth century gave us as a philosophical excuse for long factory hours and child labor.

How did it look? How did it sound? How did it read?

Was it beautiful? These tests have more validity than the kind of foot-pound measurements which are appropriate to the time-and-motion-study world.

That sounds pretty snobbish, doesn't it? It sounds as if we are opting out of responsibility and claiming to need nothing more than the touch of fox fire which glows about our special heads. Well, no one claims this—or, let's say, I don't claim it. I do know that I have learned a great deal about the theory and practice of acting since those early days, that I am proud of this knowledge and use it, I believe well—and that sometimes since then I have done a much better job—and sometimes one that didn't have half what the nervous undertaker had.

As to the business about acting vs. playing the violin, I'll skip the defensive jokes that come to mind and simply say that since musical discipline is further away from normal human experience than acting, its proportion of technique must be higher. I brought the analogy up and I get to drop it. Jascha Heifetz is a great artist, and so is Sir Ralph Richardson. Neither need step aside to let the other go first into the pantheon.

The debate about the proper proportions of inspiration —to use a useless but irreplaceable word—and technique in acting fills up a lot of debate time within the acting profession, and the only thing you don't get much of is objectivity.

Let's look at a couple of representative extremes. Here's a man of forty who is short, stout, and bald. A few touches of greasepaint, a little puff of crepe hair and—hey, presto! we have an Old Testament prophet, complete with minatory bass. The next time you see this man he is in flannels and blazer, a shy Harrow boy with an engaging cracked tenor, in love with his housemaster's wife—or, in our outspoken modern theater—the housemaster. This actor is per-

fect as Charlemagne, marvelous as Quasimodo, and nobody knows him on the street.

Let's take another sort. His harsh, inflexible voice is almost as well known as his distinctive and unforgettable
face. Years of careful handling have given his single "character" the rich bloom of a well-tended meerschaum pipe
—we love to watch him do nothing at all (remember Jean
Gabin beside the swimming pool in *Any Number Can
Win?*) because—quite truthfully—he does nothing at all in
a wonderful and exciting way.

The first actor has had to learn all sorts of special skills.
He can fence, speak several languages and the broken English versions thereof, give you an authentic anatomy-based
limp for every mishap, and he carries a remarkable assortment of character spectacles in a make-up box containing
a complex palette of greases, putties, powders, pencils, and
equipment for making every kind of scar or wound. He is
a first-rate actor.

The second of our actors uses no make-up except for a
slight sunlamp glow, and speaks no language save English,
and that with a regional accent. He limps unconvincingly
and cannot fence at all. His explanation for this is that very
few people from a Midwest farm, his obvious place of ori-
gin, ever enlisted in the Musketeers.

He has only one special skill. It is that of being a first-
rate actor.

He would in fact make a wonderful Musketeer, inept
swordplay, plowboy voice and all.

Success makes everybody mellow, but down on the
levels where most of us can be found fighting for a grip
on one rung or another, the first of our extremes is
described by some as a disgusting piece of clockwork, and
the other fellow is known in some circles as an exhibition-
ist displaying a salable neurosis.

Sit with me in a dressing room of a summer theater box-office-deep in pine cones and listen to my roommate. The three-tiered, tackle-box make-up kit in front of him is his badge of honor. He looks with hostility at the little tin candy box which holds all the stuff I know how to use.

"How many actors have the style for Restoration comedy?" he cries, in a voice that cost him a lot of money in lessons. "Do you know how to handle a five-foot cane with a tassel while you're taking snuff? Can you sit down right in one of those lousy long coats? Can you bow and do a minuet and take off your hat without disarranging your wig? Damn right, you can't. And I'll tell you something. Neither can that motorcyclist they got for the revival of *The Plain Dealer*. He thinks the Restoration is when the Catholics got even with the Protestants for Martin Luther. You know why they cast him? I'll tell you why they cast him. Because he was such a hit as the wounded pilot in *Never Have So Few*. What the hell has the RAF got to do with the Restoration? You know what they offered me after two years at Yale and two at the Royal Academy? A chance to be in the ballroom scene and understudy the old man. I told them what they could do with their understudy and the ballroom after it"—and so on until it is time for us to make our entrances in the special Campers' Matinee of *Night Must Fall*.

He is perfectly right and it is shocking how cavalier some people are about basic knowledge. Elsewhere in this book I am all on his side, but he doesn't need me on his side, he needs the producer of *The Plain Dealer*, and I am afraid that bitterness is driving him to the extreme position which argues that artificiality is the only reality. His bitterness is easy to understand if you've ever done a Campers' Matinee. They laugh at the serious parts.

Sit with me beside a lake and listen to another actor

speaking over the sound of rats gnawing the pilings under our waterfront theater. He looks at me with hostility, not because of anything I have done but because he is hostile all the time. It lends excitement to what he does onstage. "What is this crap with lessons?" he cries, in a voice that could use some. "What I got, I got in here"—business of pounding on the body which really does move with superb natural grace—"and I don't need some school-teacher that they taught her what Shakespeare had for breakfast to tell me how to play Hamlet or anything else. You were here last week. You saw what I done with that rotten part. Did you ever hear anybody get cheers in a ——— part like that? Damn right, you didn't. Anyway, who says I don't prepare? Every morning with the weights while the rest of you ———s are still in the sack or reading some ——— book about acting. Say, a little work with the weights would take some of that flab off you, buddy"—and so on until we have to make our entrances in a winter-uniform army play about a freezing patrol, which marks the open-ing of the summer heat wave beside the lake.

He is perfectly right, and they did cheer, and he did deserve it. He has something that you can't learn. If by some chance he hits it big, all that energy will be chan-neled by press agents into socially acceptable aggressions like surf-boarding, fighting with columnists, and black-belt competitions at the stars' gym. If he doesn't, the drive and energy will turn him so sour and nasty that no one will want him around. It's a pity, but really, what is so ter-rible about learning? When I asked him that, he took his hates and weights to another room, so I never got his answer.

I'd ask you to sit with me in some other dressing rooms, but after a while it depresses me, so I guess it would depress you too. There are almost as many variations of the argument as there are actors. If you want to hear my own, moderate, best-of-both-worlds opinion, come to my dressing room after the first scene of the second act. I don't have another entrance until near the end of the third.

There are times, goodness knows, when the amount of training an actor could profitably use overwhelms me, as when I was called to play a waiter on a live TV show. I was told that the part was small and simple and that the show, for a reality gimmick, would work out of a real restaurant. It never occurred to me to think what the staff of the real restaurant would think of my doing this, but I found out when I arrived. They hated me. To begin with, I had a mustache. The headwaiter, forgetting that I was only Garçon for a Day, commanded me to shave.

"Mustaches are unsanitary," he barked. "None of our waiters have mustaches. Look around you."

I looked around me and saw a ring of clean-shaven, sullen old men, flicking napkins in a menacing manner and radiating contempt. I fear I saw their point. If the part was so easy, why couldn't one of them play it? After all, it took a lifetime to learn the subtle secrets of first-class waiting, and this was a first-class restaurant. In view of what happened I wish one of them had played it.

One of the least hostile waiters was told off as my instructor. He took me through a short course in crumb-clearing and how to throw the napkin over your arm, but he spent most of our regrettably short time doing something between an audition and a reproach. While I stood slackly by, he showed how he could wave a tray through a wide angle without spilling a glass of wine, how he could gut a lobster—this was a piece of pantomime worthy of Marcel Marceau, since we didn't have a real lobster—how he could carry an assortment of round things stacked up his forearm, and other accomplishments which I couldn't possibly pick up that morning. At the end of a demonstration with rolls, too complicated to describe here, the rest of the company arrived, my education ended, and we began to get ready for the show.

The plot of our playlet involved a cab with passenger, which was to draw up in the real street outside the real restaurant. The passenger, after refusing to pay the fare, entered the restaurant and ordered from me a lengthy and —so it proved—impractical meal. While the first two courses of it were being served, the actor-cabdriver was to seek out an actor-policeman and bring him into the restaurant where he was to arrest the diner, who would depart, leaving me a dollar tip. I was to glance at the dollar and discover on it one of the serial numbers for which a newspaper was then offering prizes; and a close-up of the gratification flitting over my expressive face was the fade-out.

The trouble started when the headwaiter got back into the act. It was my idea that the actor-diner order things served in little round bowls with handles on both sides. My suggestions for the two courses to be seen on the show were jellied consommé—even I couldn't spill that—and oatmeal, which we would call something like Supreme of Gratinée Farcie. If they didn't have oatmeal I would take applesauce, or Bonne Femme de Bordelaise à la Mode de Caen.

If the headwaiter had struck me—as I thought he might do at that moment—it would have been a pretty problem as to whether I would have gone for redress to the waiters' or the actors' union. It appeared that this restaurant had never served oatmeal, served applesauce only rarely, and then only as an adjunct to pork dishes which came on sizzling platters and were quite beyond the capabilities of this thrice-damned ninny with his great big unsanitary mustache. (I never did find out why he considered mustaches unsanitary. Surely the waiter isn't supposed to *taste* the stuff to make sure it's right? My teacher didn't say that.) If they wanted to serve fodder such as this fellow described, why not set the show in a cafeteria and cease to sully the names of gentlemen's feeding places easily recognizable to discriminating viewers? He would not even hire me to stand behind steam-table French toast (his idea of the world's lowest food), but the TV people apparently found me in some way satisfactory, and there was a very nice workmen's restaurant around the corner if they wanted— well, the director of the show arbitrated the dispute as disputes between actors and outsiders are always arbitrated, by giving the headwaiter carte blanche to make me serve flaming ice cream on swords (I believe it is very big in Chicago) if he wanted, and we got on with rehearsing such secondary matters as the lines.

At the dress rehearsal the headwaiter showed me the first course, and I wished very much that like so many other actors, I had spent a couple of years at Schrafft's. On a slippery tray stood a slippery big dish with an insecure grip on the bottom of a slippery little dish on which balanced a big, footed cup of ice in which sat a small, top-heavy bowl of too many shrimps. Beside this on the tray were cocktail crackers nested in what seemed to be a skate and a glass ball full of sauce.

"This," he purred, "is how we always serve a shrimp cocktail."

While I was having a loathing contest with him, the actors on the street had troubles of their own. Real cabbies, hating the actor-cabbie, kept pulling into the parking place in front of the restaurant. The real policemen were too busy hating the actor-policeman and blocking him off from the actor-cabbie to bother with keeping the space clear. Nobody seemed to hate or envy the actor-passenger-diner, which was curious because he was the star of the show. However, the stories of the other actors can go into their books, and right now I am going back into the restaurant to the real show, the cameras pushing back and forth among the tables, I standing wiping my face with my napkin to the horror of the ring of vulture-waiters circling just outside camera range to pick clean my mistakes, and the actor-diner just coming in the door. He hurried to my table without assistance, because the management had said absolutely no to the sacrilegious idea of a actor-maître d', and gave me the order for the fatal shrimps. Now I had done it all right at the dress rehearsal, and I would have been all right now, no matter what they may tell you at that restaurant, but the director had changed the camera pattern, and it happened when I tried to step high over a fast-rising electric cable. This isn't, after all, a normal waiter's problem, and anyway it wasn't seen on camera, although the crash of all those dishes must have resounded through a million homes. The camera did register the diner's dismay and his weak smile when I served him the crackers which I had saved from the fall —I told them *one* dish, but they wouldn't listen. Quick-wittedly, he started in on the dry little things as if they were what he always ordered. He had quite a mouthful of flinty crumbs when I reappeared on the screen with a second complete order of shrimps, which the headwaiter had forehandedly had standing by. I had tried to explain to him that it was too late in the script for shrimps, but he was thinking in restaurant rather than dramatic terms, and he pushed me on. The actor gave me an agonized stare, spat the broken biscuits into his napkin, and reached for the shrimps. Just then I saw the actor-policeman come

in the door, which was my cue to serve what I called the
Osso Bucco à la Vesuvio, a name I had chosen because
it was a smoking pyramid of plates down the sides of
which ran gravy-lava. With a desperate deftness that would
not have disgraced my tutor, I snatched up the shrimps
before the poor diner could get one, vaulted the cable between myself and the serving table, placed the shrimps
before a real diner, who was delighted with the lagniappe,
whirled up the great roast, and had it in front of my man
too late for a forkful but just before the arrest.

The grinding of the headwaiter's teeth must also have
been heard in millions of homes, but I was out of his
reach and stood staring at my dollar, looking like a man
who has found the money not in a restaurant but in a
Turkish bath. In one last smear on the place's reputation
and my forehead, I took off the worst of the sweat with
the sodden napkin as the close-up camera drew near.

Later the director chided me mildly for not looking
happier when I discovered that I had a "lucky buck."

"You forget," I told him, "how much I throw myself
into parts. All I could think about was that they were
going to give me the bad tables back by the kitchen door."

Actually, the headwaiter wouldn't give me even that, but
at the last he was nice. He shook my hand and said,
"Come back any time—but only as a customer."

A while back I promised to tell more about my Broadway debut, and even though the promise was only to
myself, now seems the time to honor it.

In those first few months when the road was un-
deservedly smooth, Sidney Phillips, an MGM executive
and occasional theater investor, saw me play at Woodstock
and was so impressed with something that his keen eye
saw—perhaps a woodenness unequaled since the heyday of
the silent Western, that he suggested me to Brock Pember-

ton for the role of the expressionless telephone repairman in a play called *Love Me Long*, which Pemberton was to produce in the fall. A month or two later I went in to see Mr. Pemberton and had my first inkling of how theatrical offices operate. The elevator was jammed with assorted types, and as we disembarked into the anteroom, a keen-eyed lady inspected us carefully and said, judiciously, "No, I'm sorry there's nothing for you, dear. No, sir, I don't think there's a part which would suit you. No, you're just a little too young, I'm afraid," etc. She was kind but very positive about me. I didn't fit anything even remotely.

Bewildered, I said, "But, I have an appointment with Mr. Pemberton. He sent for me."

"For goodness sake, why didn't you say so?" said the lady. "Of course; the Telephone Man. He'll see you in a moment."

Behind me, the elevator door wiped across a row of re-proachful faces. Mr. Pemberton and I had a pleasant, in-conclusive chat, and another month passed. My wife-to-be, who had been the leading lady in Woodstock, got me a job at a theater in Putnam, Connecticut, where I was bringing a keen knowledge of Thackeray, Dickens, and Trollope—and none of Stanislavski—to the part of Mr. Hawkes, the family lawyer in *Peg o' My Heart*, when Mr. Pemberton's office called again. Rehearsals started Monday. Would I be there at ten in the morning. I was, but I had to drive all night after the Sunday performance in Connecticut, and I was a little gritty-eyed and more than a little sleepy when I walked into the rehearsal. This was the Real Thing, and I felt depressed that at the moment of achieving it, my only thought was to lie down on the cool linoleum for forty winks.

I was allowed my winks, sitting against the wall in a broken-seated, splinter-backed, bentwood chair, which, through some elaborate conspiracy, is carried from theater to theater by my enemies and has been dying under me through sixteen shows. The way things are going, though, I think its left front leg, which is badly buckled, will outlast mine, which is giving way at the hinges.

At lunch I woke up enough to be excited at the idea of eating with Real Broadway Actors and through excitement and exhaustion was so frenetic that they didn't know whether they were eating with a Real Broadway Actor, a Real Newspaperman doing an "inside the theater" story, or a Real Nut.

After lunch, when I was making the first of a million shifts in my off-balance chair, Mr. Pemberton suddenly said, "I'd like to hear Woodie read." My heart sank at the thought of failing before all those nice people I'd been to lunch with, but I did a wake-up trick I had learned on long, drowsy days in the Polo Grounds press box (knuckle your inflamed eyes vigorously; the subsequent tingle is a real tonic) and advanced to the footlights.

I got a good grip on the suddenly slippery tissue of the part, and in the manner of Penrod Schofield reciting, "I hight Sir Launcelot du Lake" at Mrs. Laura Rewbush's "Children of the Table Round" pageant, I gave what nightclub performers call "my impression of" the phone man. Nervousness lent an edge to my nasal voice that crepitated the glass in the exit signs. (Later the director, Margaret Perry, said to me, "You have a lot of problems but none of them is audibility. You have a voice like an ice pick.") When I finished, nobody said anything for a bit, and then Mr. Pemberton, in his characteristic obverse way, said, "You needn't go," a phrase which it took me a full ten seconds to understand and enjoy.

Of my eventual undeserved triumph in this role, I have already spoken, and you need not worry that I am going to take you through every step of the spinning and the peculiar manner of my chrysalis, in which I became a butterfly without ever emerging from it. The play was a failure, a fact which surprised me, lost in dreams of glory. I was never surprised again, but then I never had such dreams again. But two more incidents, kind friends, and I will let you pass on.

I had supposed that out-of-town dress rehearsals of a Broadway play would not be the shambles to which I had become accustomed in my short stock career, and I went into a deep panic at what happened the night before we opened in Wilmington. Set changes didn't work. Lights went off and on at the wrong times. At the end of the first act, Shirley Booth and her fiancé were supposed to leave her apartment and go to the St. Regis.

"Let's go to the St. Regis," said Miss Booth, getting the exit exposition over with quickly, and went to the door of the apartment set. She tugged, but it wouldn't open.

"I'd love to go to the St. Regis," she said with cheery desperation, and tugged again.

"I've just got to get to the St. Regis," she cried as she put her foot against the door jamb and pulled till the set swayed like Charlie Chaplin's cabin in *The Gold Rush*.

"Oh well," said Miss Booth resignedly, "if we can't go to the St. Regis, let's have some fun here," and advancing to the front of the stage, she did a waltz clog and sang a little song. I believe it was "Smile Awhile," but perhaps you had better ask her.

One person there, I determined, would keep a cool head and amaze the veterans. Here was a chance for Broun, the old artillery sergeant, to show the stuff of which he was made. When we got to my entrance I came on like Citation bursting out of the gate, and played my part like the

Notre Dame eleven "winning one for the Gipper," their dying comrade.

After the rehearsal I found out that the management was calm, and indeed, had only one worry. It was me.

"My God," said the director, "what were you doing up there? I never saw anything like it."

Mr. Pemberton, his normal calm badly cracked by my foot-stamping, whirling, two-fisted effort to pick things up and set them on their feet again, gave me a long, pained look, and left.

"I was only trying to act more," I said defensively. "I thought I was helping."

"Acting will come later for you," advised Miss Perry in a kindly tone. "Perhaps much later. In the meantime, just say your lines. It's very funny that way."

On opening night in New York I danced up the back-stage iron steps on Icarian wings. I stopped at Miss Booth's dressing room and, merry-voiced as a Pantomime Peter Pan, cried out, "Good luck, Miss Booth!"

With a veteran's foreknowledge of the notices, she had been thinking about Come Back, Little Sheba, in which she was soon to triumph. She turned slowly from her dressing table, looking at first like someone reproaching a chuckler in church. She softened when she saw my fatuous grin and said, "I forgot. It's your first, isn't it, kid? Well, good luck."

Perhaps we should leave my career right there on the threshold of fame, and sum up all the rest of it in a sentence.

The door to renown, like the door to the St. Regis, got stuck, and, well, here I am, dancing and singing "Smile Awhile."

Gᴇᴛ ᴀɴʏ ɢʀᴏᴜᴘ of actors together and soon the talk will veer to the venality, stupidity, incompetence, and general moral nullity of producers.

I haven't often been vouchsafed producers in groups. They tend, like the Rocky Mountain sheep, to operate alone and on very precarious and inaccessible pinnacles. I have talked to a few, however, and they seem agreed that actors are venal, stupid, incompetent, immoral, and, for good measure, childish.

This set of bad opinions arises, I think, from the fact that neither side of the desk in a theatrical office is a comfortable place. There are always many more actors than there are jobs, and as it is painful to plead, so also is it painful continually to refuse. A young man asking for a job in a bank can probably eat a good lunch after the banker says no. I find it hard to believe that a lot of emotion goes into asking for a spot in a cage full of somebody else's money. An actor, on the other hand, is asking for the fulfillment of a dream. As surgeons must develop a jovial callousness on the subject of open bodies full of clamps, sponges, knives, and hands, so those who deal with actors must develop a protective blindness cum brusqueness that will permit them a ratio of a hundred no's for every yes, a hundred slaps for every handshake.

To be a good actor, one must have a sensitive, almost skinless persona, able to absorb bits and pieces of other people and to combine them with bits and pieces of oneself, remaking them all into delicately balanced mobiles which must be carried through the wind tunnel of rehearsals to the shooting gallery that is the theater.

To be a successful actor, that is, a working actor, one must have the breezy brass of a door-to-door peddler, the coarse persuasiveness of a used-car salesman, and the beautiful, tremulous sincerity of a con man selling oil stock to old ladies.

Combining this round yang and square yin is a problem to which no answer will be offered here.

Three hundred-odd million years ago there was a creature called the crossopterygian fish which spent part of each year crawling around dry land on its ridged fins with its gills closed and its air bladder open for business. In this way it managed for some eons to eke out a meager living. A little of the old crossopterygian quality is very useful to an actor.

Consider for a moment the atmosphere of most auditions for plays. The actor is summoned to a theater with no more advance knowledge, more often than not, than the play's title and an agent's comment that "they don't know how old they want him to be, baby. It depends who they get for the lead. Wear a gray suit and give them a kind of ageless feeling. Don't stand up too straight. All the leading men they're considering are short."

Arrived at the theater, the actor finds the alley outside the stage door filled with actors better known than himself, and pushes through to a harried man with a clipboard who tells him that despite the projected precision of the time schedule—"They want you there at 2:28, baby, so take your dexedrine at 1:30"—things are running late, about an hour late. He would give the actor a script to while away the hour, but they are very tight on scripts. The actor may go away for coffee, sit in the cellar under the stage where he can hear the desperate efforts of his rivals and the steady succession of "thank-you's" from out front like thumps of the guillotine blade, or stand in the alley checking the steady wane of his pep pill.

If he is fortunate he may have a few minutes with the script, which often turns out to be a first draft in which several important changes have not been made. At last comes the moment of which he has dreamed. He is ushered onto the stage, his name is called into the darkness of the house where sits a weary group nursing butt-filled coffee containers, and he discovers that he cannot see the script very well because his head shuts off the light from the single large bulb directly above him which is the regulation light on these occasions. The script shakes in his moist hands, and he hears the voice of a twenty-five-year-old assistant stage manager speaking lines at him. The youth is playing the part of the Dowager Empress of Russia, and fifty previous tries at it that day have added nothing to the luster of his playing.

Very often the aspirant has only the vaguest idea of what the boy empress is talking about because a good many producers do not give out a whole script but only the two or three pages on which their trials are to be based.

In such cases the actor is forced to perform with the gener-
alized energy of a carnival pitchman. In any case, whether
everyone is thoughtful, kind and on schedule, or slipshod,
rude and late, the unhappy actor has the same problem
when he is cut off—what to do with all the rest of that
energy. At the moment he came on the stage his adrenalin
began to flow at a rate suitable to a football game, a fight,
or going up the hill at Gettysburg with Pickett. It is a rare
audition where he will be allowed more than one tackle,
one punch, or one step toward the Union lines. At the
words "thank you," he is left ready for anything but the
long walk back down the alley.

My own prescription for this problem is a dive into the
nearest newsreel theater, where I slowly unwind by watching divers come back onto the board, displays of spring
hats, and little boys losing their pants while boxing. By the
time the color camera shows us how the Old and the New
Mingle in Marrakech, my hands stop shaking, and when
the mouse chases the cat in the cartoon, I am ready to
identify with the mouse and laugh a little.

A casting director I know told me that sitting out front
is both depressing and uninformative and then asked me
to devise some better system. I'm sure there is one, but
I wasn't able to think of it offhand—or later—or now. If
the producer limits the candidates sharply, or simply par-
cels out the parts among those who have already worked
for him, there is an outcry that new talent is not given a
fair chance. Without the illusory activity of many auditions, actors dry up creatively, and whether there are too
many actors or not, the destruction of talent through rust
and inactivity is just plain wrong. There may not be
enough jobs for all in our rather restricted modern theater,
but anything which keeps the talent alive, even if it is only

an awful hour in an alley, followed by a worse two minutes in a shadow cave, is worth doing.

Of course, there are ways to make it easier. It is a good thing that more and more producers see to it that the actor gets to read the whole play before he arrives. It is a good thing to get at least an old lady if the Dowager Empress is going to feed lines to the candidate, even if the old lady has to put down her mop in the back of the theater. Most cleaning ladies read better than stage managers do anyway.

It is a good thing when the people out front take an extra minute or two to talk to the actor so that the sound of his own voice doesn't startle him when he begins to read the part and so that he has a moment to pull himself together after hearing the always splendid reading which preceded his.

It is a good thing if the appointment is automatically set for an hour after the time the employers expect to see you, since that hour always seems to get lost somewhere. This loss is a great mystery to all, since it doesn't seem to have been lost by spending extra time on any of the actors I know, or on me. If everybody went in and out as quickly as I do, you could cast *Hamlet* before the lunch break.

I suppose it is pretty awful sitting out front watching a series of human skyrockets from the moment of the match to the moment of the burned stick, but the flight is a short one, and it would be of great help to the rocketer if there were no conversation during his moment of flight. Nothing is more upsetting than giving the news of the czar's death to the dowager empress, while from the corner of your eye you notice that the director and the author have eyes and ears only for each other. At such moments the actor is tempted to scream aloud the words which he has been secretly saying through his whole life as an actor—"Pay attention to me!"

Some dreamers have suggested that the actors should all audition with some classic passage of Shakespeare, so that they could be exactly compared, like cultures in numbered Petri dishes—so many germs, so much agar—such and such a result. Actually this makes about as much sense as asking all candidates for chairs in a symphony orchestra to audition on the oboe.

Among their other fantasies, actors cherish the one about the overwhelming reading. In this one, a reedy youth, a little old man, or a breathless girl (depending on which category the dreamer fits) is cast in the role of King Lear because the reading was just so magnificent and magic that common sense is swept aside and a laughing, sobbing, applauding producer pushes forward with a contract to be signed on the spot. Well, maybe somewhere it's happened. Most legends have some basis in fact. Scholars say that even the unhappy Oedipus did not spring from the brow of Sophocles to the couch of Freud without historical basis. He is preceded and paralleled in all his miseries by the Pharaoh Ikhnaton.

Sarah Bernhardt played Hamlet, after all, and further strengthened the legend of the magnificent reading by gaining admission to the Conservatory by simply reciting the words of "The Marseillaise." I don't know, however, that any young actress in this country has ever tried reciting the words of "The Star-Spangled Banner" at an audition. Anyway, acting schools are easier to get into than plays. Looked at from an attitude of higher economics, you pay to go to acting school, a fact which can put an invisible orchestra behind the reciter.

Singing auditions are a special horror all their own, unless you are a singer, in which case acting auditions are a special horror all their own.

Some years ago a director asked me if I could sing, and when I said "No," he pressed me jovially.

"Surely you can sing a little bit," he coaxed.

"No, not even a little bit," I replied firmly. "My voice is thin and unpleasant, and I play parts requiring a thin, unpleasant voice."

Undeterred—and I must say I found it pleasant that the urging was on the management side—he asked me to bring a piece of music and audition anyway. I selected the hardest popular song I knew, "Who Cares?" from *Of Thee I Sing*. It is a wonderful song, which swoops high and low and leaves little room for breathing. I thought I might as well prove my point rather than sing "Happy Birthday to You," acceptably and get fired later when they came out with the grown-up song.

Arrived at the theater, I read the lines which went with the part to general laughter and approval and then placed my music on the piano, and to an expectant hush, began to sing. I sang cheerfully, reedily, and, like Jane Austen's Miss Beaty, "was good humour itself, and not much besides."

When I finished the hush was still there, but it was the hush of the tomb, and I tiptoed across the wide stage toward the wings. I had almost reached safety when a sepulchral voice said, "Don't forget your music," and I had to make the long trip back to the piano.

I was awful but not really nervous, because I had chosen not to involve myself. Some years later, after a number of lessons which had explored and laid bare why I was so bad, I did my second singing audition, this time with one of the longest of popular songs, "There Is Nothing Like a Dame," from *South Pacific*. The wings of the theater were full of barrel-chested young men humming bits from *Die Meistersinger* as they awaited their turns, and as I gave my music to the accompanist I foresaw their contempt.

They had every right to it because, as the accompanist struck a chord and I plunged in before he could begin the actual accompaniment, something terrible happened in my throat. It appeared that I possessed a flutter valve which made me sound like what is ironically called the "vox humana" on a parlor organ. My head was filled with conflicting advice—from the teacher: "Lots of confidence, now!"—and from prudence, which counseled immediate flight. The auditorium closed in on me until I was singing inside a black velvet egg about as big as a coffin. I saw no one, sang to no one, and prayed for death. Surely, I thought, they will stop me. Where is the healing, cauterizing sound of "thank you"? No one said anything, and approaching the end of the verse, I hit the lines with a desperate vigor that tightened the egg and opened the valve. My throat pulsed like the gills of a catfish on a sun-baked dock. The pianist had closed to within half a length of me, but seeing the finish, I went to the whip and drew out to a two- or three-bar lead, and fell across the last "da-a-a-a-me" like a two-pack-a-day Pheidippides arriving from Marathon with news of musical slaughter.

Everyone was so kind! Pity poured over me like salt on a flayed back.

Singers tell me they get the same feeling when speaking lines, and I came to agree with them some years and lessons later, when I was summoned to the piano again.

This time I sang first, confidently and cheerily, smiling briskly, and counting in my head—"ONE two three FOUR five six," as I told of the up-to-date wonders of Kansas City.

"That's good enough," said the director (*Die Meister-*

singer still lies ahead of me). "Now read the speaking part."

I don't quite know what happened, but when I finished there was the same stunned silence that had greeted my "Who Cares?" years before. I had reached the point of singing like an actor and acting like a singer.

I'm going to keep going, though. On one of my recent tries, I didn't get the job, but my agent reported "Oh, they liked your singing and your reading very much. They just wanted somebody else."

It made me feel like the old baseball player, Mike Ryba. For years he moved up and down the way stations of the St. Louis Cardinal farm system, playing every position including pitching and catching and throwing in a little managing and coaching from time to time. At the age of forty-two he finally made it up to the Cards as a relief pitcher and pitched an inning in the 1946 World Series. I caught him in the dressing room and asked him how it felt after the long odyssey of fried food and stuffy buses.

"Well, kid," he said, "I look at it this way. It's one step closer to Cooperstown."*

Very different from the audition is the interview, a preliminary which some producers go through because it makes them feel powerful to have people travel long distances to hear: "Thank you for coming in. We're just kind of looking people over at the moment, matching up types as it were. If you've changed your phone number, let my receptionist know on the way out."

Other producers do it because they honestly feel guilty about the desperate, unheard, unseen thousands who want so much to be actors, some of whom actually ought to

---

*I feel like a German psychiatrist explaining a joke, but I didn't want to spoil the bitter beauty of the quote. For any non-baseball fans among the readers, Cooperstown is the site of Baseball's Hall of Fame.

be. If you're a producer you know which group you belong to; if you're not, I'll tell you that there aren't too many of the first kind; it's just that I'm one of the people they always call.

Most actors take with them to the interview the attitudes of the artist. This is pure and fine and fatal. Private visions and ideals have no place there.

The right attitude with which to enter a producer's office is that of a door-to-door salesman pushing a line of ballpoints, plastic pigskin wallets, personalized gummed labels, or some other often peddled product. As you come in the door you must simultaneously be figuring out the character of the prospect and how you will persuade him that you are different from the other salesmen. In the case of a theatrical office you look first at the framed posters on the walls. Are there none? Then this is the producer's first show. For him, a fresh sincerity, a reference to the wonderful work being done in university theater, a glancing, deprecatory reference to some writing of your own for an English avant-garde film review. If you haven't, in fact, written for such a magazine, make one up. Some of the real ones look as if they'd been made up by actors.

Let us say there are many posters and almost all of them have girls adjusting a bra strap, and in big, splashy, white letters: "Naughty!"—*Trib*; "Sophisticated Fun!"—*Times*; "Warm Humor!"—*Post*. Quickly now, you are a man of the world. Crisply rattle off the Broadway shows you've been in, leaving out the one about the greed-caused mine disaster. Are you not a member of the Actors Studio? Tell a joke about the Studio. Are you a member? Tell a joke about some of the "nuts" at the Studio. Let us hear words like "technique," "craft," and "timing." You should give the feeling that were it not for the thick carpet (producers of comedies always have thick carpets) you would do a waltz clog. You are an old pro who has trouped with some great clowns. Chuckle reminiscently, and tell about a couple of them. Become suddenly serious. Remember you're a solid workman too.

Do the posters suggest high ideals and limited runs? "Somber Power"—*Trib*; "Shattering Indictment"—*Times*; "Strong Meat"—*News*. Look at your knuckles. Flex them as if you did a lot of work with your hands. Speak slowly and grope for words like "impact," "reality," and "truth." Are you not a member of the Actors Studio? Say you wish you were. You wish America were ready for Wedekind. You wish we had a national theater. You wish you didn't have to work on Broadway except in this play—but you have to eat (this lets him know that you know that your salary notions aren't as far out as your feelings).

Are the posters for musicals? "Hats in the Air!"—*Trib*; "Hats in the Air!"—*Times*; "Hats in the Air!"—*Journal*. This is a tricky one because you are going to be interviewed by a group of eight people, six of whom have no power whatsoever, and you have to find the right two almost at once. One of them will look as if he or she doesn't belong in the business at all, and in fact, he or she doesn't. However, because musicals cost a great deal of money, he or she is allowed to be associate producer and to put up $400,000. Associate producers don't know anything, but they know what they like, and it would help a lot if it was you. The best thing to do is to smile at the money while telling a story involving innumerable untraceable tent-show musicals to the other person who counts. One big, glowing "Hi!" done with a sweeping motion of the hand will do for the others.

There are, of course, innumerable variations. In a sense, I have done nothing more here than show you the four strings of the violin. Your melodies are your own.

Someone, somewhere, has just said "Tchah" and cast this book aside with a scornful word about prostitution. They couldn't be wronger. Nothing—well, almost nothing —that an actor or any artist does to get a hearing really represents selling out. Selling out is done on the stage, the page, or the canvas. An actor who, having achieved the job, upstages his fellows, or mugs for laughs, is selling out. He is selling out himself, the profession, the playwright, and the rest of the cast, which is a lot of sins for one mug, but it's true. Curiously, I have found that some of the most somber puritans in an office—"I let them know I'm a human being! I tell them if I don't like the play, and I tell them only my talent is for sale!"—are ruthless attention-grabbers onstage. "I feel that my character would be doing a little dance here while the rest of them are talking around the table. You see, my character is a neurotic narcissist and likes bright clothing . . . I have to give those little cries of pain while he's telling the story. It would be false not to."

This kind of thing, which actors usually describe as being "true to themselves," used to be called "flycatching" in an earlier, simpler day, and by any name it is a far worse betrayal than an office or audition act one puts on in order to catch the fleeting attention of those whose eyes and ears are dulled by the impact of too many smiles and too many pleas.

I am sure that before Rembrandt painted "The Night Watch" he laughed at a lot of very dull Dutch dialect jokes and slapped the backs of innumerable businessmen-sitters and behaved generally like a jolly tulip dealer or cheese merchant. He had to peddle the idea, after all, to a committee, always a tough business. When he came to painting the picture the integrity test became a real one, and he passed it, infuriating the tulip and cheese men by put-

ting them in the dark and behind each other's backs
because that's what his picture demanded. Posterity for-
gives him for saying, "Yes, Mynheer, your daughter's water
colors show real talent."

Posterity enjoys the picture.

Of course, just getting asked to the interview is a
triumph which the actor may be a long time achieving.
So sparse are the opportunities in our profession that we
give value to the meaningless in order to have any values
at all. An actor is always pleased that an actor's agent will
tell him personally that there is no employment for him.
If the agent does it over the phone it is a second-class triumph, but if he will actually let you into his office and
tell you face to face that we know no one who wants you,
the day is made. The more usual thing is that the reception lady tells you that the agent does not even want to
know of your existence. As a small safety valve, some
agencies place a pad on the receptionist's desk where the
actor may scrawl his name and phone number in the hope
that—well, what hope, really? It's just that it's better than
walking out. Still, if you write your name on six or seven
pads a day, you have at least given hostages to fortune.
You have taken time to make a specific effort. You have
made a sacrifice of your time and your self-esteem. Surely
if there are gods they will notice the offering.

Xenophon notes that when the Persians first marched
on Greece the Athenians made "a vow to Artemis that they
would sacrifice to her a goat for every one of their enemies
whom they killed, but since they could not get hold of
enough goats, they decided to sacrifice 500 every year, and
they are still sacrificing them today." You will remember
what happened to the Persians who were so foolish as to
come goatless to war. The actor tramping through the the-

ater district in the process called "making rounds" is in a sense sacrificing a goat every day—himself.

Another offering that an actor can make is the composite photograph. In a composite the actor has himself photographed in unsuitable roles to show his versatility. A boy in his early twenties will sue for attention with a glossy eight-by-ten which shows him as Polonius, Ghengis Khan, Pope Leo III, and as himself, sensitively brooding over some driftwood.

A day spent slipping these into envelopes, addressing them, stamping them, writing "Photo—do not bend," and carrying the thick, satisfying bundle to the post box, is not only a first-rate sacrifice but can give the actor the same kind of numbing anodyne that oakum picking provides for restless sailors when the trade winds fail.

Oakum is, I believe, eventually stuffed out of sight in various cracks and holes. So are the pictures.

"All right, all right," you cry. "Nobody makes you be actors! Why don't you get honest jobs and stop beating your heads against the wall."

"Soon, soon," we answer, but we are like the otherwise intelligent people caught by the one-arm-bandit slot machines. Everyone knows that the machines are about 90 per cent against the player, but that, of course, is the last player, the one who set up the jackpot for you with all his nickels. So much has gone into the machine now that surely one more nickel should—oops, could I have change of a dollar, please? I know, I know, but by *now*—wait, I found a nickel in the lining of my coat.

By the time most actors are out of nickels, there are few "honest" jobs for which they're not too old. My age, for example, is such that I can only accept top management posts, and I've still got a few nickels, so you can put your board chairmanship right back in your pocket or give it to some retired general.

Anyway, character actors' lives are being extended artificially by the aging of our audience and the concurrent stretching of the permissible age of glamour in our stars. Now that the majority of the audience is made up of what Ken Murray used diplomatically to refer to as "elderlovelies," a leading man under forty seems a little bit callow. If the role is that of a college boy, well, forty looks college age to those who Charlestoned their way through State, and so the sere sophomore with the big name is hired. What are we to do now with his instructor, fatherly Doc, who is described in the script as thirty-eight? To keep the spread with our hero, actors must be summoned who played college boys for Belasco and would have long since have earned the old Emeritus in a real college. And then there is Prexy. Older than Doc by far, he is played by an actor who remembers Edwin Booth but not many of the lines.

In our fast-moving society the years will quickly debar you from guiding the destinies of a bank, a business, or a nation but you're never too old to win your letter in the theater.

Illusions of age can be made to work both ways. In the nature-food stores you can buy books which tell how the Hunza people of Asia live to be a hundred because they eat nothing but potato peels or blackstrap root or whatever. This is one of those things that "everyone knows." Recently, a doctor went among the Hunza with open eyes and ears and discovered that the barrel chests came from rickets, the stories of advanced age from a desire to please on the part of a polite people. Told that they look a hundred years old, they always said they were, rather than embarrass the guest by revealing that their diet had made them look like centenarians at forty.

Perhaps the best and least meaningful rule about theater age was that set out by the wonderful Laurette Taylor in the case of the late Tony Ross. Tony, a splendid actor, was just about young enough to get into the Army in World War II, and his service did nothing to make him look younger. Neither did the comprehensive celebration with which he marked his release. Lying quietly with a couple of witch-hazel pads over his eyes on the day after his return to civilian life he was jangled into agonized attention by the phone. His croaked "Hello" was swept away on a crest of urgency.

"Mr. Ross, this is Margo Jones. We are making a change in the cast of a new play called *The Glass Menagerie*, and you must come right over and audition for us."

Tony's protests that this wasn't a good audition day were unavailing, he made his way to the office looking as if his army years had all been spent outdoors in the rain.

He husked a greeting, was given a script, and, on cue, read the Gentleman Caller's first line.

" 'I'm 22 years old. How old are you?' "

Tony looked up sadly and added a line of his own.

"Oh, for Christ's sake," he said, handed back the script, and started to walk out of the office. He was pulled back and made to finish the reading. Later, when Miss Taylor arrived from rehearsal, she was told about the actor.

"We had a wonderful man here," said Miss Jones, "but he was so old!"

"Who was it?" asked Miss Taylor.

"An actor named Anthony Ross. Just wonderful, but so old!"

Miss Taylor's face opened into that wonderful smile

with which she could sweep away everything including logic.

"Oh, that's all right," she said. "He's not old. He just looks old!"

The line got lost in a rewrite. And Tony went on to make the Gentleman Caller immortally his.

The great bogey to all actors is type-casting. Whenever two or three actors are gathered together this practice will be bitterly assailed. All will agree that a really fine actor—and there are two or three of them present—can do anything. Endless stories are told of summer-theater triumphs in which the juvenile did Lincoln's father to universal applause, or a twenty-one-year-old girl—the one who is telling the story—absolutely amazed everyone as the centenarian grandmother in *Whiteoaks*.

Someone will start adding the real ages of all the famous Romeos and Juliets, and it's true that you get into very big figures before you have named many of these famous presumptive teens.

Each person will have a story about how he or she was completely fooled in the theater by a piece of daring casting, and all will agree that this is the best kind of acting, indeed the only acting worthy of the name. The rest is hardly more than modeling.

My own story, and quite true too, is of how I saw an enchanting little girl in Paris play in Ibsen's *The Wild Duck* and only discovered after the play that she was the famous Ludmilla Pitoeff, three of whose grown sons were playing in the production with her.

Somewhere in the middle of this standard conversation, after a good, bracing chat about how repertory is best because you never play the parts to which you are suited, the talk will change to current employment problems, and someone will say, "I felt I was a cinch for the part. He's described in the script as a thin, stooped New England type, sort of a young Parker Fenelly. Now, if that's not me I don't know who is. I was absolutely perfect and I gave them a real baked-bean accent and wore my wire-rimmed glasses. Do you know who they took for the part? A little, smiling, fat man. You just have to look at him to know that he's completely wrong. I don't know how their minds work."

No one has ever found the first half of this conversation incompatible with the second half. In essence, unimaginative casting is the kind that gives the job to someone else.

My own career has been largely governed by the size of my mustache. When I first entered the theater I had a neat toothbrush and found myself repeatedly cast in TV shows as druggists, bank clerks, and shop assistants. My continual costume was a shapeless cotton coat. Trousers I didn't need since I was always behind a counter covered with empty cereal boxes and prescription bottles. I leaned over the counter, paced up and down behind it, sold people the empty boxes and bottles, but never came out because the camera would then reveal that the whole of my shop was the counter, standing amid similar fragments of police stations, country houses, and duplex living rooms eight feet wide.

Although my scope of movement was small, my characters ranged wide psychologically. I played a string of druggists once who had in common only the right to fill prescriptions. One of them sent his prescriptions on to Moscow. The cabalistic writing spelled not placebo, but the plans of an atomic submarine. This druggist was a fierce, menacing fellow who came within an ace of overpowering Ellery Queen when he came behind the counter. My qualifications for playing him were that the week before I had been a pathetic little wisp of a druggist suspected of filling a prescription with poison. As the show turned out, I didn't have the nerve. A maniac with a bigger part had done it.

Once, when the druggist had very specifically to be elderly, the casting director sent me regretfully away, then called back and said that the make-up man would transform my egglike face into a prunelike face, whiten my hair, and put knobs on my knuckles. "The big thing is," he said, "you've played druggists before."

I opened my mouth to make a mild jest about my lack of a Ph.G. and then thought better of it. The tide of irrationality so seldom runs our way, that we'd best be silent at such times. I said something simple, like, "That's true," and went off to be aged.

After some years of this I received a month's warning that I was to be a comical deputy sheriff in a Western. Having nothing else to do in the intervening month, I devoted myself to growing my mustache and went to the first rehearsal with a fine, ragged number somewhere between Bret Harte and Robert Louis Stevenson. Everyone was delighted, and there followed a series of deputies and town bums. The mustache grew to a full Stephen Crane, and I took on a sideline of "Living Calendar" parts. In almost every play, movie, or TV show set in the past, a character will come on very early and place you in time with a remark like, "This Colonel Washington seems a lot smarter than General Braddock," or "They say that young Robespierre is making quite a name for himself." With my mustache I had hardly to say anything at all. One quick close-up said "nineties" as clear as could be, but just to make sure, I would say something like, "Mighty cold today. Wisht I was in them Philippines with Teddy Roosevelt."

There are a lot of these parts, because our age has chosen

the nineties in the same way that earlier, more cultivated societies chose the Age of Pericles—as a daydream haven to be emulated in externals and envied in the irrecoverable equilibrium which these "giants in the earth" seem to have found.

According to the 1960s America reached a zenith some seventy years ago when stern but kindly parents and happy, hoop-rolling children ate ten-cent beefsteaks in beautiful old houses which drowsed in perpetual sunshine while everything tiresome was attended to by servants who were capable, cheerful, and cheap. Spiritually everything was at rest, and our values were examined and found good every Sunday between a fine flapjack breakfast and a succulent chicken dinner. Every Fourth of July we looked at our practical political position and found it worthy of fireworks and the flag.

All of this is said over and over again on TV and in films, and if you will hark back you will remember innumerable evocations where your time machine was halted by a thin actor with a big mustache, coming out on a front porch to say, "I seen one of them Lillian Russell postcards. Wow!" or, "That there Bryan and his Free Silver. Bah!"

In time Hollywood called the Westerns home and the demand for my mustache fell off. I trimmed it back to something between a Marshal Joffre and a General Pershing and bought a pair of steel-rimmed glasses. These permitted me to play accountants and men who are bitter because of losing out in the rat race. There are lots of these small-souled folk in current drama, and their glasses give them away as quickly and as surely as the cigarette betrayed the hidden scarlet letter on the bosom of the melodrama lady.

In the theater the dream and the nightmare are very close, or, as the Greeks put it: "Hard beside each other run the roads of night and day." The bigger the chance, the bigger the opportunity to look foolish, and the more people will see you do it.

In what I now call "The Affair of the Singing Druggist," I had the feeling that the roads of night and day went jointly down a roller-coaster slope.

It all began when I got a phone call asking if I would sing the role of Harry Druggist in a benefit performance of Marc Blitzstein's *The Cradle Will Rock*. I chuckled over the ineradicable identification with the pharmacy dodge and then explained to the caller that the whole thing was impossible because I was not a singer.

"Oh, we know that," he said airily, "but everybody thinks you're a perfect druggist. Will you do it?"

Vanity wrestled with common sense. When I heard the place of the performance, Philharmonic Hall, vanity was thrown all the way across the ring. The name Leonard Bernstein as conductor made the whole thing seem so impossibly professional that vanity was pushed right through the ropes. Then, just as in the TV wrestling matches, there came the dramatic turnabout. I saw the faces of my singing teacher, my friends, those who had heard me sing. I saw their faces as I was saying, "Oh, by the way, Lennie Bernstein has asked me to sing in an opera. Where? Oh, Philharmonic Hall. Solos? Yes, several. Well—mi, mi, mi— it's been nice—mi, mi, mi—talking to you."

Vanity came back through the ropes like a tiger and pinned common sense to the mat before I could say "Yes," and then I said it.

A nervous week later I was meeting someone who did not know what a perfect druggist I was, a preliminary director who hoped that I was a perfect musician. He handed me a thick portfolio and said, "You might like to look over the score."

"If you think it's a good idea, I will," I said, ever eager to do the right thing. "But I don't know how much good it will do. I don't read music."

He looked at me the way I look at people who ask if the Kentucky Derby is for trotters, and then, with a politeness which only imperfectly masked his contempt, asked if I would like him to play it through for me.

It sounded fine, and I was nodding agreeably to the sound of the plangent chords when he stopped and said, "That's where you come in. Haven't you been counting?"

I said miserably that I "don't count either." Throughout, you will notice that I said "don't" rather than "can't," trying to make it look as if I had once had a choice about music and had decided, after careful consideration, to do something else, perhaps more important.

I said that if he showed me where the "one" came I could do the two, three, and four, the way I used to when I played "Marching through Georgia" on the sandpaper blocks in the school rhythm band.

He explained that there really wasn't a "two, three, four" or at least not my kind of "two, three, four," because this music was in 9/8. (It's all over now, and I learned all kinds of things, but I never did find out what 9/8 is.)

When I left the preliminary coach he said, "You have nothing to worry about," with the same false heartiness with which one addresses the mortally wounded juvenile in a war picture. I gave him back the same smile the juvenile gives, showing the triumph of a sweet nature over extensive internal bleeding, and carried the score pressed very tightly against me, the title inward. I knew that if anyone saw it and asked me any questions I would begin to cry.

Common sense was everywhere demanding a rematch, but it was too late—too many people had thanked me for being good enough to do it, people who had not heard me sing but who said, "You're such a perfect druggist!"

I was passed from hand to hand. A kind lady, the concert pianist Shirley Rhodes, took me through the music over and over again. It was agreed that it was too late for me to learn to count, but that if I heard the scene enough times I would just "know." The lady said she thought I was very brave.

My own singing teacher endeavored to overcome my inability to follow what was happening by making colored crayon marks under the right words to make crayon marks under if you are singing in 9/8. Since he was not connected with the enterprise he did not have any need to be polite. He said he didn't think I was brave, but foolish, and that I had lots to worry about.

The days passed quickly, and I found curiously small savor in the game that vanity had prompted. Of course, I told my friends that "Lennie" was going to conduct me at Lincoln Center in an opera, but when they expressed amazement and disbelief, I shared both emotions to a disagreeable degree.

The concert was scheduled for a Sunday evening, and on a Friday midnight there gathered in Philharmonic Hall a cast of experienced singers and singer-actors, the conductor of the New York Philharmonic, and an actor who had frequently appeared as a pharmacist.

There has been a lot of high-flown aesthetic debate about Philharmonic Hall, but no side will be taken here. Suffice to say that on that Friday night I thought the place shockingly too big. One of my early teachers had recommended that I sing to an exit light in order to get a feeling of projection, and I sought the red glimmers in the far reaches and, on finding how far away they were, decided that the teacher had never been in a place like this. I repeated to myself, like an incantation, the story I had heard of Dame Edith Evans' first experience in the giant hall.

Dame Edith had flown from England to do two evenings of Shakespeare with Sir John Gielgud and Margaret Leighton, and after a few comfortable rehearsals in the cozy greenroom, was led onto the monster stage for a look. At first she gave the smothered gasp that well-bred persons substitute for round oaths, and then paced about the stage, peering into the abyss.

At last she cried out, "Johnny, Johnny," and Sir John came forward hastily with words of reassurance. They were not needed, however, for Dame Edith said cheerily, "You know, if you stare at it long enough, it's rather intimate."

I stared. I kept saying to myself, "It's just another theater," and answering myself, "Sure, and Yankee Stadium is just another playground, and Madison Square Garden is just another gym, and—what would happen if I got sick?"

I didn't get sick—or sick enough—not even on Sunday afternoon, when the dress rehearsal went as all dress rehearsals seem to, rather worse than the first get-together at the beginning of the production. We never really finished it, because they wanted to let the people into the hall.

The first part of the program consisted of excerpts from the Blitzstein-Hellman opera *Regina*, and some songs from unfinished work by the composer. We were to be the second half.

With some vague idea of getting the "feel" of things, I went up during the first act to a viewing box in the side wall from which, through protective netting, the artists can look down on performance and audience. The effect, at least on me, was like looking back down the Matterhorn while feeling for a grip on the slithy moss. All those heads! All those rows and rows and rows of potential scorners! "My dear, I didn't know whether to laugh or cry at that frightened little man with the ragged mustache. What did he think he was doing?" "I couldn't agree more. Such a pity when the rest of them were so marvelous." "I understand Mr. Bernstein told him never to—" But by that time I was in the rear of the box, pressed against the wall, trying to find a grip on the slithy wallpaper.

As the real singers went gloriously on with *Regina* I retreated to a small side cell and sat with a couple of people who were trying to eat chicken sandwiches before we were summoned to the stage.

I took a bite from mine, then, like Penrod, near the bottom of the doughnut box carefully placed the bite beside the cavity I had made. One of my colleagues smiled understandingly and patted me on the back.

"Cheer up," he said. "It could happen only in America, that you should make your debut in Philharmonic Hall."

It seemed only minutes later that Leonard Bernstein struck a firm chord and I took a deep breath and thought about two things—three things, actually, the last of which was the song I was about to sing, a charming celebration of how wonderful it is to own your own drugstore. The first thing I thought about was the terrible audition where my voice had fluttered. I wondered if this would happen now. The second thing was a comfort, the thought that Bernstein would somehow play notes that would make my mistakes sound like something that had been intended all the time. I know now why such people are called "maestro."

Then another glowing thought came to me. After all, my name in the opera is Harry Druggist. I thought of all the times people presumably wise in the ways of the theater had said to me, "The important thing is, you're a druggist."

"The only difference now is you're a singing druggist," I said bravely to myself, and burst, if that's the word, into song.

Everyone told me later that I sang just like a druggist. Now if someone will write a full-length work called *La Farmacia*, I will be ready to go to the Met.

It may seem that this story has no place here, but to tell the truth, now that the whole thing is over, it has a place in everything I do. Like a happy King Charles's Head, it chuckles its way into my conversation whenever possible, and sometimes when it's really not. I need not feel immodest since I am not claiming anything remarkable in the way of execution, but only, like Doctor Johnson's dog walking on its hind legs, to be remarkable for doing it at all.

However, let us now do to it what was originally done to King Charles's Head, and turn back to our theme.

Theatrical convention, false at first, may have sufficient power to make itself come true. It was the distinguished crime writer Raymond Chandler who first pointed out that movie gangsters were laughable and unrecognizable only for the first six months or so of their celluloid existence. By that time enough real gangsters had been to the movies. Fascinated by what they saw, they adopted it all, and "See if bright boy packs a heater," went from the screenwriter's typewriter to the back-alley realities of crime.

In his charming book *Stage Land*, Jerome K. Jerome describes the stage lawyer of 1906:

He is very old, and very long, and very thin. He has white hair. He dresses in the costume of the last generation but seven. He has bushy eyebrows and is cleanshaven. His chin itches considerably, so that he has always to be scratching it. His favorite remark is Ah!

Whatever their cause, once these conventions take hold they are hard to shake. The fact that I was a real newspaperman has not been of any help to me in getting reporter parts. I don't look like a newspaperman. The few occasions when I have been permitted to play one have always been of a special nature. I have been a newspaperman whose ineptitude led to a scandal (wrong picture caption), a sports reporter who could not even get the results of a neighborhood bowling tournament right and thereby caused embarrassment to many, a police reporter who made a nurse lose her job by bribing her to give improper information and then revealing the source—that's the kind of newspaperman I look like.

On the other hand, I got a job some years ago by coming out on the stage and saying to the hirers in the darkened hall, "Before you ask me any questions, I want to ask one. Who looks more like a bank clerk than I do?"

They gazed up at the slight, stooped figure in somber flannel, at the thin, colorless hair fighting for position on the narrow skull, and hired me on the spot.

On the other hand, though I bask in the belief that I look like a college professor, I cannot get the same endorsement that I did for the bank clerk. This despite the fact that I actually did set out to be a college professor and have never done anything in a bank but put and take.

The last time I was called to audition for a professor I got into the well-worn, leather-patched tweeds, filled the pockets with shabby tobacco pouch, cracked briar, and a folded copy of *The American Scholar*, stuck my finger into the traditional slim volume of verse—"Oh you don't know her things? George Meredith called her the 'crippled nightingale,' but it's true she's hard to find. This is from an edition of five hundred"—and went down to the interview.

This is going to sound like a pat joke, but the records of the Theater Guild will bear me out. They looked at this Mr. Chipsian figure, heard me read with the weary precision I remembered from so many classrooms, and then said, "Mr. Broun, would you turn to the second scene of the third act and read the college janitor for us?"

That's the part I finally played, with the weary precision I have brought to so many janitors.

There does come a moment of divine confrontation to some actors, the moment of meeting the good part in the good play. Once an actor has done this, he is made. It will do him no good to play a bad part in a good play or a good part in a bad play. These will bring him credit only toward unemployment insurance, but the good part in the good play means that he suddenly emerges as a person to be reckoned with, to have his caricature on the wall of Sardi's restaurant, to have his jokes—or his press agent's jokes—repeated in Broadway columns ("Woodie Broun postcards us to say that now that the firm of Mao-K isn't A-OK, the world looks go"), to have his opinions broadcast on TV forums ("Direct from his hilarious performance in 'Virgin Intern,' Woodie Broun will join us tomorrow night for a hard-hitting discussion of adolescent psychology"), and to be led into the rich pickings of the game shows ("Now, if Mr. Broun and his housewife partner can give alternate lines of this famous poem, a set of matched pony-skin luggage plus—").

There is one drawback to this sort of eminence. It means that the actor will play this same part over and over again. Only the name of the character will be different.

Still, those of us who have never had such a part will take it, ennui and all, if we can.

Actors at the top of the ladder, like rich nations, are inclined to a lot of grumbling about materialism and dross and the good times on the lower rungs.

Poor nations and obscure actors can only cry, "Jump, then." Peasant simplicity, the wistful daydream of modern urban thinkers, can be achieved by a simple act of bankruptcy. I'm inclined to feel, though, that it is easier for a camel to pass through the eye of a needle than for an East Side moviegoer to enter into the kingdom of the happy, dancing, singing, ouzo-drinking Greek dock worker.

Whatever is at the top of the ladder, actors cling and climb with a driving energy that could, if properly harnessed, lift the Empire State Building several feet. (I remember vaguely that the Book of Knowledge used to say that this event could be accomplished by the energy in a glass of water, but there are lots of oceans and lots of actors, and the building hasn't moved yet.)

They know how uneasy lies the head that wears the cardboard crown of fame. Once after a dinner where four current lions had been assembled by Lady Cork, a great tuft-hunter, Sir Walter Scott wrote, "If you are celebrated for writing verses, or for slicing cucumbers, for being two feet taller or two feet less, than any other biped, for acting in plays when you should be whipped at school, or for attending schools and institutions when you should be preparing for your grave, your notoriety becomes a talisman, an 'open sesame,' which gives way to everything, till you are voted a bore, and discarded for a new plaything."

Scott was the only one of the lions whose name would mean anything to anyone other than an encyclopedist today.

In most fields of endeavor a man may, after some years, learn his limitations, but since our only limitation, we feel, is bad luck, we actors will unflaggingly crowd the alleys, the agents' offices, and the producers' anterooms, when not leaving telephoned pleas with taped answering services ("This is a recording of my voice. You have thirty seconds in which to leave me a message"), or sending postcards to producers active and inactive ("Please watch me next Thursday morning at ten on 'Rocket Cadet'").

Someday, you see, they're not just going to say, "Thank you." They're going to say, "We want you to play this funny but tragic alcoholic with a wooden leg and a death scene."

And if none of this ever happens, what then? One can follow the escapist example of Twisleton Fiennes, a Regency jet setter, who said to his valet, "Place two bottles of sherry by my bedside and call me the day after tomorrow," or one can ponder the words of a Dostoevskian Dale Carnegie who shared his wisdom with me at a lunch counter.

While we waited for our thick cups of thin coffee he mumbled a disjointed mixture of misery and threat, railing against the conditions in an assortment of mental hospitals, threatening the "brass" with dire consequences if he told all he knew about World War I, refighting the Argonne, and just plain gabbling. In the middle of it he stopped and turned to me a face which was suddenly keen and urgent.

"It's like everything else in the world," he said. "You begin at the bottom and work your way out."

IMAGINE the *Queen Mary* entering New York Harbor at full speed with no one at the wheel. Imagine further that her captain, her owner, her designer, and the helmsman are stationed at the furthest reaches from the bridge, armed with baseball bats. Anything goes, and the winner gets to bring the ship into its berth.

Would you be surprised if the *Queen Mary* went aground off Albany or crashed into the base of the George Washington Bridge?

Don't, then, be surprised at all those Broadway flops. The conditions under which plays come to New York are about the same as those we set for the *Queen Mary's* unhappy landing. Instead of the four fighters we put on the ship, substitute the producer, the director, the star, and the author. For baseball bats substitute every weapon known to modern psychology. It takes a little longer to sink the play than it would to sink the ship, but the few weeks of rehearsal and tryout seem to disappear as quickly as the gap between the ship's bow and the rocks.

This is, of course, irrational behavior, but I believe that the irrationality is explained by the size of the stakes. Irrationality rises in direct proportion to the value of the prize. People run newsstands fairly sensibly, governments, armies, and big gambles foolishly. Complication isn't the answer. You can't explain Marshal Haig's campaign in Flanders or the South Sea Bubble or the Tulipomania on the grounds of the complex factors involved. There was just one factor, self-delusion, and to add another law, self-delusion rises in direct proportion to the value of the prize.

The modern theater is very big business for the winners, a kick in the head for the losers, and in a terrifyingly short space of time one is in *Life* or in limbo. Let's look at some of the stakes. A director, unless he is very well established, faces the following alternatives as a result of a couple of months of work. If the play succeeds he will receive a thousand or more dollars a week for from one to seven years. He will get this money sent to him wherever he wants it. He can count it on the beach at Tahiti, in an Italian villa, or while reading the scripts of new plays. The success of the play will bring him many scripts, and if any of them succeed he will have more thousands to go with the first lot, and more scripts and so on.

If the play fails he will go back to teaching acting in a studio on Ninth Avenue. In the summer he will direct a package production of *Under the Yum Yum Tree*, starring two television panelists.

Take a look at the author's problem. Success means the same thousands to him, plus the movie sale, plus a chance to have his next play put on. Failure means years of work for nothing, the death of something specially and personally his, and a set of reviews suggesting that, worse than

inept, he is actively malicious. He must keep, for the fore-
seeable future, his job as copywriter, house-organ editor,
or teacher of journalism.

The star can recover more quickly than either author or
director, but he usually has more of an ego problem—
hence why he is a star. Deprived, even for a few days, of
attention, applause and interviews, he begins to suffer like
a drug addict, and will often rush from the closing night of
a failure to make a movie on blocked currency in Mace-
donia.

The producer is the least involved from an ego point of
view, the most from the financial. A success can, in the
hands of the right tax man, make him rich for the rest of
his life. Thinking about how those stupid authors, directors,
and actors did him out of a fortune darkens the days that
follow his failures.

With all this at stake it is clear that each of these people
must be at the wheel. As they struggle over control, the
play, like the *Queen Mary* in our parable, may get very far,
perhaps too far, off course. The struggle may begin when
the group is assembled for the first rehearsal of the play, it
may develop later, or it may begin long before the project
is officially launched. The story which follows is quite true.
A few details have been changed to protect the guilty, for
whom I may someday work.

A writer I know was asked to lunch by a famous star to
discuss adapting an old movie into a modern play. The
star began the lunch with a few routine methods of putting one off ease, speaking indistinctly and softly to create
a sense of strain, bending forward suddenly and releasing
the famous ringing baritone when the writer craned for
comprehension, and putting out the proffered lighter with
little, outward puffs.

The actor moved onto a subtler plane when he began to

reminisce about the old movie. He recalled with pleasure the work of one actor whom we'll call Button Gwinnet.

"Wait a minute," said the writer, "Button Gwinnet wasn't in the picture."

"Oh yes," said the actor, "he played the pawnbroker who recognized the brooch."

"No," said the writer, "that was John Hancock."

"Then he played the detective sergeant who kept following the dwarf."

"No, that was Henry Knox."

"Then he played the Dutch diamond cutter, the one with the scar."

"I was about to point out," the writer told me, "that that was Sam Adams, when I noticed that my companion was leaning over the table with an intent expression, his steak knife tipped toward my heart. I had the panicky feeling that if I didn't admit that Gwinnet was in this picture he might lunge across the table and stab me. I thought the whole thing was silly and not worth arguing about. I also felt that as a civilized person I could rise above the bumptious desire to show superior knowledge—so many words to say I was afraid—so I said, 'Well, it's a long time since I saw the picture, and I guess I got confused. Gwinnet must have been the diamond cutter.' As soon as I said this he relaxed and attacked his food with little growls of pleasure.

"I realized then that the small sound which accompanied my speech was the snap of my spine. He had made me say something we both knew was untrue and he knew that from then on he would have no trouble with me. I didn't get to write the play after all, but I'm lucky I didn't have to pay for the lunch. I offered to three times."

This is only one way of gutting only one person, and the methods are as varied as the pages of a karate manual. It is interesting to me as one of the best examples of winning the duel with the pistols still in the case.

Let's take a typical first day of rehearsal and see what happens when the struggle begins there. Please believe that it has all happened. Sitting on a sagging cane chair in a half-circle of actors under a work light I have heard these words, and variations on them, many times.

It is traditional for the director to make a little speech to the assembled cast and, to make up another theater law, the length of the speech is in inverse ratio to the length of the director's career. One or two distinguished veterans start the rehearsal without any speech at all, but they are so famous that there is no power struggle in their productions, only a certain amount of shouldering for their attention.

This opening, to which I have added notes, is short but anxious.

"Ladies and Gentlemen," (our director has our undivided attention for perhaps the last time) "you are about to begin the wonderful experience of living with a truly beautiful play. I know it's beautiful, because Jimmy and I have been living with it for a year, and we looked at it from every aspect. We know that it's beautiful early in the morning and late at night, and even without all the help that you talented people are going to give it by bringing it to life on the stage."

(Here, with the speed of a pickpocket, the director is claiming co-authorship. Has he not "lived" with the play for a year, working with "Jimmy," the author? Jimmy is a rather dignified man named James, too dignified to say, "Don't call me Jimmy!" too unschooled in the theater to realize that, like the professor in *Die Blaue Engel*, he has just had the first egg broken on his forehead. The business about how good the play is without the actors reminds them of their secondary roles in the operation. The star senses this and interrupts.)

"May I say a word, Sludge? When this script was first sent to me I said no. I loved the play, but I felt the part was so powerful that anyone who approached it honestly would have ten years taken off his life. Our producer is a persistent man, however, and he kept coming back, so last month I took the script out to the ranch, turned off the phone, and really read it. I want to tell you the more you read it the more beautiful it gets, so here I am, ready, willing, and—I hope—able."

The interruption begins with a request for permission, at once shows its superfluity by proceeding without it, employs the masher's intimacy of the unsolicited nickname— did anyone ever call Belasco "Dave"?—and proceeds to point out that the play must need him or he would not have been repeatedly solicited. The reference to the ranch suggests those useful bargaining backups, Hollywood and money, and "approached it honestly," "shutting off the phone," and "really read," show him to be the kind of intelligent, integrity-laden actor who *must be listened to on rewrites.*

He will want them, probably in the form of jokes—which put years back on his life—and a big, sympathetic scene where he can be extra-honest. The modest note at the end shows his emotional balance and mental health, in case anyone was going to claim different.

"Thank you. That kind of loyalty will mean a lot to Jimmy and me in the testing times ahead." (In judo one uses the violence of the enemy's attack to undo him.)

"Now today we aren't going to start putting the play on its feet. (He hasn't decided how to do it.) I want us to read it through a couple of times, and I want to talk to each of you a little bit about your characters. (Perhaps the actor has an idea he could use.) These are real people, and we must get inside them, every one of them. Some of you have worked with me before and know that my reputation as an ogre is rather overdone. The only thing which makes me angry is a lack of dedication to the play. I will be quite harsh if I sense that, but otherwise I am only too happy to hear your suggestions and to work with you after rehearsal on anything which is not clear to you. I would hope that during these first few days you won't ask too many questions because I think many of them will be answered when I show you the structure that I have in mind for the play."

(The vagueness of the business about getting inside real people is calculated. It is an excuse for any criticism. "No, no, baby, you're still outside. You've got to clothe Jimmy's wonderful skeleton with your own flesh and heart's blood!" It means nothing except that the actor had better come up with an idea because no one else has one. "Some of you have worked for me" suggests that if you keep your nose clean he may use you again, the ogre part reminds you to be afraid, and the stuff about suggestions is to lure you into a spot where you can, if necessary, be accused of lack of dedication. "Don't ask questions until you see the structure" means wait till it's too late.)

"I believe our author wants to say a few words, so I'll turn the floor over to him for a few moments before we take a break so you can talk to the Blue Cross people and the wardrobe department.

(Lumped thus with fitters and statistics collectors, the author sustains his second egg, tries to make solemnity do the work of strength.)

"This play is a statement of something I feel very deeply about. I hope all of you do too. I am ready for all kinds of changes. I know a play is a living thing and has to be worked over, but I'm going to fight like a tiger to keep a clear line to what seems to me a very important idea. If the play fails it will not be because of the unsoundness of the idea but because we haven't done it justice. I very much hope that we will, and I think you're just the bunch who can do it. Thank you."

(This is the hedgehog defense. It lacks any threat to the others and is therefore merely a confession of weakness. The "clear line" is in for a hard time. The last stand is the invocation of the Dramatists Guild contract forbidding any changes without the author's consent. The answer to this is the producer's threat to close the play forthwith, and faced with closing or crippling, most playwrights vote for crippling. Their punishment is that the New York critics make notes of all the new lines the playwrights didn't like and quote them in the reviews.)

The appearance of exaggeration, for believe me it is really all true, is due to the short span of the whole operation. Speed up the film and you appear to have hysteria; slow it down and you have a corporate board meeting. The one person we haven't talked much about so far is the producer. He is the reason, really, why the whole thing happens.

Remember the oft-quoted passage from Conan Doyle's "The Silver Blaze"?

"Is there any point to which you wish to draw my attention?"

"To the curious incident of the dog in the nighttime."

"The dog did nothing in the nighttime."

"That is the curious incident."

The quotation is apposite to our discussion of producers because the producer, like the dog, should be expected to make the most noise and, curiously, doesn't.

When the actor-manager ran things we had a very different state of affairs. Men like Booth and Forrest in America or Beerbohm-Tree and Forbes-Robertson in England were no more engaged in maneuvering for position than was Louis XIV. They put up the money for their own productions, put their names to the theater leases, and headed the program. Sometimes, to finish things off, they wrote the play too. It is not my argument that all this produced the greatest theater ever, but simply to say that in such circumstances there wasn't any doubt about who was running things, and no time was wasted on finding out.

Even later producers who did not act or write their own material still were the sole proprietors of their shows and were entitled as the financiers to a respectful ear from all, whether what they said into it was nonsense or no.

Today a producer is too often a young man who discovered at the Yale Drama School that he didn't have it as an actor, writer, or director, and decided that ordinary business was just too dreary.

He brings to the theater a sense that it ought to be pleasantly challenging and an apartment big enough to hold backers' auditions in. He is a subscriber to a number of avant-garde theater magazines, swears by Bertolt Brecht and Eric Bentley, believes our theater should have "something to say" and will, unless stopped, wreck a production trying to make all the changes suggested by out-of-town critics, ticket brokers, and the ladies who book plays for theater parties. This latter group seems always to make the same suggestion, "Make the end happy and get Henry Fonda."

Even the older producers who are at least competent businessmen have had to give up much of their control. Since backers are for the most part persons with tax problems, clouds of accountants surround the producer's head like so many mathematical mosquitoes, droning out special conditions. Very often the producer hasn't time to attend the rehearsals, so busy is he with amortizations of the sinking fund on a five-year-level-term basis to be computed on a last-in first-out system as to subsidiary income.

His moment comes when the group is sitting in a Boston hotel suite reading bad reviews and wondering how it all happened. It is then that the producer recalls other occasions when all looked black. "And then they decided," he will say, "that *Away We Go* was a terrible title, and somebody said why not call it *Oklahoma!*" He will then tell the writer that Shakespeare used jokes even in *King Lear* and tell the star that he is glad the play was put on if for no other reason than that the world should see the star's performance. This kind of thing, done with a lot of energy when the others are weakened by a long struggle and a critical clout, can often give a producer control of his show in a single day. When this happens the director eventually becomes sulky and sits in the far left-hand seat in the last row sending messages to the actors by someone called the "production assistant," who, before he became the messenger, was the one who said, "How many regulars and how many blacks?"

Sometimes the struggle, like a particularly savage civil war, exhausts everyone so completely that a pretty good play is destroyed. I served in one such, where the author and director were locked in an artistic Indian Wrestle for six weeks. Neither gave any ground, and as they alternated in telling us how things should be done, we began to feel like those pigs at Cornell who were driven mad by being given alternating stimuli. Unlike the pigs, however, we were unable to relieve our feelings by biting the experimenters.

The director would urge us to bring a warm, natural realism and humanity to our roles, and after a ten-minute break, the author would speak to us of stylized comedy and the brittle beauty of controlled exaggeration. Agreeing to everything, we gave performances of a friendly, uncertain artificiality, reminiscent of the Corn Exchange Players having a shot at Chekhov.

After six weeks the director's knuckles hit the table and he departed suddenly, giving way to another director who, under a banner labeled ENERGY drove us to a pitch which, with a little more practice, would have won the Yale game. Too soon to find out whether this was the answer, we opened in New York, and too soon thereafter we turned in our suits and went home.

To read, it had been an exciting and promising play. One could understand the enthusiasm of those who backed it, and one could later understand their bewilderment and disappointment at what happened to it.

There is just so much time, just so much energy, just so much imagination. If all of it is used co-operatively, a play just might succeed. If it goes into a game of King of the Castle, the chances are dimmed. A fist fight among four watchmakers isn't much help to a watch, and a power struggle among the makers of a play is in the same class.

So much for being smug. It is, of course, fatally easy to be wise down below. That's why all the really good war memoirs are written by enlisted men and junior officers. That's why actors like myself always know exactly what's wrong with the play and with the theater itself. The funny thing is, of course, that we really are right. We do know what is wrong with the play and what is wrong with the theater. It's just that our knowledge will begin to blur if we are given any chance to use it.

Friends of mine are impressed that I always know whether the plays I am in are going to fail or succeed. I try to explain that I am not wiser than those at the top, it is simply that I have less at stake. At my salary, realism is not such an accomplishment. Tell me that success means a big check every week at American Express in Capri and my judgment might go to pieces.

So much, also, for being humble. Nobody really means it. At least, nobody in the theater does. Theater people share a quality with race-track gamblers. Coming back on the train from a losing day at Aqueduct or a losing play in Philadelphia will produce conversations which are philosophically parallel. I have been on both trains many times and the conversations I now quote are honestly representative.

Here we are coming home from the track. The speaker is sitting behind me on the train. As the years go by I begin to believe that it is always the same man, but when I turn around to look, it appears to be at least a different face.

"Ya know sumthin'? I had eight winners today and I din't cash a ticket. In the first that Beeby's Baby is a stickout. Hasta win. So what happens? The boy gets himself caught in a pocket going around the turn. How ya gonna win then? You gonna run the four-minute mile in a subway rush? You gonna beat a bunch of bum horses when they're like guards around ya? So in the second my figures make Jolly Jerry a cinch, and he was. Only thing he din't have no blinkers on so he went onto the outside where it was soft and run an extra half mile. Whyn't they put blinkers on him? In the third I had my best bet, Laughing Ada, and that's the one that really makes me mad. Yeah, I know she was last all the way. To run that bad she musta bin sick. How come those crooked owners don't tell you a horse is sick? If I had've known that Laughing Ada was sick I would of bet on the winner," etc.

So it goes, all the way to Penn Station. Infinitely wise, infinitely put upon, the speaker is a spiritual winner, a temporal loser.

Let's say that *The Soft Impeachment,* a play about academic life, has just been left in Philadelphia, and the company, according to its union contract, is being transported back to New York, "the place of organization," if organization is the right word. The star is speaking.

"I told them again and again, you've got to have someone to root for. If my character loses his integrity by accepting the associate professorship, then we've got no hero. I told them exactly how to make it into a hit. 'It needs one scene,' I said, 'a scene where I denounce the dean and force him to cancel the girl's expulsion, while outside you hear the students beginning to demonstrate for me.' It wouldn't have cost anything. Everybody who's offstage could have been yelling, 'Professor Moulson for prexy,' or something like that. That would have given me a new dimension, and they would have had another *Male Animal,*" etc.

The author says, "They never seemed to realize that the play was symbolic. When the set designer brought in plastic ivy and a sample of that rubbery stone wall, I knew they just didn't get it. They seemed to think it was a college musical without songs or something. We did it at the university theater with just black drapes, and that was the production that excited everyone. If Broadway had any understanding of simple honesty," etc.

The director says, "They never backed me up. I said I can't function as a director when a middle-aged baritone is allowed to direct himself in the role of a young intellectual. He's forgotten what young is and he never knew what intellectual was. He's supposed to be a professor and he kept bothering wardrobe to get him a fraternity pin. Still, if they'd put me in complete charge I'd have gotten a performance out of him. Didn't I get one out of," etc.

The producer said, "They don't know their craft. It's the unions. It's high costs. In the twenties we'd have kept this on the road until it was good. We wouldn't have been afraid of a good laugh, either. What's wrong with laughter," etc.

The battle for control has now given way to the struggle to get out of responsibility. No one was wrong and everyone was wrong. They all had a winner and didn't cash a ticket.

The trouble with this kind of thing is that nobody learns.

Scars are one thing, experience another. If all one learns are some new holds and grips for the next battle, then all we are doing is teaching our watchmakers to kill.

Cynics, of whom I am not one, are fond of pointing out that the less there is at issue in a political campaign, the more savage the campaigning. If you look up the elections of James Monroe and William Henry Harrison, you will see what they mean. So, they argue, the very bitterness of the power struggle is an indication that power is all there is to fight for. If our theater was making all kinds of "statements," the artists could rally 'round the flag, but as it is, the only flag to rally 'round is the Jolly Roger.

Certainly when we were discussing what was at stake earlier in this essay, we didn't mention chaplets of laurel leaves or anything like that. It was mostly money.

Theater people add to their discomfort by pretending that this isn't so. We are always talking about what a bunch of devil-may-care nonconformists we are. As it sometimes seems that every priest passed up a chance to be a big-league baseball player, so it sometimes seems that everybody in the theater has given up either a fortune in series TV or something important in the commercial line in order to stay unfettered, honest, and able to express himself. The difficulty arises from the twin goals of beating the bourgeoisie and persuading the bourgeoisie to pay $6.90 a seat to see it done.

The result seems to be an endless series of comedies about a businessman who defies his boss and a boss who admires him for doing it, while his wife: "Oh, Jim, I'm so proud! And darling, I'm just going to love going back to a little kitchenette, and making the beds myself, and darning your socks. I'd rather be plain Mrs. Jim Michaels, than the wife of Mr. Michaels, our sales manager. And Jim, I've got a surprise for you. I've saved your drafting instruments all these years."

However, let's have one dragon at a time. The badness of scripts deserves a lecture all its own. Let's return to that day when the company sits around reading the Boston blasts. A whole painfully erected structure called "reality" has just been swept away. Those ecstatic post-curtain self-congratulations are revealed as painfully silly. If the critics are right, a lot of smart people have been very wrong. There are a few people in the theater who react to this kind of thing with cheerful determination and minds unclouded by fear or anger. There are a few people in other fields who do the same, but not many anywhere, and in the theater the speed, the size of the stakes, and the temperaments involved, bring the scum to the surface of the boiling stew very quickly.

For now the struggle often re-erupts with extra virulence. Panic has ground a sharp edge on the knives. Urgency is the excuse for the bludgeon which we pad with the word "frankness."

Here the author, who has up to now been either shut out or coddled, depending on whether or not he tried to fight for power, becomes the center of things. He is fought for, as in other wars men fought for the Eagles of the Legions or the banners of the Old Guard. Possession of his ear, or more important, of his mind, may be the key to victory. There is a fixed belief in the theater that an author can, in two weeks in a hotel room, do what he was unable to do in two years in his study—make his play work. It is believed that he can do this despite the fact that he himself is now too frightened to have good judgment and that the instructions he receives from his associates are insanely conflicting. Sustained on chicken sandwiches and toothglasses of whiskey, he sits staring at hotel-room water colors and his typewriter. At the previous night's performance he will have been visited by at least two very distinguished theater people. Objective, unconnected with the play, they will have told him how to fix it very simply. The first one will have suggested that the first act is perfect and that the second act will be okay when the death scene of Professor Moulson's wife has been eliminated. The second one will have told him that the second act is reminiscent of the mature Pinero and that the troubles are in the first act. They can be eliminated by making Professor Moulson's wife die early, and using the strong death scene to hypo the middle of the opening act. The director will have given him a talk, mostly recriminatory, about suggestions ignored last summer when they were "living" with the play, the acceptance of which would have fixed things up long ago. Indeed, to listen to directors is to wonder why there is a dearth of good plays. All of them are such wonderful writers that if they would just stop directing for a while and go to the typewriter, the Athenian theater would be with us again.

One is reminded, though, of Jane Austen's Lady Catherine de Bourgh, who remarked comfortably of music, "If I had ever learnt, I should have been a great proficient."

When a playwright is continually asked for changes he becomes hysterical even if he is a playwrighting machine. I know this because I appeared in the only script I ever heard of that was written by a playwriting machine, an IBM computer programed to turn out a Western pantomime script for showing on television. Certain rules of logic were fed into the machine, that men desire gold and whiskey, that whiskey makes you shoot poorly, etc. Two characters, a sheriff (me) and a badman, were the protagonists, and the props were two guns, a bag of gold, a bottle of orange pekoe rye, and a glass. Prodded by its programers, the machine turned out endless variations of the simple drink-shoot-die-money-grabbing formula. Sometimes Jack Gilford (the badman) got at the whiskey first and in the subsequent struggle only wounded me while I, the abstemious sheriff, got the bull's-eye and the money. Sometimes the lawman was instructed by the robot writer to have another shot and died after inflicting what Penrod Schofield, in his novel *Harold Ramorez*, called "only a flech wond." Indeed, the scripts were about on the level of the adventures of Penrod's penciled picaroon, except that we swore no "vile oths" as the guns banged, the glass and bottle clinked, and the money jingled.

The computer crew showed us the actual scripts as they had come from the machine, neatly thought up by banks of tubes, neatly typed by metal fingers. We recorded one in which the sheriff triumphed and one which saw him fall, and then the crew showed us one of the last pieces the machine had written. After turning out a whole series of perfectly logical, satisfactory little plays it had responded to a request for one more variation with a petulant farrago of nonsense. In it I took the gun from the badman's holster, while he pointlessly spun the cylinder of mine, which he in turn had taken. In a desperate humor (can you anthropomorphize about a bank of vacuum tubes?) it had written over and over again, "Sheriff drinks, sheriff drinks, sheriff drinks" ("Note," says the psychiatrist, "the machine's need to blacken the name of the authority figure!").

We performed that version too, and when it was over I sought the scientists to find out whether the machine's last words had been an appeal to get in touch with the Dramatists Guild, but they, alas, had returned to their transistorized Bard, which may, by now, have progressed to the atomic *Hamlet*—"But I have that within which passeth belief."

The star has an advantage over everyone else at this point, the health gambit. Deprived of a song in a musical or a joke in a straight play, many stars react like rats deprived of vitamins in medical experiments. They droop, shrink, lose their skin tone, and bite anyone who comes near them. Miraculously, the restoration of the missing material will soon have them scurrying about as bright-eyed and glossy as before, or perhaps a little more so with the knowledge that no one will try deprivation again.

When the medical rats become disabled as a result of the experiments, the scientist has only to pick up the phone and call the white-coated Pied Piper in the cellar. The difference between experimental animals comes out as small variations in sexual desire, food hunger, and intelligence about mazes.

When a star droops as a result of deprivation, the whole production is in jeopardy. There is nobody to phone except the star's agent and then only to plead for help.

The weapon of illness is powerful, almost too powerful.

Like the atomic warhead it can, if used too often, destroy the bomber. One doesn't want the reputation of being a troublemaker. Better a few coughs, a slight warning hoarseness, a droop as one crosses the stage, than the open rebellion of taking to one's bed and announcing that the play—in its present form—is too exhausting.

Back to our author. He has half finished his chicken sandwich, and after all, nobody ever finishes a Boston hotel chicken sandwich, but he hasn't half finished the new scene, because usually he doesn't know if it is necessary, or, if it is, whether it ought to be funny or sad, nostalgic or nasty. After all, when he wrote the play, he thought it was just fine. He paid to have it mimeographed, and he was told only four weeks before that it was "a truly beautiful play." Why now these cries for change? Well, the audience, through its representatives the critics, and through its own failure to laugh at the funny parts or sit still during the dramatic bits has indicated that it doesn't find the play "truly beautiful." A novelist can brush all this sort of thing aside and wait for the judgment of posterity. But for a playwright, as for an actor, posterity is every night, and it ends when Mr. and Mrs. Posterity don't buy enough tickets to keep things going. Of course, this doesn't mean that novels are better than plays. When the group experience of the truly beautiful play works—when actors, writer, and audience are all caught up in the wonderful rightness of what is happening—it's a great deal more exciting than chuckling over Thackeray in an easy chair or following James Bond to bed on the printed page. It's just that the opinions of yesterday are no help tonight.

Still, granting that the audience is the test, it is also sometimes as hard to read the results as the chicken entrails which misled the Romans in 409. Laughter alone is no test. Nothing is easier than to make an audience laugh.

If an old character lady in a watered-silk dress says, "Well, I'll be a son of a bitch!" it is a sure-fire shriek (which is why old character ladies seem to be saying it all the time), but if there is no real reason for the line, the audience, which rocked and roared all night at jokes of this sort, will repay you at the curtain call with a scornful spatter of applause and a hasty exit.

So also in our current theater of the Analyst Boys at the Grand Guignol you can get very satisfying gasps and rigid attention while you describe a rape or reveal a quirk— "My God, your own brother!"—but by eleven o'clock, if these things have not had a purpose other than shock, the audience is in an uglier mood than the hero's mother. Sometimes a modern audience will convince itself that such a bad time must be cultural, but we'll get to that later.

Let's burst in on our playwright again. Has he solved that little problem? For whom? For himself, the star, the audience, the director, or the investors?

Since no one is sure what really ought to be done to the play except "improve" it, many out-of-town changes are as characterless as a housewife's trip around a living room before a party. When she is finished, the ash trays are all in different places and the ice bucket has been put back of the bottles, but it's the same old room, and none of the guests have a better time. But sometimes, for well or ill, something really big is demanded.

The problem for every author in this spot is where integrity ends and stubbornness begins. Is his objection to the big change the unrealistic childishness of one who lacks the maturity to accept help? Is he even self-destructive and desirous of punishment through the death of the child of his invention? Does he fear to admit his inadequacy as a writer? Or—wait, now wait. Does he alone have a vision which rises above grubby fears? If he holds out now, will everyone thank him—at the anniversary party—for the steadiness of purpose which brought Truth through storm and mutiny?

How can you tell? There is no answer to that one—not even later when the whole thing is over. There are as many "if-onlies" in most plays as in a Mary Roberts Rinehart mystery story. But there in the room, in an atmosphere with the worst features of a pressure cooker and a grave, something must be done very quickly. The actors have to learn it, the stage manager has to change the routine of the show, the electrician wants to get the changes into his light plot, the costume lady has to get different clothes, the carpenter has to rehang the upstage door so it will open inward for the big new entrance which—"They're all waiting on stage for this, Jimmy. For God's sake, can't you write any faster than that? We only have three more days before the Philadelphia opening, baby, and if you thought they were mean here in Boston wait till you—all right, all right, I won't distract you. I'm just trying to tell you that this is no time to make like Shakespeare. What you need here is some of that TV technique. Those guys write a show a week. So what's so hard about a couple of lousy scenes? Moss Hart rewrote the whole of *Light Up the Sky* out of town. A whole new act every week. We don't want that much. Anyway, why are you always kicking when we ask for more sympathy for the hero? He's your hero, after all. He's a college professor, not Benedict Arnold. You got to have somebody to root for or you're—well, you don't have to bite my head off. Hey, speaking of bite, would you like a little something to eat? We could send down for sandwiches."

Few twentieth-century authors have the toughness of Henry Fielding. When David Garrick complained to Fielding that a scene in his new farce, *Wedding Day*, ought to be cut for fear of demonstrations in the audience, Fielding replied, "No, damn them, if the scene is not a good one, let them find *that* out."

When they found it out and reacted accordingly, the bruised Garrick retreated to the greenroom, where, according to an eighteenth-century chronicler, he found Fielding "Indulging his genius and solacing himself with a bottle of champagne. He had by this time drunk pretty freely, and cocking his eye at the actor, while streams of tobacco trickled down from the corner of his mouth, 'What's the matter, Garrick?' says he, 'What are they hissing now?'— 'Why the scene that I begged you to retrench; I knew it would not do.'

" 'Oh, damn them,' replies the author, 'they have found it out, have they?' "

Such talk is surprising from a playwright, though not from a man who chews tobacco while drinking champagne.

But when the author of *The Soft Impeachment* has acceded to assorted wishes and made something to fit the new clothes, the new entrance, the new door, the new light plot, and the new approach—what does he do if it works less well, as is often the case, than what he had before?

Then it's back to work and a black eye for the one whose suggestion won the last time. Sometimes the author rebels or collapses and then there appears that formidable figure, the Play Doctor. Unbeknownst to the author he has been watching and taking notes for several days before his public appearance before the company. He knows just what to do but makes a great show of being no more than a humble penwiper for the faltering genius.

"The only reason I consented to come, ladies and gentlemen, is that I believe that you and Jimmy have a truly beautiful play here, a play worth all our best efforts.

Mine will simply be to do a bit of carpentry, a bit of sharpening, a shift of emphasis. I'm sure you all know, as theater people, that a very little polishing can mean a great deal to a gem."

No one pays any attention to this ritual, for all know that this simple carpenter carries not a hammer but a hatchet. The only questions are whose name is on the hatchet handle, and whose skull, or skulls, the hatchet will cleave. Is he the creature of the producer, the director, or the star? We will know very shortly, when we find out whose previously ignored ideas are being sharpened, shifted, and polished.

Sometimes the doctor is a new director.

"I'll be talking with each of you individually, but right now I want to say that what we are all going to strive for in the short time remaining to us is high style. You must think of this play not as a naturalistic examination of college mores but as a Restoration drama in tweeds. Don't be afraid of artificiality. Think of the older meaning of the word artifice, a skill. I know you all have skills that haven't been used as yet, and it's going to be very exciting bringing them out. We have a truly beautiful play here whose impact has been muffled. Ladies and gentlemen, we're going to take the gloves off!"

And off we go to Philadelphia! The three days since the new man took over in Boston have proved that a couple of actors can't manage high style and new lines in four performances, and we eye their empty seats in the parlor car with a mixture of fear and relief like so many World War I fighter pilots. We, of course, have Von Richthofen right in the car with us, oiling his twin Spandaus in the drawing room. We stare at industrial Massachusetts through the grimy train windows and try to think how to say lines like, "Personally, I feel a professor should stay out of politics," with high style.

In Philadelphia we get the new actors, the author gets some new water colors, the star gets a new throat doctor, and the play a new chance.

If the right person has won our battle, perhaps things will turn out well. There are some plays each year which succeed, after all. It just seems such a pity that there always is a battle. It isn't true as some claim that this healthy competition of tooth and claw is a creative process. The only thing habitually written in blood is a pact with the devil.

Henry James said to Compton Mackenzie, "I once wasted ten—indeed, twelve precious years in foolishly supposing that in the light of experience I could grope my way towards a more—towards that always elusive—in short, that I could add yet something to what, when it was written, I had given all that I could give at that time."

They don't give you ten years in the theater and "always elusive" goes double when the hands which are seeking the elusive are clammy with fear. Still, who wouldn't be afraid? Philadelphia is the last chance. If it doesn't work here, there will be that awful meeting in the hotel sample room when the producer begins—

"Perhaps you're wondering why I canceled the rehearsal call at the theater. Well, I guess you've all seen the Philadelphia papers. I want to say that I don't think I've ever been with a more talented and hard-working bunch in my life than you all, and I hope and pray that we'll all be together again someday. We still feel that we had a fine play but you have to face reality—" and so on down to the gloomy business of the distribution of railway tickets and the mysterious call for us all to turn in our scripts. I often wonder what they do with them. Some-

where in a warehouse there must be a kind of theatrical
Arlington where they are piled, but what the producer of
a failure wants with the now illegibly marked-up copies of
his mistake, I don't know.

Once, when I was in a play which closed so quickly that
they didn't have time to ask us for the scripts, I spent a
dollar mailing it back. Scripts, the man at the post office
told me, aren't books and don't get the cultural benefits
of the book rate. This one certainly wasn't a book or a
play, but they had written me and asked for it. I thought
of sending them the dollar, which might have been more
useful, but like most actors I live in the illusion that the
producer of a failure really will hire me again, and I try,
standing in the rubble, to please even those who are buried
under tons of bills and bad reviews.

Assuming that our play is not beaten to death in Philadelphia, the knuckles whiten again on the handles of the
baseball bats and the principals have one more try at beating each other to death.

The time of dainty deadliness is over. For the rasp of
rapier on rapier we substitute the thud of fist on chin.
There is wailing and rending of contracts.

There is a wonderful new word in the business vocabulary which covers situations like this. The word is "Associates." "Partners," that old-fashioned word, suggests
men with an obligation to each other—and indeed, legally
partners are liable for, and to, each other. "Associates"
suggests a group of Balkan guerrillas banding together
briefly to win a small battle, then splitting again into
Marko's men against Stoyan's men with some help from
Kyril's group—until, of course, Stoyan is destroyed at
which point Marko will have it out with Kyril.

In Philadelphia, hunting cries echo through the halls of
the luxury hotels where the Associates club together, but

the echo is the problem. Where does it come from? When you are alone in your room, are they all alone in theirs too? Or are they all in one room planning how to get rid of you? Well, there's one way to find out, and the house phones ring endlessly and the doors are tapped continually. Then, of course, if you find someone alone and stop for a chat, how awful it is to have the next one come along and think that the two of you are plotting. Sometimes you do it just because it's expected.

I remember once finding my director wandering in the lobby of the Hotel Taft in New Haven. It's hard to hide in New Haven, because there is only one hotel and one outside restaurant which are of executive timber. But the rest of the contestants had managed to hide from the unhappy director. And on opening night too.

"Come and have a hamburger," he said. I was embarrassed because my part was of such a nature that we hadn't got to know each other very well.

"Take your hat off on that line," were the only words he had ever previously spoken to me. It was clear also that a role of that size does not entitle one to the director's company.

"I know what you're thinking," he said with the sweet smile of St. Sebastian waiting for the arrows to stop hurting, "and it's true. I've called every room they could be in and gone across the street and looked for them there. When a director can't find producer, author, three stars, or a gaggle of agents on opening night in New Haven—well—"

Neither of us alluded to the subject again but wandered into a happier past before we had either of us got in the theater. He told me about his boyhood in England, and I gave him some inside dope on the newspaper business.

I think that with considerable gallantry for one now off

the expense account, he paid for my hamburger, but I'm not sure. I know that I never saw him again.

I've often wondered where they hid. In view of the shortage of hidey-holes, a good guess would be that after he left me and went to his room, they erupted from a linen closet and hurried away, leaving someone to give him a one-way ticket on that post-theater train to New York, which, unlike the one in the spiritual, carries innumerable liars, gamblers, and four-day creepers.

As the mortality rate among the talent rises, the creative activity tends to dwindle. It is said that one of the reasons for the downgrading of Josef Stalin was an effort to persuade Soviet scientists and artists that originality didn't mean exile.

When a play is on its third director and second play doctor and is minus four or five of its original cast, you will find that save for those actually onstage, the actors are hiding in the lounges appropriate to their sexes, provided they have not been made into headquarters dugouts by the campaigners, while those onstage are endeavoring to be inconspicuous until they can get offstage. The creative process? "Listen. Just say the lines loud, say, 'Yes, sir,' when he speaks to you, and get lost. The last one that made a suggestion got a fifteen-minute talk on how the play wasn't about him and a five-line cut for a climax . . . Whatever you do, don't say hello to the author. They're going to bar him from rehearsals, and you don't want to get known as a friend of his . . .

"The company manager said he wanted to see me after rehearsal. I wonder if he's going to give me the money for my dry-cleaning bill or a ticket home. It's hard to concentrate, but I'm afraid to ask him . . . I hear George was here last night and that he's taking over the direction . . . No, no, he said it couldn't be saved . . . I heard they're going to book four weeks in Detroit and get a director from the Coast . . . Our producer asked me for a Dexamyl this morning. I don't suppose he'd have asked me if they were all that dissatisfied with me. I mean there are others he could ask."

And on the upper levels? "I'm just going to tell you one thing. The public thinks college professors are communists and after eight weeks in your play I think this one is and so are you . . . Jimmy, don't pay any attention to him. I've been for you right along, and I tell you we'll be in good shape if you'll take my rewrites for the end of the first act. For God's sake, am I asking for co-author credit? Not that I don't deserve it . . . When I started in theater we dealt with ladies and gentlemen. Can you imagine Robert B. Mantell calling me a son-of-a-bitch? Well, in those days can you imagine me taking it?"

Somewhere under it all there are the bones of a "truly beautiful" play, and sometimes these bones rise again, polished white by the tides of acid. Sometimes the same tides melt them.

> As we wax hot in faction,
> In battle we grow cold;
> Wherefore men fight not as they fought
> In the brave days of old.

The Romans on that occasion were united by the Etruscan invasion, but I think a theatrical Horatius might have more trouble. Who would stand at the right hand and who at the left? The center of the bridge is the star spot, after all. Nobody ever calls it Herminius at the bridge or Spurius Lartius at the bridge. It might well end up with Herminius and Lartius sinking knives in Horatius and throwing him in the Tiber while Lars Porsena, blessed by the Nine Gods (there were more newspapers in his day) marches in and closes Rome by the end of the week.

Let's leave *The Soft Impeachment* in Philadelphia, its leaders endlessly locked in struggle, like the two moose in a glass case at the Natural History Museum. If I remember correctly a pack of jackals or hyenas or something nasty wait eternally on the edge of that power struggle too. I suppose it's the nature of the moose to lock horns with any other moose he can find. It may be that it is the nature of the theater person to behave like a moose, but I don't believe it is inherent.

Once when I was driven to protest what I thought was unfairness to me in a tryout (I got fired), the author took me by the arm and said, "My boy, when people are frightened, fairness is the furthest thing from their minds." Perhaps that's so, but the question of why everybody is so frightened comes first. Of course, a play cannot be done with the same comfy busyness with which one hooks a rug or makes a blockhouse out of matchsticks. When Joe McCarthy managed the New York Yankees he wouldn't let the players smoke pipes. "Pipes make you contented," said Joe, "and champions aren't contented." Neither, of course, are creative artists. Adrenalin is the fuel of creativity. At the same time, it has to be said that where fear may drive one forward, terror—and it is terror that I have been talking about through most of this essay—stops everything right up to breathing. I remember some photographs taken by a German psychologist. They were of nursery-school children in a situation where both activity and inactivity promised punishment. The children rolled themselves into balls on the floor. I have often seen theater people lying in orchestra seats in the same foetal knots. When I see it I switch to the Number One breakfast without an egg and ask the hotel to move me back to a room on the courtyard without a bath.

To say, "We must all be braver," is as pointless as writing one of those books for failures about how a little confidence will make them rich. (They buy a lot of the books, though.)

With that in mind, I give the following advice to all factions in the theater.

Never let fear cloud your judgment, nor jealousy distort your attitude toward your fellows. Use every minute of the working day in work, without any time off for temperament or tries for personal aggrandizement. Be generous in victory, philosophical in defeat. Listen to those with talent and be kind to those without it. Enter into the job with a selfless devotion to the total production. In being true to it you will be true to yourself.

There could be more, of course, but the broad outlines are there, and I guarantee that anyone in theatrical power who follows the above rules without exception, will end up as the producer, director, author, or star of a Broadway smash. Perhaps you had better read over them again.

PSYCHOANALYSTS do not use the word "cure." They promise nothing and suggest only that they may ameliorate a condition, perhaps make the non-functioning function after a fashion.

There persists, however, a legend among psychiatric patients that if you can get the right man, you can hop into his office a toad and emerge a number of dreams later as a happy, laughing, fearless demigod, who will shortly be rich, famous, and loved. If this isn't what you're getting, you don't have the right man.

Theatrical producers have something in common with analytic patients—indeed they sometimes are analytic patients. They believe that you can take a toad of a play, a toad, moreover, which has spent time beneath the harrow, and after a number of days in Boston, Philadelphia, Washington, Wilmington, New Haven, or any other town with unbelievably selective audiences representative of main currents in American thought, emerge with a happy, laughing, fearless hit which will soon be rich, famous, and the recipient of a Pulitzer Prize.

Admittedly, for many plays, the out-of-town tryout is no more than a shakedown cruise in which the adjustment of a few bolts will make all shipshape. It is not, however, the efficacy or validity of the preliminary tour that will be talked about here, but the kind of life the average actor leads from the moment he files into the parlor car, to the moment of return to New York for the final throw of the dice or—if the play has died on the road—the trip to reactivate his unemployment insurance book.

In the week before the entrainment we have taken the first step by inspecting the list of available hotels and making known our wishes to the show's press agent by signing up on a sheet where, from what we have chosen, a pretty good guess may be made as to our salaries and also our hopes for the play. When too many actors put down the YMCA it is time for a producer to think twice about the whole project. I do not know, however, whether the producer ever sees the list. I sometimes have wondered whether anyone saw the list, while facing a supercilious desk clerk who says he doesn't know anything about our little show, he only knows about the Princeton game and why don't I try the ones down by the depot.

Once in Washington I stayed at a hotel apparently made entirely from brown linoleum and inhabited by retired civil servants in bad repair and the senior classes of rural high schools. A sign in the lobby encouraged these latter with the words, "Our cafeteria specializes in mass feeding."

Another time the whole company received brochures from a place in Philadelphia with wonderfully low rates and the slogan "The Hotel Where the Stars Stay." I found out later that the stars were a couple of famous but demon-hunted playwrights who had gone there to drink in a little of the rich atmosphere of decay and despair. I fell for the brochure and for the lobby, which was as clean and inviting as the entrance to a trapdoor spider's burrow. I registered and left my bag with a desk clerk who, without showing me the room, told me jovially that its last occupant had been a princess.

I began to be doubtful when, returning from the theater, I got a look at the elevator and its operator. Surely the place where the stars stayed could do better than that unshaven old man in the collarless neckband shirt. He was senilely annoyed that I interrupted his reading of a magazine whose very title would get this book banned, but showed a little grim amusement when I told him my room number. He looked like one of those unsympathetic people in Gothic stories who direct you to the haunted chamber. I felt respect for him, though, when the old elevator began to claw its way upward at such an angle that both of us lay against its once-gilded left wall. A man who would ride in it many times a day didn't lack grit. As I emerged into the hall, a damp slot carpeted with—but I never took a second look and I'm not really sure.

"If that there princess left any of her pitchers behind, save me one," said the elevator man with an ugly approach to animation. "She was dancin' down the street at the strip club."

Terrible smacking noises of relish pursued me down the hall. When I opened the door—have you ever noticed how much more terrifying the old ghost stories are than the creepy stuff on television? It is because they leave something to the imagination. The screen shows you an efficiently constructed electronic monster or an actor in some nasty make-up, but the old stories let you shop among your own fears with something like, "What I saw when I opened that door burned itself into my consciousness for a frightful moment before the brain fever took my reason. Today, white-haired at thirty-five, I live in a quiet seaside cottage to which my ruined health drove me. Even in these peaceful surroundings I sometimes wake at night screaming so loudly that kindly neighbors come to comfort me. I cannot tell them what I saw. I can never tell anyone."

Let that paragraph describe my room that evening. I don't wake up screaming, but on subsequent trips I have tried to wake up in peaceful, comfortable surroundings no matter what I thought of my play.

But come now, if I keep on this way we will be as late for the train as our ingenue, who always goes first to Penn Station. In time critics will call her "a shimmering will-o'-the-wisp," but the stage manager has another name for her. My own name for these breathless, big-eyed creatures in uneven felt skirts is chocolate-covered razor blades.

The executives and the author go at once to the drawing room, and if you hear a typewriter tapping in there it is a bad sign. It means that last night's run-through for the actors' friends went badly, and when you can't get enthusiasm from actors' friends you are in desperate shape.

The rest of the company produces books, chessboards, crossword puzzles, and other evidences of cultural elevation, but there is a certain amount of exploratory eddying in the aisles.

For the weeks of rehearsal in New York our connection with each other has been just in working hours and the lunch breaks. We have all had our own homes and families and personal lives. Now for some weeks we are going to have a home, family, and personal life all encapsulated in the production. We examine each other with new eyes.

Who would we like to spend time with and who would we like to avoid without hurting feelings and how can it be done? What are any of us going to do about the desperately lonely old character man with his murmured dirty stories and his endless and detailed descriptions of dinners in the 1920s? He is a marvelous actor and quite a good-hearted man, but we find ourselves almost hating him because he suggests what we may become. Who likes us and who doesn't? There are enough rebuffs in our professional lives without risking another with a suggestion about dinner. Sex enters into this but not to the degree that people outside the profession steamily imagine. Aside from moral considerations, which weigh as much with actors as with anybody else, there is the practical dictum which a veteran male star put this way: "It's okay to be onstage with the ones you're not sleeping with, but there's always trouble from the ones you're not sleeping with any more, so why not visit backstage at some other show?"

Rank within the play means almost nothing. There are a few stars who do not like to have more than the single, symbolic democratic luncheon with small-part players, but for the most part, since the need is social, the test is social, and that old character man fails it, even though his death scene in the third act compels the admiration of all of us. When we are not admiring him we are avoiding him. How easily the poor man sees through our evasions about going back to the hotel to wait for a long-distance phone call, and yet how fatal to let pity grab you by the ankle and drag you down into that stagnant pool of old conquests, old programs, and old menus.

On arriving in the first town, usually New Haven or Wilmington, the actors hasten the business of getting settled so they can hurry over to look at the front of the theater. Whatever shape the play has taken in the dark

privacy of rehearsals, it has an outer shape indicated by billboards and pictures which everyone wants to have a look at. Even those whose contracts guarantee that their names will appear in certain places and sizes will reassure their suspicions and comfort their self-loves by standing for a time in front of the houseboards drinking in the magic words "With Heywood Hale Broun"—well, those are my magic words. You can supply your own.

The smaller players have been guaranteed nothing but are always hopeful of crumbs. They know that somewhere on the wall of the lobby, there may be a list of everybody, but how prominent is it? Is it one of those bland but really disappointing alphabetical lists where one's eminence is simply due to having the name Aalborg? Or is it one of those where you can grind your teeth because you come two names after that dreadful phony and console yourself that that pompous poop is ahead of only that theatrical tweenie, the general understudy.

Having once been the general understudy, I know that the pompous poop can have no satisfaction in finishing ahead of this never-to-be-transformed frog prince. In the play *Point of No Return,* where I filled this minor office together with a three-line part as Second Bank Clerk, I had my first chance to "go on" for someone, but there was no excitement, no congratulations, and no interest on the Coast. On the day in question, our star, Henry Fonda, was out with a sore throat. A featured player took over for him, the First Bank Clerk took over for the featured player, and in the bank scene I walked across the stage two additional times looking judicially at a check that I had made out to myself in the sum of $8437, signing it in the name of the president of Belmont Park (return on an imaginary daily-double ticket).

And yet, to return to what I said about the lack of caste

in theater social life, it was in that play that I was admitted to the friendship of three very distinguished actors: Frank Conroy, Colin Keith-Johnston, and Robert Ross. (Frank and Bob are gone now, but what all three taught me in the long sessions around the dressing-room teapot is not forgotten. This little alphabetical listing is less of a memorial than I owe them, but I try to tell some of the things to other actors, now terrifyingly younger than myself, so that, as Samuel Butler said, "We shall meet as all men meet, on the lips of other men.")

When the actors have read all the names, they look again at the whole billboard, which is, in a sense, the banner under which they will march. All those names and the big title give a new reality to the up-to-now amorphous enterprise, as the regimental guidon gives symbolic identity and cohesion to the troops.

Now it is time to go into the lobby and look at the rehearsal pictures that will make do until the set is up and we are photographed in costume. Are you in any of them? Well, I think this headless figure in the background is me. It looks like my tweed jacket—and yes, here I am, full face, and half an inch high in the fight scene. Here are the star, the author, and the director, smiling chummily over the script, a pose they probably will never take again, unless it be at a prize-receiving party.

And now inside to look at the list of dressing rooms. The wiser actors have approached the stage manager days before with requests about dressing with their friends. Bearding him on the first afternoon in New Haven is asking for a shriek of rage, because he has been there two or three sleepless days ahead of the company, trying to find out why the setting, which slid back and forth so ingeniously in the cardboard model, is now groaning and splitting at every tug.

We inspect the set and shake our heads over the furniture ("You mean I have to climb up on that little table?" —"That's the chair I have to carry out on the porch? They better write in a butler to help me."—"This is the only Long Island mansion ever furnished out of the Salvation Army." etc.). If the stage manager ever hears any of this he has many ways of getting even, so it is only a discontented murmur, like that coming from a beehive when rain washes the flowers clean of nectar.

On the call board is a sign which tells us all to be at the theater, ready to go, at a mid-afternoon hour. In the many times I have been out of town this has never but once been accurate within three hours of the actual starting time. You're thinking I'm going to say that was the one time I was late, but I'm too timid for that. A lot of actors were, however, and caught hell even though the stage manager admitted it was the first time in his experience that everything was ready on time.

Now we go back to the hotel for the unpacking and the placing of the portable lares and penates. In my own case, I would not dare to undertake a part, no matter how trifling, without having on my dressing table a museum figurine of a Tibetan gentleman who was so perfect in life that he was chosen to receive Buddhahood. I also take him to contract signings in hopes that his serenity will soothe me as I read the terms.

On my bedside table at the hotel stands a little, flat-hatted Japanese sage in ivory. He is a traveler like myself, as shown by his staff, wallet, and bottle, and his comfortable smile suggests that he enjoys his wanderings. On difficult mornings I look at him for quite a while before I rise.

Then comes the small shelf of books, the traveling clock, which spares me asking the desk clerk for such a decadent

waking hour as noon, the portable radio for football games
—"I have an entrance. Tell me who scores the touchdown,"
—and the family snapshot to remind me that, agreeable
though hotel life is in short stretches, I will not become,
like the old character man, a sojourner in coffee shops and
corridors.

I think that most actors have a real feeling of exhilaration at these outset moments. There will, of course, be
all sorts of difficulties, but they will be difficulties connected with a single specific goal, the success of the play.
The day-to-day horrors of "Where am I going? What is the
shape and meaning of my life?" are, for a time, put aside.
There are no household details. No one will ask you to
get the laundry, buy another chop, or help with homework.
These are comfortable tasks in normal times, but as you
cannot ask a 100-yard-dash man to tell you the time in
mid-race, you cannot ask an actor for much diversion of
attention during the critical days of a play. Even if the
play is bad, the actor worthy of the name will put aside
his objective judgment and fight to raise another Lazarus,
or at worst to see that the body is laid out becomingly.

If the play is one which needs only tinkering, the actor
will be working very hard on refining and polishing his performance. Freed of the need to learn new scenes every
day, he can find the more satisfying tiredness of checking
and rechecking his timing, removing hesitant half steps
from his movements, and studying the gestalt of the person whose name he bears every night from 8:40 to 11:10.
(Sometimes it is from 8:40 to 11:40, and then there is
the problem of unlearning the material which the reluctant
author pares from the part.)

Few actors care much for cuts in their parts—"But that
line really tells something vital about Joe's attitude"—but
the distress is greatest when the part is least. Many a time

I have heard an actor say mournfully, after losing a line, "There goes 20 per cent of my part."

Once in New Haven a three-line cut cost me 100 per cent of my part and left me a depressed piece of living set dressing. A three-line addition to my role—the same three—in Boston, made me almost as happy as Richard Burbage on the day Shakespeare said to him, "I've got some new lines for you, Dick. They're to show that the Prince is wondering whether he ought to go on living or not, and whether death might be preferable. I think you can do something with them."

When the actors assemble at the theater and when at last a technical rehearsal begins, there is, at best, controlled chaos, at worst, chaos. The actors are unusually cheerful and compliant, however, because they are the only ones who know what they are doing, and this rare state of affairs gives them the condescending good humor of so many Mr. Darcys. They will stick to it till all hours, not caring how many times a cry of "You mean my wife and child were on that ship?" is interrupted with a shout about how the bastard ambers shouldn't be on the balcony rail.

Getting into costume has a great deal to do with this gaiety in the trenches. It is particularly strong when the costumes are really costumes—plumed hats and ruffled capes or panache of any sort—but even the old suit you sold to the management as an appropriate garb for an accountant is somehow inspiriting. It is not your old suit any more; it is the accountant's old suit, and it feels very different from the rehearsal clothes, which were always yours and therefore a little uncomfortable for the accountant.

I have one old suit that I have thriftily sold to several managements on a run-of-the-play basis. Each time I put it on in New Haven, however, it has a brand-new life unconnected with me or with any previous character in which I have clothed it. It is, in short, my *costume*.

Make-up gives excitement to some, particularly the young, who enter the dressing room looking fresh-faced and radiant, do an underpainting that makes them look like Fauvist portraits, cover it with basepaint mixed in a dish from three different tubes—"The 26 absorbs light, the 27 gives basic tone—and the 28 defines features," draw lines and apply shadows and come out looking fresh-faced and radiant and a little too red around the corners of the eyes.

Even I, who try only to bring my small, sunken eyes to the surface with a smear of brown under them, a smear of yellow over them, and a little play with an eyebrow pencil, am always a little pleased with the unexpected keenness of my gaze in the mirror.

Throughout the rehearsal the stage designer sits in the middle of the orchestra with a plywood desk spread over the seats around him and murmurs changes and corrections into a PA system, which, for reasons I have never understood, seems quite inaudible to the people backstage but very clear to me, sitting in the last row of the orchestra nursing a coffee container, unable to do anything about cues 32A and 33, and heedless of the warning on 34 and 35.

Exhaustion and the unions bring the proceedings to a halt after a while, and the stagehands, who are sensible people, go off to bed. The actors, who are not, range through the town in search of waffles, pancakes, and loosely scrambled eggs with crisp bacon. In our free-enterprise society a big enough demand will always produce a supply, and in New Haven, at hours when the last Yale man has stopped studying, you can always get a waffle.

Moss Hart once described New Haven as "a stretch of pavement connecting the Taft Hotel and the Shubert

Theater, entirely surrounded by what appears to be a small city," and there is no doubt that the people on the bridge of our theatrical ship don't have time for more of the town than that. Those of us who are not in the first or second or third act as the case may be, sometimes extend ourselves beyond that stretch. I think I know more about New Haven's urban-renewal project than the mayor does. He likes it and I don't, because it deprived me of the finest string of old book and junk shops that ever whiled away an afternoon.

Musical shows often spend a whole week dry-running before their openings, but straight plays content themselves with two to four days, and then, one night, the lobby is not thinly populated with actors going for coffee and reading their names but full of people who seem amazingly calm and cheerful, considering that this is opening night. You will see a few nail-biters as you make for the alley to the stage door, but they are our commanders, kept at their staff posts, unable to go over the top with us and obviously sure that we are the least promising troops since the Hessians were here.

There is more genuine unselfishness around on opening night in New Haven than in the whole of Foxe's *Book of Martyrs*. Whatever feuds may develop later, and granting the doubled and tripled tensions of the New York opening, this is the first time we have all done it together for real, and nobody having the slightest idea what is going to happen, the whole cast will, when not onstage, sit on the stairs or out of the sight line in the wings, listening and praying for everyone else. They will clap silently when the company boor gets a big laugh, and raise their hands in silent prayer when the impossible star launches into the big speech about integrity. When the old character man dies, they cry and then bury him in kisses and handshakes after the curtain. On that night they may even ask him to come for a waffle. More likely it will be a little judicious whiskey. It is not so much that you need intoxication, of which you have had several magnums onstage, it is more that you need an excuse to behave in a noisy, boastful, foolish manner. A glass in your hand gives you the comforting illusion that you are not slightly mad but only slightly drunk.

Despite the fact that the production has traveled at great expense to get away from New York, many of the people in the audience have made the long trip from the city. Some of them are theater professionals, some of them are people who like to be "in," some are friends and relatives, and some are jackals in search of carrion to take back to their Broadway burrows.

Most of them play the game, however, and come backstage to say effusive, insincere things, and I think this is as it should be. It has been complained that such stuff only confuses the actor, takes away the worth of real praise, etc. On opening night, however, we are too vulnerable for criticism, constructive or otherwise. One should as soon tell a mother that her new baby has big ears, as tell an actor on opening night that he could fix up this or that by doing that or the other. He may thank you but he will hate you. Nobody wants medicine poured in his mouth while he is crying "Excelsior!"

As to the reviews in New Haven, there are two attitudes, positive and more so. If the notices are good, they show that all concerned have worked hard, and builded well, and should be happy. If they are bad, it is even better because it guarantees that there will be no dangerous smugness, no letting down in the steady march to victory.

Let's listen to a typical New Haven morning-after speech. Bearing crumpled newspapers, coffee containers, and faces, the cast is huddled on the shrouded furniture of the set when, with the cheery determination of dental surgeons, the Big Boys arrive, each carrying a folded New Haven paper so no one will think they are smiling out of ignorance.

"Folks," says the chosen spokesman, "I want you to know one thing right away. There isn't a single criticism in these papers which some of us haven't been aware of for days. If the critics hadn't agreed with us, we might not have had the wonderful unanimity which we now have about the way to fix things up. We don't want any of you to be discouraged or panicky. I, personally, think of these reviews as a good old-fashioned tonic, and I welcome them, do you hear, I welcome them!" (His whitened knuckles as he grips the paper suggest that welcome is a funny word.)

"We will play this same show in New Haven, and believe me there is no reason to be ashamed of it, and on the train to Philadelphia you will be given some vital new scenes which our author is working on now. Some of you may have thought that his absence this morning showed that he was discouraged or angry. If you think that, you haven't read our script carefully. This play was written by a fighter, a man who isn't going to be scared or discouraged by a couple of smart-aleck hick newspapermen who want to be known as 'the Connecticut Menckens.'" (Confused murmurs from several young actors who want to know who Mencken is and is it good to be one.)

"The stage manager wants you to stick around and run through some of the scenes where the lights were a little imprecise last night, but before we leave I want to tell you the essence of our thinking. What we have here, ladies and gentlemen, is a real package of dynamite, make no mistake about that. The only thing we have to do is find the right fuse for it. It shouldn't be hard if we all pitch in, as I know we will." (An actor has the thought that another name for a package of dynamite is a bomb and grins, drawing a hard stare from the producer, who has just thought of the same parallel.)

So you play out the week in New Haven, and if yours is a fashionable show which has sold all the seats in advance, you do it in a peculiar atmosphere of success which resembles the bright-eyed rosiness of a fever victim.

If you are depending on your notices to sell tickets, you will have the terrible making-love-to-a-closed-door feeling that actors get from empty houses.

During this period there will be a certain amount of busy work. As soldiers are kept busy digging holes and filling them in so that they will not begin brooding over the outcome of the battle, so theater people are drilled in slight changes of staging, cuts of words or phrases, and how best to climb on the new table, which replaces the one that broke on opening night.

The train to Philadelphia leaves on Sunday morning, and standing on the platform, gripping their Sunday papers, the actors will begin to talk about food, a subject which will take almost as much time as the play over the coming weeks. There is only one good place to eat in New Haven (I sometimes eat in the other, so I will name no names), so that the great restaurant discussion can't really get started there, but waiting for the train, the veterans will start talking about the gustatory delights of Philadelphia with all the savage relish of the Sultan's troops discussing Byzantine women while waiting to storm the walls of Constantinople.

I suppose psychiatrists have long since figured out and written monographs about actors' preoccupation with eating during a tryout tour, but I am not on the mailing list for any of these monographs, so I will give you my own theory here. It seems to me that in times of danger, we cling to simple, pragmatic pleasures with extra intensity. Plays succeed and plays fail, and do both for reasons which no one can quite pin down, but you can always pin down a broiled lobster, and for those minutes in which you are rending it and dipping it in butter and mashing its springy sweetness against your palate, you are in a world where success is as easy as cracking a claw.

If you are the lucky actor whose play is riding the triumph trail and has already sold six months of New York tickets, you may not have quite the same fierce pleasure, but you have the gentle joy of eating lobster you know you can afford. Actors in putative failures find that pleasure ends with the arrival of the check; actors in guaranteed hits can produce their credit cards with a smile and add a cigar to the total.

The Philadelphia opening has its stresses and strains, principally the "vital new scenes" which almost always turn out to be nightmare mosaics from a memory point of view—of new dialogue and old. This means that the actor can confidently follow the synaptic tracks he made in the past weeks up to a line which is suddenly not quite the same and goes off in a very different direction for ten seconds, returns for eight words to the beaten path, then comes to a dead halt at a place where there used to be a broad and well-traveled paragraph. What faces him now is a thicket of little-known words through which can be dimly descried something that is familiar but used to be found half an act back.

It is more like a siege than a battle, however, and it lacks some of the fire of the first skirmish in New Haven and the assault on the heights which is to come in New York.

The siegelike atmosphere is compounded by the fact that the stay in Philadelphia is almost always at least two weeks and sometimes, with musicals, may run to four. Philadelphia is to my mind a charming city, however, and for those hours when rehearsals are not scheduled it possesses the pleasures of splendid museums, miles of *ancien régime* gaslit streets that take you far from the clangorous realities of modern theater, and Leary's Bookstore.

An hour in the musty, vaulted caves of Leary's, where the top rows of books are only to be reached from a towering ladder, can solace me for the loss of lines, a banderilla from the director, or being saddled with one of those "let's-just-try-it-tonight" jokes that sometimes signal the death agonies of a comedy.

Once, in Philadelphia, I remember, I was with a comedy that acquired a play doctor to whom the sight of a roll of toilet paper was the signal for merriment. Bathroom jokes flowed rapidly from his pen, and being given the most luridly specific of these at the end of a day's rehearsal, I made my exit, slammed my fist against the door frame as a substitute for doing something mature, and went off to Leary's, sucking the blood off my knuckles.

There I thought of what I should have said, said it to myself and dismissed it, and discovered a rare copy of *Lyre and Lancet*, by that genial comic Victorian, F. Anstey. I read a third of it perched on the ladder and was ready to say the line that night as if it were good. I did, and it wasn't, and I lost it but kept the book.

There are two aspects of Philadelphia that I find a trifle melancholy, but neither is the fault of the city itself. I went to college in the suburbs of Philadelphia—"Thee we praise with songs of gladness, name thy glories o'er. Hail to thee, our Alma Mater, Hail, All Hail, Swarthmore"— and sometimes, when I am pacing the streets trying to memorize a toilet-paper joke or thinking of the general merits of the enterprise which currently engages me, I think of the high hopes of the far-off days when all I had to worry about was what happened to my botany drawings, and I feel a *nostalgie de ciel.* By eight o'clock, however, I prefer going in a stage door, no matter what's going to happen inside, to my old teaching ambition which for tonight might have included correcting thirty-five blue-books on "Contrasts and Comparisons between Wordsworth and Browning."

Philadelphia was also a frequent stop for me in my baseball-writing days, and sometimes now I step furtively into the great glass and plush lobbies of the hotels where I used to stay at someone else's expense, contrast them with my clean but modest quarters as an actor, and feel a *nostalgie de luxe.* Clubhouse men to carry your baggage from the train! Merrymaking in the road secretary's suite! Having the planked steak dinner or the lobster—both halves—and signing for it! Certainly a great deal was lost when I went off with the raggle-taggle gypsies, oh, but then as I enter the stage door at eight o'clock I remember that at this hour in the old days I was, if a night game was in prospect, sitting in the press box trying to shuffle the monosyllables I had collected on the bench into a lively, colorful background story to run in the early edition, a story that would be scrapped a few hours later and replaced with my hastily written account of the game.

Assuming Philadelphia to be the middle stop on a three-town tryout tour which will end in Boston, it is likely that the power struggle, which is discussed elsewhere, will reach its peak of intensity here.

Like children listening fearfully to their parents quarreling in the library, the actors hang about the door to the theater's ladies' lounge—which because of its commodious-

ness is usually made the command post—listening to the
fierce sounds of combat drifting up the stairs. If the noise
becomes loud enough to be clearly audible, the stage
manager, like nanny, will herd the actors away and set
them to playing some game or other such as "Running
through the Curtain Calls" or "Clearing the Sightlines in
the Party Scene."

After a while the big folks will emerge from the lounge
trying to pretend, like Mummy and Daddy, that it was
mostly joking, but inclined to take out some of their
frustrations on the children.

We can tell who won this particular round by where the
protagonists sit. The ones who settle into the back rows
have had a hard time of it, and the ones who go back to
the hotel have had a major reverse. Sometimes, indeed, the
hotelgoers become stationgoers and are never again seen by
us. Sometimes we get the truth about this, and sometimes
we get the same kind of cream cheese the children get
when they hear that "Daddy is going on a long trip."
These are the times when you will hear that the star has
been called to an unexpected movie commitment, con-
tracted for long ago, or that the author wants the peace
and quiet of his farm in order to give us something really
special, or that the director has been stricken with mononucleosis and must rest for many months. Of course,
directors do sometimes get mononucleosis, and the other
stories are sometimes true, but if you heard what was
coming out of the ladies' lounge you are inclined to doubt
them.

Despite the fact that producers think a new director is
very often the solution to everything, the statistics would
seem to indicate that this idea is as fallacious as the idea
that a new baseball manager will bring a team up from
the depths. When directors can act and write—when man-

agers can pitch and hit, these notions will have some validity.

Certainly for the actors a change of directors out of town is a time of trouble in which they are usually too frightened to accomplish anything at all. A new director like a new colonel in the army, feels the need to take hold with a few strong gestures.

"More close-order drill," barks the colonel. "This outfit is going to have some of the lard sweated off it! And another thing. I walked down the company street last night and noticed that the men were very lax about saluting. From now on—" etc.

The first couple of rehearsals under the new director will see actors continually scurrying for the shadows, anxious to avoid notice. They all know that a standard gambit of the new chief is to pick a patsy. This poor devil will be somebody with a medium-sized part—it is dangerous to poke the star, and picking on the small-part people makes you look like a bully—and his performance will be taken apart before his eyes. Like the rebellious noblemen who were shown their own entrails on Tower Hill, he will be carefully kept alive. When he begins to shiver and grow white the director will stop for a few minutes and talk to the lighting man, but in a few minutes the rehearsal begins again, and the actor is inspecting his own pancreas—"What were you thinking of, Mr. Broun? Did that seem funny to you? Don't you know that comedy is organic and is not achieved with funny voices and grimaces? Please feel free to speak. If you have some reason for this way of doing the line I would certainly be glad to hear it."

There is, of course, nothing personal about this, and if the new man had happened to start on another scene you would be as organic as the best, and he would be dissecting another actor. The director's purpose is simply to show that he can make things very uncomfortable for those who don't hop to it when he speaks. The patsy didn't fail to hop. He was chosen before hopping time began.

It may be that years of experience have shown this to be a sound method of taking hold, but I don't remember that the regiment improved much (the colonel did become a general, though), and I find that the first few performances after the directorial change look like those old, old animal acts where the dogs went through the flaming hoops all right but never took their eyes off the whip. The crowd felt uneasy and were glad when the jugglers arrived.

Sometimes I have been the patsy and, despite all the foregoing philosophy, have found it very painful.

The best way for the actor to handle it is the soldier's way. Expressionless but alert, listen to the order and obey it with alacrity. Don't say anything but "yes, sir—no, sir—no excuse, sir," and keep your feelings off your face. The director will soon think you a fool or a friend (you aren't one, but there's no reason why you shouldn't eventually be the other) and turn his attention to somebody who was foolish enough to say something like, "But it always gets a laugh," or "Perhaps if I told you my motivation—"

Once a new director, baffled by my perfect dormouserie, was reduced to a final prod. "You're not making those moves because you feel them," he cried, after changing them eight times, "you're just making them because I tell you to." Everyone waited for me to shout "Of course, I am. My God, what else can I do!" but with the iron control of a thirty-year man with six stripes whose next trip to the pay table will be for a pension check, I wheeled smartly, returned to my original position, and said, "I'm sorry. Would you like me to try again?"

"Miss X," said the director, "why are you doing that little sidewise move on Mr. Broun's first line? Did no one ever tell you that pointless movement blurs a play? Do you think this scene is about you?" A small iron ball melted inside me, but I indulged in no smile of relief and simply withdrew in good order, carrying my equipment and my wounded.

Sometimes a play gives up in Philadelphia, or to use the current euphemism, "is withdrawn for extensive revisions and recasting." Since the whole effort of everyone is geared to the opening in New York, these premature closings leave scars of frustration on everyone and a terrible urge to do the thing somewhere if only to complete the cycle. Little boots it that the trip to New York will only mean the humiliation of jeering reviews, the simultaneous opening and closing, and a lot of unwanted sympathy from people who had previously thought you honorably unemployed. However rusty and foul the ship, the crew want the chance to sail it into New York, the only proper place for it to sink.

There is also the practical fact of the extreme provinciality of the New York theatrical community. It does not matter that agents and producers have journeyed out of town in droves to see a play in which you give a brilliant performance. For hiring purposes, for prestige purposes, that performance is considered as ungiven unless it is given in New York.

Once I went to Philadelphia in a play which did not even complete the time it had scheduled there, ending its brief, unhappy life after the first of two scheduled weeks. It was supposed to be an unsparing play about miserable people, and the audiences laughed, at first uneasily and then uproariously, as the miseries tumbled awkwardly on top of each other.

Our last matinee took place on the afternoon of the Army-Navy game, and as we fought through the scene where the characters gave a numb little party with rolled-back rugs and dancing, I noticed that one of the actors kept peering into the vast 1600-seat theater as we shuffled through the mambo. After the scene he told me that he had been counting our audience and it consisted of 47 people. Throughout the rest of our march to doom, both as characters and as a theatrical enterprise, both of us had to fight a terrible desire to laugh insanely. So much work, so much pain, so much rewriting and relearning and all for this, for a demise without the dignity of notice, a death rattle drowned by the cheers of the midshipmen and cadets.

What were we laughing at? It seemed better than the alternatives, which were crying or thinking. Let an actor think too much about theatrical life and his uncertain part in it, and he will soon be an agent, a teacher, or a trainee in a brokerage house.

I can, on sleepless nights, imagine what the New York critics would have said about that play, and yet when our closing notice was posted, I honestly felt no relief, no release from a near impossible task which I was not performing with any particular distinction. I felt like the boxer, bleeding and helpless, who tries, when the fight is stopped, to push the referee aside so that he can be punched some more. This is not masochism, it is dedication, and we only laugh at it when it fails to bring off the miracle it seeks.

From the first day of rehearsal my objective judgment had told me that we were going to end up stone-cold dead on Market Street, but no matter how bravely you bare your breast, the knife is always a disagreeable surprise.

Till the last moment, however, we enjoyed the special pleasures of tour life, telling each other about wonderful places for snapper soup—I believe our leaders were on broth, however—and spending merry evenings in the Variety Club after the performance.

The Variety Club exists in a number of cities and supports an impressive roster of charities with contributions from its members, most of whom are, I believe, connected with motion-picture distribution. Its club rooms are open to actors, and here we sit till all hours, exchanging gossip and news with actors from other plays in varying states of readiness and solving each other's problems. (With staggered matinees we usually see each others' shows.) Using sugar lumps, we restage scenes, and between the lighting and the stubbing of a cigarette add crispness and pungency to several pages of dialogue. Between refreshing sips we junk sets, redesign costumes, and hire and fire stars—"So he'll want a couple of thousand a week more than the guy you've got now. Give it to him. He'd make that second act seem funny without changing a line, and as to the third act all you need is to take the action into the captain's cabin and throw away that lousy stretch of promenade deck. It looks as if it was cut out of a big bathtub boat."

Somehow nobody ever runs out with any of these suggestions and down to Rittenhouse Square, where, in hotel suites which soften suffering, the big conferences and confrontations are taking place.

Occasionally the officers will come down from the bridge and relax with us at the Variety Club, but then we only tell them wonderful places to get snapper soup.

When the club closes its door for the evening, it's time to anchor our flying fancies with waffles, and everyone goes next door to a hospitable all-night griddle which thoughtfully provides, as did Squire Trelawney, an apple barrel. Many a provident actor breakfasts on one of these apples and a couple of toothpicks he gathers up with his change.

Assuming that Philadelphia has neither given us a medal nor stripped us of our buttons in a hollow square of critics, we will be off to Boston for clam chowder, Indian pudding, and the last set of revisions.

There are not many ways in which Boston resembles Paris, or wants to, but they have one splendor in common. There is an inner city of concentrated beauty as yet almost untouched by the stainless-steel fingers that tore the heart out of New York and replaced it with a glass and metal pump that circulates but never sings.

Clustered around the Common as around the Cité in Paris, are blocks and blocks of the Real Thing. Of course, in Boston, as in Paris, a good deal of the antique beauty is just a façade, and the Emerson behind the gracious fanlight is the Emerson Mailing List Service, Inc., but to the casual observer, the actor on a lunch hour, Boston is still the town that married poetry to commerce and made it work at least as well as most marriages.

Boston is the site of my favorite theatrical hotel, where the clerk, instead of finding your reservation on a punch card, after a little difficulty about misspelling, simply hands you a bunch of keys and says, "Here you are. Pick yourself a room." I always take the one with the catty-corner fireplace.

I would name the hotel except that then *you* would take the one with the catty-corner fireplace.

We haven't dropped around to the theater for several pages now, and a lot has probably been going on there, even if it is only the kind of treadmill-running dear to producers and hamsters.

At this late stage in the proceedings, attitudes have begun to harden, and the most difficult thing to come by is a fresh approach. Vaguely, subconsciously, everyone knows it and knows also that to ask for it without defining it is to reveal that uncertain hand on the rudder which is bad for discipline as well as for navigation.

This is the time when a director will try to get invention from his actors by what I call the Expressive Hand Method. Calling the actor to the front of the stage after watching a scene run-through the director will say, "Do you know what it lacks, baby? This." And he will hold up his hands with the fingers interlocked.

"Right now it's more like this." The hands are pulled apart and travel away from each other in sinuous loneliness. "If you give it some of this"—palms are pressed together—"I think we can come closer to a real"—fingers locked in the original position—"without the danger of this"—fingers pull suddenly apart in hopeless disarray.

This kind of thing can go on for minutes at a time and is one of the best ways we know of saying, "Baby, I'm stuck. Help me!" without sacrifice of dignity.

The actor's proper reply is some sage nodding and some fast thinking. Here is a chance to try something of your own if you've been thinking of it, and if you haven't, ask for a chance to go the the bathroom and try for a quick inspiration. If the new approach doesn't work there will be more finger demonstrations, but at the moment, if there is one, when the director claps his hands together and cries, "That's it! Now you've got what I wanted!" you are entitled to the secret smile of the éminence grise. You have done your first directing, and if you're good at it, perhaps someday you can sit out front interlacing your knuckles for somebody else.

You can, if you wish, stand on your right to be directed, but it is not a good idea. The health of the play is too important for this kind of insistence. Only if you are more detached than an actor is, can you say, "Just tell me what you want."

Many years ago I stood in the vestibule of a train with the late Mel Ott, then manager of the Giants, and the

late James P. Dawson, who covered the New York club
for the *Times*. Mel was a shrewd manager and a kind man,
but perhaps sometimes too kind to deal out the heartbreak
that comes with demotion on a ball team. He was con-
templating a change at second base and wanted a little
encouragement for the disagreeable job.

"Jimmy," he said, "you've been around a long time and
you've been with this club all spring. Who would you put
on second base?"

The magisterial Dawson paused for a moment and then
said, "Mel, how much do the Giants pay you for managing? Just a rough figure, Woodie won't tell."

Mel named a round sum respectably up in five figures,
and Jimmy said, "The *Times* pays me a fifth of that for
writing about how you manage. Make your own decision,
Mel."

Dawson and I weren't on the ball team, though, and we
wrote stories whether the team lost or won. I suppose it is
unjust that a man who gets a great deal of money for being
a decisive and inventive genius has to get some decisive
ingenuity from a man who is getting a small amount of
money for looking and sounding like a janitor, but however hard the lonely eagles at the top of the power struggle
may go for each other's livers, the actor is one who wants
very much to be on a team, and he will always pretend
that the fingers mean something.

Going back to our first moments on the train, I told
you how we begin casting about for dinner companions
before we have been out to the first New Haven sandwich.
Actors have to be part of a team even to take their meals,
and watching the logistics of assembling a four-person
dinner group from four different hotels and from four
different rehearsal schedules, shows to what lengths we will
go to keep a team together.

"Jim will pick up Mary in the bar of her hotel, and they will wait for Joe at the stage door. I will get a table for four in the bar of Durgin Park and put hats on the other chairs until you come, then one of us can get into the restaurant table line while the other three have a drink. If Joe is held up he will call Mary's hotel, and she will have me paged at Durgin Park. In that case, since you can't get in there at all much after six, the three of us will leave word at the stage door for Joe as to where we have gone."

Boston night life is sparse but extremely varied. There are dignified, leathery-oaky bars, neon-lit plasticy-vinyly bars, and there are joints which make the Marseilles waterfront look like Disneyland. There are also all-night cafeterias which have armed guards, although whether in expectation of a riot or a robbery, I have never discovered. I have always found Boston cafeterias as damply decorous as the poached eggs (called in Boston "dropped" eggs), which are a staple of the local diet. Because Boston hotels are as soundproof as interrogation cells, a good deal of the post-performance partying is in Joe's room, Jim's room, or Mary's room. So thick are the walls that even the actor-folksinger who brings his guitar—increasingly a feature of such parties—cannot be heard next door, a fact that often makes one wish he were next door.

I must record here a famous next-door incident from which some Bostonians may not yet have recovered. A couple of years ago before a Boston opening, announcement was made to our company that the author and management were giving a cast party at the Ritz. I walked over with another actor, sent him up to the party while I called home to tell how many laughs I had gotten, and then asked the desk clerk where the Bloomgarden-Hellman party was taking place. He sent me to the second floor and there I found our stars, about half our company,

and a lot of chilly-looking people in evening dress. Actors
are used to seeing chilly-looking people in evening dress at
opening-night parties and always assume them to be dissatisfied backers of the show. This group seemed extremely
dissatisfied, but after looking at the buffet I thought perhaps it was more a matter of indigestion. Spread on a table
were platters of that concentrated, expensive, disturbing
food made from surprising parts of exotic animals, together
with some cheeses of great age and advanced inner life.
There was no sign of the simple, hearty stuff that an actor
wants after a hard evening's work and no sign of my friend.
I wondered uneasily whether he had been written out or replaced and, being informed of this, had run out into the
night, but no one remembered seeing him at all. I wondered too at the absence of our hosts but guessed that they
were having a strategy session (latterly, I imagine these
sessions to be devoted entirely to the problem of who
should be hired to replace me) and would shortly join us.

Meantime the actors traveled speedily along the road to
heartburn, scooping up the pâtés like so much oatmeal and
treating the old cheeses like blocks of Velveeta.

There wasn't a great deal of liquor, but we got what
there was, the chillies having gathered into a corner some
distance from the bar. At some point after most everything had been eaten or drunk or left under a chair, a distinguished comedian was sent up to join our cast party,
and one of the dinner jackets recognized him and, coming
over, said he was surprised to know that our guest was a
member of the Boston Friends of Chinese Art, whose
annual "do" this apparently was.

Such a round of apologies! Such bursts of nervous
laughter! Such good manners and reassurance from the
Friends!

One of our stars assured the Friends that we would call

the maître d' and order another round of rare viands to replace our depredations. Alas, said the Friends, lances of pain piercing their gentility, the rare viands were irreplaceable. The Friends, connoisseurs of foods as well as of Middle Ming glazes, had spent months assembling this regal delicatessen from the four corners of the globe. Some devoted members had made specialties themselves. The spread could be reassembled, of course, but just about in time for next year's meeting.

With feeble smiles and broken murmurs we made our way out and up to the third floor where we found the rest of the cast wondering whether we had been replaced. Here also was a long table of foods more suitable to nervous stomachs, foods with which we at once tried to encapsulate the pirated treasures, which sat like fifteen dead men on our chest.

It was suggested by kind hearts among us that the delicious noodles steaming on our buffet would make an appropriate palliation offering to the mandarins on the floor below, but someone else said that noodles were peasant fare in China and to offer them to the aristocracy would be like handing kippers to the Queen. Someone said what if the Queen liked kippers, but in the end we ate all the noodles ourselves.

Somewhere near the end of this last stop on the tour will come the magic date when the play is "frozen." This is the day after which no changes are to be made, and the company is just to act, without prodigies of mosaic memory. "Freezing" is a good sign and indicates that you can start thinking about ordering opening-night tickets for New York and stop worrying about the summons to the hotel ballroom. This call, which always means the death of the play, has a certain superstitious aura about it. No one likes to kill the play actually in the theater, although, of course, in New York there is no place else. On the road, however, a neutral ground is always chosen for the killing.

Assuming that the play is going in, the last few days have a special exhilaration. The creative struggle is over, and for a very brief time we are united. There is now nothing left to do but fix bayonets and run up the hill, doing or dying without the exhausting anxiety of reasoning why.

On our first train ride we gathered into those small groups which by their very exclusivity shut out the idea of chaos. Now on our last train ride we are gathered into one group which has come through chaos to find—well, we'll know what at about 1 A.M. on the day after we open. If we win we will describe chaos as creation, and if we lose—but let's hope that this time we won't.

I CONSIDER that a man's brain originally is like a little empty attic, and you have to stock it with such furniture as you choose. A fool takes in all the lumber of every sort that he comes across, so that the knowledge which might be useful to him gets crowded out, or at best jumbled up with a lot of other things, so that he has difficulty in laying his hands on it. Now the skilful workman is very careful indeed as to what he takes into his brain-attic. He will have nothing but the tools which may help him in doing his work, but of these he has a very large assortment, and all in the most perfect order. It is a mistake to think that that little room has elastic walls and can distend to any extent. Depend upon it there comes a time when for every addition of knowledge you forget something that you knew before. It is of the highest importance, therefore, not to have useless facts elbowing out the useful ones."

The speaker is, of course, Mr. Sherlock Holmes, and whatever the psychologists may think of his theory, it has a wonderful neatness, which may be why so many of us read Conan Doyle. How much all of us would like to see a little neatness in that bone-bound attic! Even if we can't have a neat one, it is a pleasure to know that one is possible, and how we envy Holmes his ability to dismiss, as he immediately after that speech did, such a disturbing fact as that the earth revolves around the sun. Most of us can neither dismiss it nor understand it, despite all those explanations involving grapefruit, oranges, and hatpins.

As a boy I tried to dismiss algebra on the grounds that it was not a tool which would help me in my work (at the time I was planning to be a beekeeper on a small, beautiful Mediterranean island), but I was not able to remove the tool from the attic, but only to break it. Even now I sometimes stumble over the pile of twisted and cracked X—Ys, X+Ys, and ABs which gather dust on the floor along with some badly gnawed Latin grammar and a plane geometry from which the Euclid is missing.

Of course, even Holmes couldn't keep out all the odd bits which make the attic difficult of maneuver. Watson, in totting up his fields of learning, had put down "Knowledge of Literature, nil," and yet Holmes appeared well supplied with quotations. In the first four stories of *The Adventures* the great detective has reference to Flaubert, Hafiz, Horace, George Sand, Richard Baxter, and some Latin, which my own literary imperfections kept me from recognizing. I can only assume that his attic was one of those spacious Victorian models that could contain a whole modern luxury apartment with room left over for ten horsehair trunks full of poetry, pressed flowers, painted chicken-skin fans with one broken slat, dance programs, and Aunt Edna's diary of a winter in Florence.

At the time that I was trying to lug algebra out of my attic I was committing to memory almost the entire contents of an encyclopedic volume called *The ABC and XYZ of Beekeeping* by A. I. Root. To this day I can spot at a glance evidences of European Foul Brood. (In case it's any use, you too can detect it by looking for larvae of a ropy, viscid appearance. Call the state bee inspector at once. There is no cure.) I know all the bees from the largest (Giant East India) to the smallest (Pygmy East India) and the odd varieties that spray acid on you instead of stinging.

Since I gave up the daydream of the Mediterranean island, this knowledge has been more useless to me than Holmes's rudimentary astronomy was to him, and if his theory is correct, this collection of arcane tools should be removed from the attic along with the first four syllables of a nonsense series I learned as the subject of a psychology experiment in college (Cak, Sib, Nup, Kev. It has taken twenty-six years to get the other eight in the series out of my attic, and I'm afraid that some night when I can't sleep, they may come back), a collection of baseball records that my son tells me has been entirely superseded by modern practitioners, three verses of a fraternity song based on the Russian Imperial Hymn, the telephone code names of all of XIII Corps Artillery (Hello Clinton, this is Lockman. Over), all the verses on the advancement cards in the Uncle Wiggly Game (In the woods an ice cream pops, and Uncle Wiggly takes five hops), how to assemble and disassemble a hand-operated ice cream freezer, President Polk's middle name (Knox) and about ten million other things which are keeping me from doing anything useful in the attic.

Indeed, my mind seems like less an attic than like a beach onto which are washed and piled the scraps the sailors threw overboard, the fish that couldn't make it, and the bottles that contain no messages.

"It is of the highest importance, therefore, not to have useless facts elbowing out the useful ones."

President Polk's middle name, could it be eliminated, might make room for the license number of my car. Could I forget "Over the fence is out, they say. This helps Uncle Wiggly six hops on his way," I might be able to remember what I did with the garage key.

Still, there is one hitch when you try to apply Holmes's dictum to the theater. The profession of consulting detective requires a neat and logical approach: "All life is a great chain, the nature of which is known whenever we are shown a single link of it," said Holmes in the magazine article which Watson called "ineffable twaddle," thus starting the great chain of explanations.

To the detective, life may appear like a chain, but to the actor it looks more like baled barbed wire on a battlefield. What exactly do we need in the way of tools? What collection of facts, carefully docketed and stored, can be brought out to solve our problems? Some people with a vademecum complex tell us that we have only to know the contents of a book by Stanislavski, or even the precepts of Hamlet's advice to the players, although the last two Hamlets I saw might better have listened to them than said them. No attack on either Shakespeare or Stanislavski is intended, but I do feel that after you have mined your soul for inner truth and spoken the result trippingly on the tongue, you may yet have more to do before you can step aside and say, "There it is—my masterpiece."

If all the world's painters continually worked on self-portraits, we might after a time get a little bored with the narrowness of the approach, and yet we seem inclined to accept this from many of our actors.

"I believe this role suits me," is a typical interview beginning. "My own father was a good deal like the old duke, and I plan—" This is nonsense. His father wasn't like a duke. Nobody is like a duke except another duke, at least in those important ducal qualities which made the author choose to give him this rank.

If the straw actor I just set up were allowed to argue with me he might say, "Well, my father was the mayor of our town, its leading merchant, and had been a colonel in the Spanish-American War. The townspeople worshiped him, and he treated us kids very badly. Doesn't that sound like the right psychological pattern? People have always been the same, after all. Anyway, what are you? Some kind of a snob that believes that birth makes a real difference in people, and that the nobility are something special?"

Considering that I'm playing chess against myself, that's not a bad argument, although I'd be a little more careful with the phrasing if I were putting the words in my own mouth.

Our young friend deserves an answer, in fact several. The old colonel may have occupied a position of power, but no one ever called him "Your Grace"; he didn't wear a coronet on public occasions; nor did the people weep with excitement at his very presence, as the Burgundians did at the very sight of Duke Charles the Bold.

The colonel may have been a much better man than your average duke, and of course there is no average duke. There are brave dukes, cowardly dukes, brilliant dukes, dull dukes, and every other pair of opposites you want to mention can be brought in and mingled in different combinations with the previous pairs. When you are all through, however, all your products will be dukes, men who behave in a rather artificial way in certain situations because they are among the few human beings whose reality includes a certain amount of ritualized fantasy.

As to the personal reference at the end of the actor's argument, I believe that birth makes a real difference in people who are constantly told that birth makes a real difference. One may collapse under the implied responsibility of "birth" and become a raffish duke who is always being thrown out of night clubs, or a recluse duke who wears eccentric hats and walks exact distances every day at exact times, but each is reacting to "birth," and so of course it makes a difference. Whether it should, which is what is really behind the question, is another matter and not germane to an actor's problem.

Are the nobility something special? Perhaps not now, but obviously at one time, else why bother to create one. You have only to read Dickens, or Trollope, or Thackeray, or any one of a dozen nineteenth-century writers to discover what transports people went into at the thought of shaking hands with a duke. This is bound to have an effect, very possibly deleterious, on all but the most level-headed of dukes, but people just don't feel the same way about meeting the town's leading merchant, and as a result he doesn't either.

The phrase "people have always been the same," has too little precision to have meaning. Certainly the varieties of human behavior, both individual and societal, even over such a short time as 900–1900 would suggest that though man's stimuli may be few and universal, his responses are not always equitable with those of twentieth-century actors.

Questing through his jargon-jungle, pursued by fierce phobias and packs of slithery neuroses which draw close round the campfire at night and slaver for his ego, armed only with a handleless Freudsword, it is no wonder that the modern actor has begun to believe that his is the only grail search that counts. It must be, because it seems so much more beset with difficulty than any previous one.

Our interview actor is prepared to do any play as if it were set in the town of which his father was leading merchant, and will make Polonius out of the town clerk and Hamlet's indecisions out of his own uncertainties as to whether to go to the state university and study business or go to New York and try for the theater.

It can be said for this approach that at least some part of the performance will have reality, whether the author's truth is served or not, truth will not be completely absent from the hall as it is when a group of scholar-actors are doing the Restoration with neighing vocal distortions and a lot of handkerchief play. There was a good deal more to the seventeenth century than saying, "Yars, mlud," and acting like a sissy. When our sample actor is on stage he will be finding a truth of his own, however irrelevant it may be.

Going all the way back to the Holmes attic theory, I argue simply that there is almost no fact, theory, or work of art that an actor should not try to jam into his attic. The oddest of bits may come to his aid at the oddest of times. I am not now referring to concrete bits of social knowledge such as how they bowed at the court of Francis I, or how to walk upstairs in armor. I mean that the actor wishing to show a certain kind of terror for theatrical purposes will probably do better thinking about William Blake's illustrations for the Book of Job than he will recalling how he felt when his coaster brake broke on Uncle Ned's hill. I mean that when we use our private griefs as a spur to help us simulate grief, we may feel it without showing it, but that I reduced summer-stock audiences to tears for a week by thinking as I heard the news of Mr.

Roberts' death, of the wonderful phrase in Henry James's letter to Edward Marsh on the death of Rupert Brooke. There was nothing to do, James said, but "to stare through one's tears." The helpless immobility the phrase suggests, the reaching through for something which can never again be reached, the very blindness of the reaching—all these seemed to me as useful as any personal memoir. The other chess player will say that this is bloodless, secondhand stuff, while his own experiences are fresh, varied, harrowing, and not prettied-up.

From the length of time it takes to get one's memories sorted out and freed of distortion in the psychoanalytic process, I don't know that he is right, and in any case—. Here I was going to make the checkmate move, when a third player entered the game and won it by using the modern means of playing chess, kicking over the board. It was Conscience, and he said, "Broun, whether any of this is true or not, the fact is that you spend many hours when you could be doing something useful, sitting over a book with a slack jaw and a curved spine. You are now simply pretending that all this opium smoking is a part of your professional preparation. You're saying, in other words, that while Jascha Heifetz was practicing for a couple of hours on his violin last evening in order to keep in trim, you were doing the same thing from a theatrical point of view by reading *Maigret in Montmartre*. You hand me a laugh, Broun. I suppose you could claim that the Maigret book gave you some useful material on playing pimps, but what about the Tarzan book last month? Don't you think you're a little old for that part? Or was it Edgar Rice Burroughs' social message that kept you glued to the book?"

Of course, this kind of generalization from the particular is a cheap weapon and typical of the level on which Conscience operates. I have known actors whose Holmesian attics were like treasure houses, others whose attics held nothing but thousands of pages of diary, and a few whose attics resemble rifled tombs.

I honestly think the treasure-house crowd are better actors. It is our duty, after all, as actors, to bring to life something more than ourselves. Present-day drama tends to be intensely personal and to concern itself extensively with the thesis that we are not listening to each other. Indeed, this is so overriding a theme that you wonder why anyone bothers to write a play when he is so sure that it will go unheeded. There are other kinds of plays still around, however, and, God willing, future dramatists will put down the violin and pick up the trumpet, or even begin again to conduct the full orchestra.

Whether it is helpful for actors to read a great deal or not, they certainly have considerable opportunity to. We are sporadically employed to begin with, and even when we are working there are a good many hours in the corner waiting for them to get to you, hours during which you can, according to the state of your conscience, absorb a broad and humanistic education that will enrich your every performance, or kill time with a book.

Whichever of these I'm doing, I fear that I tend more to prepare for the past than for the future. My particular passion is for three-volume novels about whether a younger son with £200 a year can afford to marry the doctor's beautiful daughter who will have a reversion of £50 a year from her mother's marriage portion on that lady's death. He is tempted by a plain heiress, and the doctor's daughter is nearly talked into becoming the *petite amie* of a handsome duke. After another thousand pages and a number of sub-plots involving servants, the younger son takes Holy Orders, gets a £200 living with rent-free vicarage attached, and the resultant £450 finishes the duke and the heiress, and makes possible one of those serene and happy lives that extend outward and undescribed from the final pages of Victorian novels.

There aren't nowadays many plays about that far-off world whose moves were as rigidly controlled by money as one's progress around a Monopoly board. Earlier ages have more to say to us, for they share with us, and I suspect will share with those to come, a lot more questions about the why of humanity, than will be found in that wonderful stretch that began in the sootless world of Jane Austen and ended somewhere in the soft-coal coziness of Charles Dickens, for whom life was earnest but not real. Mind you, Dickens' life seems real when you're in it, but it is what you might call reality by consent, the same kind of thing that used to let audiences enjoy melodramas of the wildest sort. Who wants to question all those coincidental meetings in *Oliver Twist?* It is enough that they were necessary to Oliver's survival. To carp at them would be to carp at the order of the world, and a world which contains Mr. Pickwick, the Crummleses, Magwich, Wegg, and, oh, so many others, all glowing with the extra vividness that artificial light imparts, should not be dissected.

Dickens was himself a sometime performer, and his work is a lesson to every actor in the art of employing exaggeration to provide that dimension of excitement which provides more-than-reality.

I begin to smell chalk dust now and realize that in another moment I will be off on a lecture which nobody asked for. The worst of enthusiasts is that they squeeze the life out of the flowers they're trying to show you. I'd just like to say for Dickens that *The Pickwick Papers* carried me through the first seven days in the Army, those days when, if unoccupied, you sit around a depot speculating on your cowardice and remembering the barbed-wire scene from *All Quiet on the Western Front*. He also saved me from the fantods when, summarily dismissed from a play after the opening night in Wilmington, I came home with a pair of badly battered items—my ego and a junk-shop copy of *David Copperfield* I had bought while waiting for the train.

For four days I became young Copperfield. His tribulations were mine. Indeed, there were several incidents involving his cruel stepfather, which seemed almost exactly to parallel—but the time for bitterness is over now. When at last David had finished his suffering and begun to see the light of happiness shining out of the end papers, I felt a great deal better and, with lightning change of fortune usually found only in novels such as the one I'd just finished, went out and immediately got another job.

Then and on other occasions I thought of the words of Virginia Woolf, "I have sometimes dreamt, at least, that when the Day of Judgment dawns and the great conquerors and lawyers and statesmen come to receive their rewards, the Almighty will turn to Peter and will say, not without a certain envy when He sees us coming with our books under our arms, 'Look, these need no reward. We have nothing to give them here. They have loved reading me.'"

For different theatrical situations, different sorts of reading are indicated. Long runs in small parts are for Proust and Tolstoy. In one of my plays I had twelve entrances and could rarely get up to my dressing room in the nosebleed altitudes above the flies. Crouched on the iron stairs, I kept one ear on the stage and both eyes on the successive India paper volumes of the pocket *War and Peace*. A few moments before my entrances, Pierre, Natasha, and all the gang would hide in my back pocket while I got ready to dash onstage.

I cannot say that any of the great Russian's awesome character building has been of use to me in the kind of parts I play, but his theory that battles are won by not fighting them has a beguiling sound to the actor facing a day of job-seeking. Inaction is dangerous, of course, but in the theater impatience is worse. The actor who gives way to despair after an unsuccessful reading for a part will soon be as etiolated—ah, there, crossword-puzzle fans! —as an acid-bath victim. Survival must be the cake and fame only the frosting.

The British Army in World War I used to give the troops a medal for every year of survival on the Western Front. They simply bore the names of the year: 1914–15 –16 –17 –18, and a chestful of them was a rare accomplishment.

At this writing I hold the theater's phantom medals from 1949 to 1964, and the other day I heard one TV stagehand say to another as I went by, "There goes one of the real old-timers. He goes back to 'Lights Out!' and 'The Web.' "

It would be nice if he had said "There goes one of the finest actors in the business," but half a Borodino is better than none.

For rehearsals, reading should be of a rambling and episodic nature. The play's plot is still too complicated and unabsorbed for you conscientiously to travel on the side with any great minds. In any case, the quality of many plays in an average season is not such as to stand comparison with classics. Reading a comic master like George Meredith while rehearsing a keyhole view of suburbia can lead to schizophrenia.

I find the best material for this time to be those chatty, genteel memoirs that well-bred English writers turn out when they've run out of novels. They are the kind that be-

gin "The first mention of our family name occurs on the
rolls of the Worshipful Company of Wool Merchants of
Dorset in 1387. We have been an unadventurous lot, stick-
ing pretty close to both wool and Dorset ever since, although my great grandfather served with modest distinction in Pitt's coalition cabinet, and my great uncle was
decorated at Talavera by the Iron Duke, then, of course,
Sir Arthur Wellesley."

There follows a chapter on what a hard time he had at
Eton and another about what a good time he had at Oxford and soon we begin to hear amusing things said by
other literary men at clubs and country houses.

The atmosphere of good cigars, mellow port, and comfortable leather chairs tends to blank out the ambience of
the rehearsal hall, which usually has the uncomfortable,
impermanent air of the visiting room of a maximum-
security jail.

At the same time the essentially trifling nature of the
material makes it possible for you simultaneously to pay
intelligent attention to the progress of the play, to pick
up the jargon of the director so that you can use it when
he gets round to you, and to be generally in that state of
suspended animation displayed by baseball players in hotel lobbies and Hindu holy men on beds of nails. This
state preserves the vitality of actors, ballplayers, and holy
men and gives them strength for the bursts of energy
which, in their different callings they must from time to
time call forth.

Musical-comedy dancers, who are perhaps the most se-
rious-minded people in the theater, tend to works of Oriental philosophy. I must say that some of this stuff reads
like Elbert Hubbard in a turban, and I wonder about the
enchantment of distance and whether in far-off India, temple dancers go to rehearsal carrying *A Message to Garcia*

bound in limp leather as a balance to all the Americans with copies of *The Prophet* by Kahlil Gibran.

For the grinding misery of a play in trouble, for those days when every morning sees the distribution of new pages which should "clarify the motivations in the second act" and every afternoon the abandonment of those pages in favor of "a really vital new first act scene which will place the second act in a whole new frame of reference and which we'll have ready for you tomorrow morning," there's nothing like the works of Anthony Trollope to keep you on an even keel.

Wonderful, methodical Trollope never threw any pages away, wrote twelve of them every day, one every fifteen minutes, and published them all. He defined the ideal novel as "a picture of common life enlivened by humour and sweetened by pathos," and wrote more than forty such novels. He said of writers, "Let their work be to them as is his common work to the common labourer. No gigantic effort will then be necessary. He need tie no wet towels 'round his brow, nor sit for thirty hours at his desk without moving—as men have sat, or said that they have sat. More than nine-tenths of my literary has been done in the last twenty years and during twelve of those years I followed another profession. I have never been a slave to this work, giving due time, if not more than due time to the amusements I have loved. But I have been constant—and constancy in labour will conquer all difficulties."

Now, you may think that is a lot of balderdash and a primer of mediocrity, but when you are steeped in panic and are watching people trying to rewrite a play with broadswords dipped in blood, the firm placidity of Trollope is better than a steel helmet.

As things progress, if that's the word to describe what happens in Philadelphia and Boston, one may feel the need for more acid in the diet and can turn to Robert Smith Surtees. Following the adventures of that master cheat, Mr. Soapy Sponge the horse trader, makes you feel that the world isn't really going to hell in a handcart but that in fact it has always been there and that some people have managed to find comedy in this state of affairs. Kipling called Surtees "Dickens with horse dung," but there is no sentiment in this chronicler of the Victorian jet set. He makes unsparing irony seem not cruel and destructive but perfectly proper and even rather graceful, which is a comforting notion to an actor on the tilting treadmill of a tryout.

Surtees' Jorrocks, the sporting grocer, once described fox hunting as having "all the excitement of war with only twenty-five per cent of the danger." That isn't a bad description of the theater.

But come now, things aren't always dark. What does one read when things are going well? What makes the sunshine brighter, softens the seats of dressing-room chairs, and lends enchantment to theatrical hotel rooms overlooking the freight yard?

I don't have to tell you. You know as well as I that Jane Austen can make the freight yard seem like the high street of Bath at the peak of the season. She was—but I smell the chalk dust again and will only append here what her nephew wrote of the time right after her funeral.

"Her brothers went back sorrowing to their several homes . . . and each loved afterwards to fancy a resemblance in some niece or daughter of his own to the dear sister Jane, whose perfect equal they never yet expected to see."

Still I find I cannot leave her without reference to a sentence which everyone connected with the arts should engrave on the inner front of his head. Because the arts are

cloudy, tricky, amorphous, and emotional, they cannot
be discussed in the precise manner that one uses in discussing bridge building, whether over rivers or between
teeth. This means that despite all our efforts to adopt a
precise vocabulary: "Workshop, tools of the craft, tuning
the human instrument, giving inner structure to the approach," and the like—we are all just trying to catch lightning in a bottle. Sometimes we do catch it, and then
bridges seem so footling as not to be worth discussing, but
there is a great deal of egregious nonsense talked in our
process.

Egregious nonsense is defined as opinions other than
yours or mine, and fighting it is exhausting business. We
would do well to remember Elinor Dashwood in *Sense and
Sensibility* who was being bothered by an oaf at a party
who filled her ears with his oatmeal opinions. "Elinor
agreed with everything that he said," wrote Miss Austen,
"for she felt he did not deserve the compliment of rational
opposition."

Remember that. Think of it often. It is the way to dignified muteness. I don't know how many times I have opened
my mouth in the dressing room to protest some tosh, then
thought of Miss Dashwood and closed it into a small,
superior, silent smile. Think of it when summer-stock character men tell you that Laurence Olivier is a fake, when
ingenues tell you all about themselves—a subject which ingenues consider to be of consuming interest—when the
baffled director is reduced to talking about "sincerity,"
when the tour veteran gives you a minute description of his
dinner together with an itinerary of its subsequent adventures, think of it and smile—and be thinking about something else.

A few lines back I had reference to summer stock, which
carries me on to the most special reading problem of all,

the summer package tour. In these junkets the cast performs the same play, carrying it to a new town and an even more impractical stage set every week—"But, my dear man, there must be a door in that wall. That's where the lover hides when the husband comes in this door; I don't care how late your girls were up last night!" From Maine to Maryland we go, stopping in resort towns where the stores sell film, balsam pillows, sunglasses, funny straw hats, pennants, pine-cone salt cellars imprinted with the name of the town, and a host of other necessaries, but rarely anything you would want to read. There is almost always a book rack, but the gaps in the wire slots and the curling covers of the available matter give warning that it is going to be one of those grim assortments running from *Linda Lomax, Student Nurse* to *Sin Town Nympho,* with a few books on home canning and building your vocabulary in between.

Obviously you must bring a carefully selected all-moods parcel with you to the very first bus station.

Aldous Huxley once wrote an essay on the special needs of the traveling reader. He confessed that he at one time took such weighty stuff as Burton's *Anatomy of Melancholy* and Hobbes's *Leviathan* on his long journeys, believing that sealed in with nothing else to do, he would finally get round to reading them. In fact, of course, traveling is very tiring, and he returned home with the *Anatomy* and the *Leviathan* still on his conscience and his reading list. Eventually he developed the habit of taking any odd volume of the India paper edition of the Encyclopaedia Britannica. The articles were short, informative, easily read—and easily forgotten if that was your wish after discovering more about, let us say, the Bessemer Process than you wished to keep in your attic.

I don't know that the sum of the world's wisdom is growing much, but certainly the sum of its knowledge is swell-

ing our encyclopedias to a size which makes throwing an
odd volume in your bag require the removal of all your
shirts and the sponge bag. I do have a set of the edition to
which Huxley refers, handy little volumes full of beautifully written information about the constitution of Montenegro and the new development in aircraft, the biplane. I
refer to it in a superior way as "the Scholars' Edition," but
I don't take it on trips with me and doubt that I will until
Montenegro is independent again.

The selection of the tour library is a tricky business,
however. The only constant on the trip is the text of the
play. There will be lively towns where the frivolity of the
long, beach-ball afternoons will run over into your evening
reading, and you'll want nothing more than a "Not since
Evelyn Waugh gave us *Vile Bodies*—" On the other hand,
there will be hideaways in the deep woods where the audience comes slipping through the trees like Hurons in Da-
cron, and in these remote spots one often wants to have
another shot at *Walden* or chew through a good loaf of bi-
ography.

There are theaters so depressing that only Wodehouse or
Anstey will save you from the shakes, and there are one or
two worthy of Miss Austen. Obviously it is difficult to
cover all eventualities without pulling an arm out of the
socket, but there are a few ways to keep the weight down
without too much loss of variety. To begin with, there
are a few novels, which, by being funny and serious, shallow
and deep, exciting and soothing, are a veritable table
d'hôte. They naturally are not very well organized and were
not favorably spoken of in "The English Novel. 4 Units.
Prerequisite, Freshman Composition," but they can for a
precious hour make you stop wondering why you are carrying the banner of banality through Massachusetts. To list
them would be to climb on the lecture platform again, but

I'll give you a hint. A good example is Wilkie Collins' *The Moonstone*. The actor or actress sending in the best list of nine more such works will receive a contract to go up the Monongahela in a floating production of *Tunnel of Love*.

Still another aid is the omnibus volume. There haven't been many of these gotten out in recent years, but in the thirties a publisher with a lot of lapsed plates around the premises would get out something called *The Voyager's Companion* or *The Bungalow Library*, containing two novels, twenty-three short stories, some short poems, and some long essays, all by first-rate writers and all in different type faces and pagination, making it pretty murderous to lose your place. These books, of which I have a complete collection waiting for the Call to the Cape, contain very little cornstarch filling, and running as they do to two or three thousand pages, are as close to the universal food as anything since the Ten-in-One Ration of World War II.

Should you be omnivorous, however, and get through your *Round the World Reader* by the fourth of seven theaters, there is one more resource. Actually on the set of your play, if you are in "a Long Island living room facing the sound" there will be bookshelves filled with volumes procured by the pound from the Methodist Rummage or the Library Fair. Don't pass these by uninspected. Here, neglected, stand Grandfather's favorites, and he wasn't such a fool as all that. Here, undoubtedly, will be the funny-sad novels of Leonard Merrick, who wrote better about the theater than anybody. Here will be the old romancer Jeffery Farnol, a trifle rococo perhaps, but when a woman's eyes gleam in the candlelight while the rapier blades snarl against each other and the stamp of feet and the gasps of desperate men fill the smoky, low-ceilinged room, I find that the pale green walls of my paying-guest aerie—"Please do not use more than one towel—no more than six inches

in the bathtub—turn out light on leaving—magazines are
for your convenience; do not deface—no breakfast served
after 8 A.M."—fade away and I am vagabonding down a
Regency lane, usually accompanied by a philosophical
tinker and a beautiful gypsy girl whose regal manner be-
trays that there is some mystery connected with her birth.

Here will be Edith Wharton, unfairly left behind in the
summer cottage because there wasn't room in the trunk
for both her and Henry James, and here will be Booth Tar-
kington, who came a little later but would never have left
Edith Wharton behind. I have a whole shelf of his work
gathered over the years out of prop rooms and the bookshelves of many a canvas Long Island living room. They are
stained with scene paint and wrenched out of shape by the
sullen fingers of the apprentice girls who came to the theater with dreams of glory and stayed to stack books and
Coca-Cola cases, but they are all wonderful and all free, and
each made my dressing room into something special, like
the Schofields' back yard, the Baxters' front porch, or the
ballroom where the masked Monsieur Beaucaire appeared
in white satin.

There are books here that will show you that some literary tricks are older than you thought. Perhaps you believed
that the pseudo-realist war book was a development of
World War II. If you plow through the works of Leonard
Nason and Arthur Guy Empey, and many of them can be
found in the summer-theater Sargasso, you will find that
the formula of pain without despair, ugliness without horror, and strong language without hate, was all the crack before the Pulitzer Prizes began. Among the most charming of theater book finds are the ones you couldn't possibly
have bought again, but which you want very much in a
furtive way. For me this includes a number of cheap boys'
books, which I loved before I ate the apple of education

and learned to be ashamed of Tom Swift and the Boy
Allies. Someone else became ashamed—or moved away—or
died, and now here they are to be found on the shelves of
"Noel de Mason's library. It is a sophisticated room filled
with silver-framed photographs of the famous, first editions
of their work, and some sketches Matisse did for a costume
party which Noel gave on Cocteau's birthday."

Well, let's see what Noel has on the shelves next to the
silver-framed photographs of Bonita Granville, Toby Wing,
Joel McCrea, and two actors from last week's show. Here is
a first edition of Leo Edwards' *Jerry Todd and the Waltzing Hen*. I was nine years old when I found out about the
Jerry Todd books and I think I read four of them in a
week. *The Waltzing Hen* was the first that I got. I remember there was *And the Primrose Cat, And the Dinosaur
Egg*, and, and, well, I can't remember, but here anyway is
The Waltzing Hen. Noel de Mason has so many books he
won't miss this, and he won't miss—no, that's the sea Boy
Allies. I only like the land Boy Allies, Hal and Chester.
They served in every one of the Allied armies in World
War I after starting out as civilian travelers in Berlin. Despite their youth they ended up as full chicken colonels in
the American forces, and neither they nor I had a dull day
from 1914 to 1918. Wait, wait, here's a special find. *The
Flamingo Feather* by Kirk Munro, *illustrated by N. C.
Wyeth*. I hesitate to take this, because it was not only an
excellent book but was pretty expensive with all those color
pictures. Still I know Noel de Mason pretty well. I ought
to, my character has been his literary agent for twenty
years, and I tell you if that crazy galoot would stop drinking and chasing after girls he'd have a Nobel Prize inside
three years. Noel is too much a man of the world to get
much out of *The Flamingo Feather*, so I'll add it to the
bag, and just to show I'm not some eccentric fighting his

way back to the nursery, I'll take along this Ring Lardner. Noel wouldn't like Ring Lardner. The samples of his writing we find in the script show that he wouldn't like Ring Lardner. They show Lardner wouldn't think much of Noel either.

At Noel's and the other summer-theater places, the removal of the books is easy, and they may be quite openly taken from the shelves. There are always more back in the prop room, and the apprentices, deep in Salinger and Golding, couldn't care less what happens to that antique stuff in stiff covers.

The problem is somewhat different on a TV show or a film. It is not that professional stagehands are fierce against actors or in favor of books. I think it is simply harder for NBC, CBS, and ABC to get hold of those old books for lining shelves than it is for a summer-theater proprietor. There are very few rummage sales and library fairs in New York City, and the old books on Fourth Avenue are all priced at two dollars and up and can't be bought by the pound.

I have found, however, that if, like the pack rat, I leave something behind, the most possessive of prop men can be mollified. I take with me, therefore, a partially finished detective story, finish it while waiting to be made up in the morning, and then trade it for something old and good on the set. In cases where I have only one book to trade and desire to take two, I do a kind of literary three-card monte, shuffling them back and forth until no one is sure whether I brought two and took one, or brought one and took two.

Movie studios, for reasons unclear to me, always have lots of books but none worth taking. If you have wondered what happened to all those old government publications, the annual surveys of the Fish and Game Commission, the Budget Director's Projections for 1924, et al, you need wonder no more. Silent and somber, occasionally dressed in a bright jacket which seems to fade slightly at the corpse-touch from within, they crowd the shelves of motion-picture settings. I don't know what the movie companies give the government in exchange. Perhaps a full set of the promotion material for the Andy Hardy series would be a good swap.

To be fair, it must be said that treasure caches like de Mason's library are not all gems, any more than were the mines of Opar where Tarzan got all those jewels. You have to dig through a certain amount of clay to find the emeralds. The book buyers on the summer-theater circuit at one time, for example, had an overwhelming fancy for the works of Hall Caine, Warwick Deeping, Marie Corelli, Honore Willsie Morrow, and Ruby M. Ayres, to name a few that I find unreadable, and then in one rummage sale they all emptied these writers from their shelves, and they all ended up down at the playhouse, where for all of me they still are, along with the second volumes without the firsts, the inspirational books, the *Jests for All Occasions* books, and all the muff kids' books, the kind you were always given, like *Black Beauty* and *Heidi*. (Please do not write and tell me how wonderful these books are. I didn't just pick the names to be smart aleck. When I was quarantined in school for the whooping cough, I read them, and I will, after thirty-five years, stand by my judgment.)

Sometimes you get something more than just a souvenir. There are a few no-joke rare books that found their way into the greasepaint world and out again. They pose a moral problem as to whether you are maybe actually stealing and not liberating, but when you find, as I did, a first edition of Jerome K. Jerome's *Three Men in a Boat* jammed under an end table with two Zane Greys and a phone book, what can you do? Take it to the producer and tell him what he has? Would he know after you told him? The first summer-theater producer to send in the names of the three men in the boat will be given exclusive summer rights to Jerome's play *Passing of the Third Floor Back.*

So should you leave it, maybe to get cut open to hide a little gun or a flask in the way they are always doing with books in plays? No, you must preserve it for the future as monks did with manuscripts in the Dark Ages. Someday someone's life will be brightened by reading about Harris and Jerome and Montmorency (don't be fooled, producers, Montmorency is the dog) and the can of pineapple, or the chapter about putting up the tent over the boat, and all because I saved the book from oblivion between Zane Grey and the phone book. In the meantime I am delighted to have it, and in order that the theater shall have a little of the glory for saving this cultural ort, I have written on the flyleaf the name of the production and where it was playing when the volume was saved.

Through all of this you may get the idea that I do not give a production its money's worth. I seem to be so busy stealing books, reading books, when do I get around to sharpening the tools of my craft, and all that. Even if reading is good for the actor, as I claim, should I be reading all through the rehearsals? Should I not be trying to find what the whole play is about? Of course I should, and so, of course, I do, to the best of my abilities. On a very few occasions I have worked for a great director—yes, sir, I mean you, but let's not tell the others—and in such cases I have spent every hour of the rehearsal period watching the director, because whatever he is doing with any actor at any part of the play is instructive and interesting and valuable. It is also true that you can learn something from watching people's mistakes, and to that extent one can profit from the other directors.

I have worked with great performers—yes, of course I
mean you, sir/madame—and watching them is always better than reading a book, but it is also true, as Pepper Martin, the baseball player remarked, "You can take an old
mule out and run him ragged every morning, but he still
won't win the Kentucky Derby."

In cases like that, the relaxed actor with someplace occasionally to hide is probably better able to do his share in
keeping the flag above Fort Zinderneuf for as long as possible.

There are a number of directors who for reasons of—but
I won't speculate about their reasons—don't let the actors
watch the rehearsals at all but seal them up in the cellar
where they sit about like so many *ci-devant* aristos guarded
by a doorman who rather resembles Madame Defarge but
who is too sleepy to knit, until from time to time a stage
manager summons them to appear before the tribunal
above. The rest, sitting on broken cane chairs or leaning
against the lime-washed walls while the cold seeps up from
the dusty concrete floor, would be well-advised to have
brought something in the way of solace. Whiskey affects
your performance adversely, coffee after a while gets boring,
but a book—say *Treasure Island*, can make you forget all
but the *Hispaniola*. No wonder that it has always been a
favorite book of children. The wonder is that adults continue to let them read it. What is the special fascination of
Stevenson's book? That Jim Hawkins, a boy, disobeys almost every direct order he is given and each time by his
disobedience saves the lives of the grownups. Jim slips
ashore when he shouldn't and discovers the whole conspiracy of the pirates. Jim goes over the wall of the stockade against the express wishes of Dr. Livesey, and before
you know it he has freed the ship, shot Israel Hands, and
pulled the square old folks out of trouble again, as he is to

do once more when he accompanies the pirates on the treasure search.

Of course, Jim conventionally mentions what a heavy heart his disobedience is giving him, but we all know that this is just the kind of thing you say to appease the grownups. Without it, they might not have printed Jim's story, and what a loss that would be. I don't suppose there is anyone anywhere, not even Tom, the fun-loving Rover, who can touch Jim for constructive mischief. Too much of the work of Huck Finn, Tom Sawyer, and Penrod Schofield fails to win the name of constructive for them to qualify against him. He has a possible rival in Frank Fairleigh, the Private Pupil. The critic Bernard Darwin confessed that he had read Frank Fairleigh far more often than he had read Hamlet. He didn't deny the superiority of Shakespeare, he said, it was just that Frank Fairleigh was so much more fun. I endorse his view, but I must say that Frank's straightforward, manly pranks, though they frequently routed bullies and cads, never saved a shipload of mature clothheads from death, as did Jim's adventures in the apple barrel, the coracle, and other places where Captain Smollett, the squire and the doctor desired him not to be.

Indeed Jim's only rivals are a couple of grownups who would be flunked by any modern psychological testing service. They are cousins of Jim Hawkins, if that's the proper relationship for persons born of the same inkwell. One is Prince Florizel of Bohemia, whose antics so enchanted us in *The New Arabian Nights*, and so irritated the sober Bohemians that they overthrew the throne and reduced him to operating that charmingly titled emporium, a cigar divan, by the time we met him again in *The Dynamiters*. Even the Prince's faithful aide, Colonel Geraldine, pleaded with Florizel not to join the Suicide Club, but you could no more do anything with the rackety prince than the elder Stevensons could do with R.L.S. He went to architecture school as his father demanded, he won a competiton medal to show that he could do great things in the bridge line if he wanted, then he turned his talents to the great bridges of imagination and threw away his drafting tools. As Jim's other cousin, Michael Finsbury, the merry corpse-hider of "The Wrong Box," remarked, "Nothing like a little judicious levity."

Perhaps there has been too much of judicious levity here, and you no longer believe that I am serious in my claim that reading helps the actor, but come with me on a brief visit to E. M. Forster who says: "In daily life we never understand each other, neither complete clairvoyance nor complete confessional exists . . . But people in a novel can be understood completely by the reader if the novelist wishes their inner as well as their outer life can be exposed . . . For human intercourse, as soon as we look at it for its own sake and not as a social adjunct, is seen to be haunted by a spectre. We cannot understand each other except in a rough and ready way; we cannot reveal ourselves, even when we want to; what we call intimacy is only a makeshift; perfect knowledge is an illusion. But in the novel we can know people perfectly, and, apart from the general pleasure of reading, we can find here a compensation for their dimness in life. In this direction fiction is truer than history, because it goes beyond the evidence, and each of us knows from his own experience that there is something beyond the evidence, and even if the novelist has not got it correctly, well—he has tried."

Taking my earlier example of duke study, it is not a bad idea, of course, to watch dukes moving about in newsreels or on TV in an effort to get such externals as the walk, but perhaps the closest we duke-apers can get to our subjects is in novels. Certainly, I now feel ready for a ducal trial onstage. If I am not up to Trollope's Plantagenet Palliser, Duke of Omnium, who was "a perfect gentleman," I can certainly do Doyle's Duke of Holdernesse, who had "a thin face, a nose which was grotesquely curved and long," and a certain weakness of character.

Those arts, which depend on individual genius and incommunicable power, have always leaped at once from infancy, from the first rude dawn of invention to their meridian height and dazzling lustre, and have in general declined ever after."

The words are Hazlitt's, and the arts of which he spoke were poetry and painting. The application I wish to make is to live theatrical television, that short-lived art which had its rude dawn in the late 1930s, leaped to a meridian height and dazzling luster in the late 1940s and early 1950s, declined thereafter, and now exists only for the dissemination of daily soap operas.

Desperate, fear-driven, immediate, it was an art practiced by wet-handed actors—"In this shot, Woodie, I want you to come running across the room, stop in these footmarks, see the body, and give a terrible scream. As you do, drop your left shoulder about six inches so we can come in over

you with camera three. Then, when you see the gun pointing at you from the window, jump two and a half feet to
the left and crouch down. Don't go further than that, baby,
or we'll be shooting past the end of the wall"—harried
directors—"Oh, my God, camera one just blew out. Somebody get out on the floor and signal the actors to stay close
together, because I won't be able to manage any cross
shots with two cameras. Two and three will have to divide
one's shots in the fight scene. We'll try to work it out during the commercial"—and confined writers—"You're not
writing for movies, Joe. You've got an actor getting out
of a full-dress suit and into tennis shorts during the middle
break. You better write a scene where he talks through the
door while he's changing. You know, he says what fun it
is to play tennis or something like that."

Half-hour shows were put on in four days, hour shows
in six or seven. The last day was a full one, running as
much as twelve or fourteen hours of technical drudgery—
"Better go a half step left. No, that's too far. Go back again
to the line: 'You say Mother is dying—'" culminating
somewhere on the dark side of exhaustion in an all-out
one-chance-only performance for some millions of people.

On the front of every TV camera is a little red light
which glows when that camera is transmitting what it sees
out to the forest of aerials across the country. Sometimes
the camera rolls so close to the actor that he almost feels
the glow of that light warming his cheek, and he knows
that some millions of people are staring into his eyes. This
can be an unnerving thought, particularly if the thought
behind those eyes is, "My God, what do I say next?" The
wise actor learned after a while that thoughts about the
forest of aerials do not help the heart, and managed to
achieve, if not calm, at least a concentration on the job at
hand which shut out the presence of the unseen millions.

Still, underneath, he remembered them and used the fear as urgency.

Ideally one might suppose that the camera should be ignored as well, but the danger there is that some great moment of acting will be lost because by ignoring the lens one has moved out of its narrow range or because by turning one's expressive features to the left instead of the right one is giving one's all to a little red eye that is closed. The watching millions then, like the people at the wrong tangential spot of a theater in the round, can see only as much of your feelings as you can transmit through your haircut.

The TV actor then, could not, in the grand theatrical manner, rush into his role with the fiery abandon which takes the whole stage by right. Some part of his brain had to stay detached to think in practical terms of chalk marks, of angles, and even of artificial changes of pace. These were indicated to the actor by a man crouching just out of camera range. If it appeared that a little too much brio was bringing the show to a close a minute or so early, the man would make taffy-pulling motions with his hands and some poor actor about to launch into a breakneck speech of denunciation would, on the spot, have to find a way to do it with slow and solemn majesty. If there had been a little too much solemnity and the show looked as if it might run too long, little circular gestures showed the actors that the philosophical pipe-smoking scene which had been planned to unfold like a beautiful flower, would have to be shot from a gun.

Also to be remembered were all the last-minute line changes dictated by the discoveries of the dress rehearsal an hour before air time, indeed sometimes only a few minutes before air time.

"Woodie, cut out the first two sentences of your fourth speech and blend the third sentence with the beginning of

your fifth speech, since I am cutting out everything in between. The sixth speech, because of what was left out
doesn't make any sense, so we've written you a new one
—got a pencil? I'll give it to you in a minute—and the
seventh and eighth are a blend with the last sentence of
the seventh and half of the first sentence of the eighth left
out. We have to save two minutes, folks, so move it right
along."

All the carefully shored up canals of memory are thus
broken down, and there is every danger that the material
will run out and make mud of your mind as the blasted
canals of Flanders turned the battlefield of the Somme into
deadly soup.

One famous director gave his cast such a talk about pace
just before the show that despite all the taffy-pulling they
finished a half-hour mystery drama with five minutes to
spare. Fortunately, it concerned itself with the murder of
a jazz musician, and the surviving members rounded out
the show with a jam session presumably in celebration of
the triumph of justice. Not every show had a band, however, and all of us had the nightmare that some day we
might be called on to recite something apposite while the
clock crawled painfully to the appointed hour of ending.

At the same time that one part of the mind had to be
set aside to take care of all these mantraps and spring guns
in the artistic path, the other part had to make sure that
none of this showed. It is possible for actors of grand manner on the stage to count the house while bringing thrilling
meaning to Lear's "Let me not be mad," or Hamlet's "O,
that this too too solid flesh would melt," but the little red
light looks into the "window of the soul" so closely that
the right things must move behind those panes even as,
in a closet, something is saying "Oh God, was that the
fourth and fifth speech or the fifth and sixth?"

The limitations of live TV gave it, somehow, a special and exciting form. For all that it scattered its image across the country, it had a peculiar intimacy. Movie cameras could go almost anywhere, could watch mobs from towers, peer up through oceans, sweep the horizons from airplanes, and through special effects go entirely outside the natural world. Time was plentiful, and screens were large. The film took the epic to its wide-screen bosom and left to the stage the excitement of the direct rapport between audience and actor, the 3-D, living color of actuality and the sense of structure which comes from seeing the whole shifting balance of a group in one sweep of that best of cameras, the human eye.

The clumsy TV cameras could make only horizontal creepings and a little limited booming up and down. Because an hour show had to be done in an hour they could not pause for regrouping and had to be careful not to photograph each other crisscrossing desperately about the studio.

Forced to look at the world through a knothole, the directors and writers of this shortest of golden ages created a kind of sonata form which drew intensity from the very simplicity of the materials at hand. Because the illusion was so limited, words and acting had a larger part to play. Shakespeare wrote scenery—"But, look, the morn, in russet mantle clad, Walks o'er the dew of yon high eastern hill." And although I don't remember anything quite up to that in what I did or saw, the TV pioneers made a great deal out of a couple of two-walled rooms, a cardboard front porch, and a short stretch of canvas street.

Actors were found and developed who could keep the two minds of practicality and dream in simultaneous operation, and if it was never easy, at least they never let you know it.

It would be silly to deny that all this ingenuity was very often used to project piffle, but the real miracle of the fifties was how much first-rate and near first-rate stuff was done under the handicaps of censorship, insufficient time, and an insatiable demand for hours and hours and hours of novelty every week.

The censorship was not only the obvious political nervousness of one of our less attractive decades, it seemed to spread to every group which bestirred itself to send a few postcards. Sometimes it seemed as if even the subject of murder might have been banned if only a few lifers had written in to complain of the unsympathetic light in which their specialty was sometimes put.

I remember the first reading of a TV play where an actor came to the line, "Don't be an idiot," and the producer stopped him and said, "Better make that 'Don't be a fool.'"

"Are the idiots getting angry?" incautiously inquired the actor and was crushed under the stern answer, "When you consider what a large percentage of American hospital space is given over to problems of mental illness, you realize that the word 'idiot' might easily give offense."

I can only imagine that it is the nature of foolishness not to recognize itself, as I did not hear that there were any postcards from fools.

"When I come in talk on a blank wall of stupidity facing me," wrote Logan Pearsall Smith, "why do I rush stupidly on to break my bald head against it?"

After a while, TV people managed to get their heads, bald or no, around at least some of the blank walls, and even the small victories gave a pleasant sense of daring.

Once I was given a script containing eighteen of what the older novelists used to call "vile oaths."

As we read through it for the first time the "continuity

acceptance" man, to use TV's wonderful word for censor, wielded his blue pencil like a sword and the serried ranks of "damns" and "hells" were cut down until only a single "dammit" was left. This latter had been saved by a plea on the part of the director, author, and star, who argued that, having given way seventeen times, they were entitled by any reading of the laws of Team Play to have their word once.

The censor gave this the wrinkled brow which indicates Mature Consideration, and at last allowed the fairness of the claim. When he had left us to the routines of putting the show on its feet, the director, star, and author, with a conspiratorial chuckle, confessed to us that the seventeen fallen oaths had never been intended to survive but had been added to give the censor a sense of a job well done somewhere short of the one they had wanted in the first place, and had, in fact, been allowed to keep. They had wanted it for the good and proper reason that an actor expected to fly into a rage finds "doggonit" a soggy springboard.

The early blues singers managed to make their meanings clear by describing the unmentionable in a special and superficially innocent language.

"'Anybody here want to try my cabbage,'" sang Bessie Smith, "'it's the best in town.'" And we all knew what jelly roll was and the vivid symbolism of the coffee grinder —"It has a special grind."

Television in those days often attempted to make its forbidden meanings clear by the Significant Expression. Close-ups of an actor and actress looking at each other could make crystal-clear the existence of adultery on a show where you couldn't say "hell."

Sometimes you would hear a director say, "Now kids, in this section where you are talking about perhaps not going dancing tonight, I want you to let them see that you are tiring of each other, are beginning to feel that soon you will end the affair. Don't give me too much disgust, though, because in the next scene when you meet by chance in the hotel lobby I am going to have a shot of the clerk recognizing you, and when I cut to you I want you to show—when you are talking about Jim's new job—that you would like to register and go upstairs once more."

It was another of the remarkable demands that live TV made on the actor, and for the most part the actors met it wonderfully, saying one thing, thinking another, letting you look into their thoughts, and hoping that they could manage the costume change faster than they had on the dress rehearsal when someone who was presumably talking to them had had to rephrase a question three times into empty space before they appeared and gasped out an answer while hiding a shoeless foot behind a desk.

In the role of a tailor I once rhapsodized over the fit of a suit which at that moment was being struggled into on the other side of the studio. I slowed down a bit as I went into the beautiful break of the trouser cuffs which was my coda, but I saw no one and heard only a few muffled cries from the dressing area. I started again with some gabble about the snugness of the collar and was taking up lapels in depth when he at last appeared, looking, naturally enough, far from the macaroni I had been describing.

Well, if it was all so terrible, you may say, why am I mooning on about it as if it were a big loss? Modern taping facilities give you all the continuity of performance and free you from the fear of saying —— by accident, failing to make a costume change, forgetting a line, falling down while running across the studio, or any of the other fears that used to flit through the head after the director had said, "Sixty seconds, everyone. Have a good show and spaceman's luck." (This last was a line from a daily children's space opera and was frequently used as that bit of wit which ought to loosen the actors up a little. It did not.)

Taping is done as continuously as possible, stopping only for major changes of set and costume, but in the event of grievous error, the act is done over again.

The difficulty lies in the decision as to what constitutes grievous.

There are occasions in a taped performance when an actor makes a small error, and he and his colleagues decide at that moment that no one would go to a great deal of trouble to correct it, and so they play on at full tilt and with every bit of energy they can summon, only to be told, "Sorry, folks, but one of you said custard instead of pudding, and since there's reference to pudding later we're going to have to do it again."

There is, of course, a little less energy this time through and when someone else makes what seems a larger mistake, the whole cast pulls up and plays at rehearsal energy level in order to save themselves for the third taping. It is this piece of group lethargy which is immortalized, however.

"Don't worry, folks, about that place where Joe fell over the couch. It makes a nice touch. The playing wasn't as good as the last time through, but it will do, and you were right on the nose for time. Make your changes for the next act."

And there you are, forever dreary.

Some years ago a historical series was launched with considerable fanfare and a full hour of Founding Fathers all talking as if they knew they would some day be on the stamps and the money, was to be taped in color. I played a discontented bricklayer who led a bunch of riff-raff in sneering at Hamilton—later we sneered at Jefferson to show how changeable mobs can be, and I remember the desperation of the fathers as time after time a fresh reel of tape began to unroll because the fog hadn't worked in the streets of Boston or the cardboard cannon had fallen off the two-dimensional ship with a thump which less suggested ordnance than an economy roll of paper toweling. After all, how many times can you say in what is supposed to be casual conversation, "The tree of liberty should be refreshed from time to time with the blood of patriots and tyrants," without becoming not just wooden but wearily wooden?

Late that night a group of us sat around with the director, all looking like survivors of Valley Forge, although only a couple were playing those parts, and he told us that he was supposed to be upstairs looking at the umpteenth tape to see whether the last act should be done again.

"I am not even going to look," he said. "It has to be okay. Nobody has the strength to do it again."

Hoarse from singing revolutionary songs, I stared at my perspiration-soaked wig and wished that the first take, quishy cannon and all, had been used. How well I had sung on that long ago morning when, like the new nation, we had been fairly bursting with hope and vigor.

If we had done it in the live days, the audience could have had a good laugh over a mistake or two, but they would have seen a bunch which looked plausible as the conquerors of King George and all his men.

Movies, of course, shoot things over and over again but not in sustained stretches of half an hour to an hour at a time.

Even the piffle of which I spoke earlier had its moments for the actor. Some of it, like the daily space opera, permitted, nay, encouraged, really shameless acting. I even saw a distinguished member of the Actors Studio flourishing his red plastic disintegrator gun with wild gusts as he snarled like someone telling about the bears in a bedtime story while herding some space cadets off to the plutonium mines of Arcturus II.

I had sentenced them to this work in a kind of galactic magistrate's court, where, for reasons of dash, the prosecuting attorney and myself were dressed as Roman charioteers, complete with short skirts and ribbon headbands.

The DA, whose lines came right out of the New York State Criminal Code, confessed to me later that as he paced up and down before my bench speaking the kind of material which usually goes with a double-breasted blue suit, he glanced down occasionally at his bare knees and had the terrible thought, "I'm naked and the judge is going to cite me for contempt."

Then he would look up and see His Honor pushing ribbons out of his eyes with a gavel, and feel better. What fun we all had, though, making faces we hadn't dared to use since playing war games in the back yard!

I am told that the children thought the show was marvelous, and the star, relentless scourge of space crime, won a decision from the tax court that he should be allowed to deduct cab rides from his income tax since his presence on the subway would break the hearts of his fans who could not imagine why he was strap-hanging on the humble rockets of the Transit Authority, when the previous evening he had been light years away.

The few theatrical TV shows which are still seen live have lost the daring fiber of the past, and as the actors go through their parts, men with large cardboard pages thrust the script at them from just outside camera range. These pages are called cue cards or idiot cards (that word again!) and the men are skillful enough so that you can appear to be staring into the girl's eyes while reading the words "I love you" over her shoulder; but people don't really look the same when they are reading as when they are wooing, and the more conscientious actors, even doing the shows every day as the soap operas are done, try to learn all but the medical jargon which makes up such a large part of these shows. Such stuff sounds as if it's being read even when the surgeon says it while reaching for the scalpel.

Even before the cue-card days some actors used to scribble a reminder or two on the floors, the furniture, and the walls; one man I knew spent hours transferring the whole of his part to every flat surface on the set. Even in a show where he had the single line, "Man Overboard!" cued by a sound-effect splash, he inked the cry on the ship railing where he was to lean.

"Why take a chance?" he said, but then, he is the actor who, on hearing that a dog was to be used in one scene, said, "Get a big white one so we can write on him."

The only means of preserving any of the prodigies that were performed in those full and frantic years was the Kinescope. This process consisted of setting up a movie camera in front of a television set and filming what appeared on it. The set was what is called a monitor. It is directly wired to the transmitter and being right there in the studio gets a better picture than the shadowy snow-bound sets in homes; but still a picture of a picture has a remote feeling, giving you, like a sepia-tone engraving of the Sistine ceiling, more an idea of what you've missed than anything else.

It soon became obvious that some better way had to be found to preserve and reuse TV shows. A way had also to be found to make sure that they were made without any of the mistakes big or small that sponsors were increasingly unwilling to accept as they paid bigger and bigger bills for their castles on the air.

Film came first, film which in the beginning had supplied TV with the stuff that was no longer acceptable for second-run children's morning matinees in small towns, Western movies in which the heroes still wore white hats, and animated cartoons in which innumerable and identical cats and mice made endless war.

The studios began to turn out dehydrated B films to order and fitted them up with hosts (a host was a passé movie star in a fancy bathrobe who unflinchingly summarized the plot of what you were about to see) and "formats" in which groups of these little pictures were tied together: "Great Stories of Passion," "Classic Theater" or —if the star who did the introductions was famous enough —"Derek Raythorne's Favorite Tales."

I shall never forget one of these in which an actor looked up from a fireplace in which a glass blaze flickered soundlessly and introduced to us a modern version of De Maupassant's "The Necklace." Presumably in order to make it one of his favorite tales, it had been fitted out with a happy ending.

" 'If we had not spent all those years slaving to buy the new necklace we should never have discovered each other, my darling!' "

" 'Oh, how right you are and what a happy accident it was' "—or words to that effect.

There is in Hollywood a square white house with a square foyer. A staircase with square railings runs up the left side wall of this foyer, and I have been in the house hundreds of times during the second half of double bills. Wholesomely zany families lived in that house, and they did things you wouldn't believe. At least, I never believed them.

When the movies began to decline the house was shut up for a while, but when TV moved to the coast, the funny families moved back in and began to do the half-hour series that were to make some of the performers more famous than presidents, prime ministers, and kings.

Here was the beauty of the filmed series. It could be shown again and again, and when it had reached a peak of popularity, its elements could be extracted and made into plays, novels, and full-length theater movies, an example of the reuse of material unequaled outside a termite hill.

There was an explosion about this time in the number of TV sets sold, so that the new shows, no matter how hastily or badly made, were guaranteed a rapidly growing audience.

I am not attempting a history of television entertainment, however, being both unqualified and biased. TV's *Drang nach Westen* was as historically inevitable as was, according to Tolstoy, Napoleon's March to Moscow, and my nostalgia for exciting chaos is too unrealistic to be pursued here.

A last anecdote and we will say farewell to the netless acrobatics of live TV. A director who had used me a number of times as a comedian summoned me to play a man driven mad by anxiety—perhaps something in the way I told my jokes suggested me for the part—and the script showed that the audience must know from simply seeing me sitting wordlessly as a legal conference, that I was about to go down the dark slide.

Later I was to have a splendid mad scene, but it was important to know that this was coming, and I had about three seconds of close-up in which to foreshadow it. Dur-

ing the last half hour before the airing of the show, I sat
alone in a corner of the studio and visualized all the possible disasters that might happen. I reviewed the difficult
camera work. If I were to make one excessive move while
thrashing about in my breakdown the watching millions
would see past the end of the wall of the Long Island
drawing room not the formal garden but a forest of cables,
"No Smoking" signs, water pipes, and paraphernalia from
a children's show that was to be seen the next morning.

I went over my lines, discovering how many words could
be mispronounced in such a way as to sound obscene. It
seemed as if a farrago of filth could be released by the
slightest twist of tongue, and I tried a few shockers, as one
touches a tender tooth to feel the premonitory pangs of
coming dentistry. They would certainly be television firsts,
and as I heard their harsh sound I felt the first film of
perspiration starting on my brow. I went on to review the
general inadequacy of my performance. Was not my lunacy
the unconvincing capering of a Little Theater Macbeth
trying to see Banquo's ghost? Was it not self-conscious and
embarrassing? It was, it was, I thought, and began to
breathe with rasping irregularity. Around me I heard the
studio begin to stir for the last minutes of preparation, and
in imagination I seated myself at the window of a commuter train and visualized the endless tangle of aerials
over the housing developments. My eye muscles began to
twitch, and I left the train and flew across the country in
an airplane, endeavoring to see all the stops on the network. My eyes started out of the fluttering lids, and my
stomach closed in an iron knot, somewhat discommoded
by some corned beef and coffee cake it found in its grip.

I tottered over and sat at the lawyer's table, and a couple
of minutes later the camera saw a man in hell. Some who
saw the show told me that they would remember my face

on dark nights when the wind blew around their seaside cottages and would hear my voice in the mad scene. In it I avoided the unforgivable, even though I was foaming slightly at the corners of my mouth.

I don't really know what happened in the scene, except that somehow I never led the camera into the Children's Village and that I acquired a couple of large bruises from rattling against myself. I don't know what happened because I really went mad for a couple of minutes. Constantin Stanislavski calls this kind of acting "diving" and commends it as a dangerous but essential weapon in the actor's arsenal. I am not the man to achieve it often, but the fears of that evening sent me off the high board in what I like to hope was at least a nine-point dive.

Tape, which now shares with film the job of bringing order to TV, has some of that dry-mouthed urgency, but, as I've shown, or hope I've shown, it is danger with a difference, and the difference, though sometimes comforting, is sometimes a little too comforting.

Precision, which knits up the raveled sleave of a TV sponsor's care, reaches fantastic heights in the making of the commercials that remind you from time to time of who is springing for all this entertainment.

Making a one-minute spot with live actors in a full day is possible, but two days is a common span for the polished sixty seconds of selling. I don't know how long it takes with the animated packages and talking pill bottles, but the technical complexity of some of them suggests that they take as long as J. S. Bach needed for a cantata—Sunday to Sunday. Whatever I may think of commercials as a viewer, I am, as an actor, inclined to regard them as our equivalent to the foundation grants which support some of our poets, painters, and musicians.

It's true that there aren't enough commercials to go

around and that they are awarded after endless auditions by standards of performance that few can understand, but then, this seems to be true of foundation grants as well.

In any case, an actor who does a commercial that is shown repeatedly on television will receive a fee for every one of these uses, and should he manage to get two or three of these grants in one year, will have a financial cushion which will permit him comfortably to appear off Broadway in parts that he really likes, to refuse roles that he doesn't like, and generally to behave like a Renaissance artist who has secured the patronage of a cardinal.

It is frequently bemoaned in the thinking press that the artist has been marooned out of reach of the rewards of the affluent society and that as the great golden galleons sail by, he can only come down on the beach and shout unheard like the men left behind when the *Hispaniola* took the riches of Treasure Island back to England.

The painter who goes in for illustration, the musician who writes film scores, the writer who does popular magazine pieces, the actor who becomes a member of a zany TV family, manage to get some of the rewards but at cost of what they really wanted to do. This kind of thing takes up most of their time.

Only the foundation beneficiaries and the actors in commercials receive both the pieces of eight and the peace of mind which comes from spending most of your days on absorbing work.

I do not speak as one who has received many of the soap-chip Guggenheims and beer-bottle Fulbrights, but that is partly the fault of my theatrical image. I have spent so many years playing scenes of low life and the sour cynicism of janitors and cowardly deputy sheriffs that I did not leap to mind when casting people were thinking of actors to play characters to be made deliriously happy by a new kind of dehydrated noodle soup or a soda pop that would help their bowling scores.

Here, however, the inexplicable standards of commercial casting proved me wrong a couple of years ago. Summoned to read for the role of an electric-razor salesman at an advertising agency which had already many times found me wanting, I went through the copy like a hung-over lieutenant reading the Articles of War on a hot parade ground and left after mumbling some casual thanks.

To my surprise I was summoned back the next day and asked to read it again. The slight approval indicated by a second chance put a pitchman's lilt in my voice, and I peddled razors with sprawling eagerness.

"No, no, Mr. Broun," said the agency man, "I had you back because I wanted my colleagues to see that dry, uninterested quality you showed me yesterday."

Hastily I extinguished the light in my eyes and tried for a now artificial despair. I must have done a good job, because a week or so later I was summoned to a department store in Stamford, Connecticut, which was to be the setting for our razor drama.

We had to work in the evening when, unhampered by real shoppers, our hired shoppers could move through the choreography which preceded the pas de quatre for two ladies and two escalators. The ladies were to emerge from two crowds, one at the top and one at the bottom of a pair of escalators and, joining their endlessly revolving mechanical partners, were to exchange some words about what to get for a husband's birthday and arrive at the magic name of the razor when they were exactly thirteen and a half feet apart or some such impossibly exact figure. The lady coming downstairs was then to walk over to my counter, and I was to tell her about the razor in the manner of one of those English tailors who make you take things by suggesting that perhaps you shouldn't.

For hours the crowds milled, the ladies escalated and called across the gap about Jim's birthday and the need for something special and arrived at the revelation of the special thing and were told to try again because they were fourteen feet apart. I believe that along about midnight someone discovered that although the ladies were metronomically constant, the escalator was not, and I think at this time a halt was called for an inspection of its worn cogs. I'm not sure of this, however, because, too apprehensive to sleep and too bored to stay awake, I was stretched out in the Cabaña Fun display hearing almost nothing except my sales spiel running through my head with the mindless intensity of Noah Brooks's "Punch, brothers, punch with care. Punch in the presence of the passenjare."

Certainly there was a hammering sound from the escalator area, but it may have only been angry agency men kicking the machinery with those heavy cordovan shoes which are the combat boots of Madison Avenue.

I know that at about 2 A.M. I was summoned from beside the glass swimming pool and faced with a wan lady who had been trying for five hours to get something for Jim's birthday and now faced five more hours of having it sold to her.

The executives closed in around us. There was the director, the account executive, the man from the home office, a group of Ministers without Portfolio, and the Impatient Man. I have done a number of commercials since this and have discovered that there is almost always an Impatient Man. The executives won't talk about him, so I have not been able to discover what place he fills in the hierarchy, but his job on the set is to look at his watch a lot and call people over to give them a wigging about how things are going. He does not talk to the actors but points at them a good deal while talking to executives in corners. When he comes closer he will stand a foot or two away from the actor, summon the director, and say to him, "He's not holding the razor right," with a jerk of his thumb to show who "he" is. The director will then turn and say, "You're not holding the razor right," while the Impatient Man goes back to his corner.

I don't think he's a vice president because the others— although they always listen to him—don't make any fuss over him or ask him to lunch. (He has unappetizing things sent in.) I think he is one of those ritual figures who are used in highly structured societies to keep down complacency, like the man who runs in front of a newly elected Pope burning straw to remind the Pontiff of the transitory and insubstantial nature of human glory.

Neither does the Impatient Man exercise any ultimate power. He is just there to crab. In my case a subterranean struggle broke out between the agency man who had liked my chilly selling, and the director, who favored the kind of razor peddling which is done from a collapsible suitcase in Times Square. Neither of them would speak to the other, but each of them took me aside and told me to pay no attention to the other while pretending to do so.

I felt like an intelligence agent who has lost his code book, and I looked desperately at the Impatient Man for guidance. He told somebody I was letting light reflect from the razor case and committed himself no further.

Eventually I did the sales message like the man whom Max Beerbohm described as "crawling on his knees while shaking his fist," but I had a sloppy tendency to do it in fifteen seconds rather than the requisite fourteen and a half. Once, without losing a consonant, I set a course record of thirteen seconds but that pleased no one either.

I don't know if any of the Popes ever growled, "Enough with the hay-burning. Get lost!" (it would sound more magisterial in Latin), but I know that at five o'clock in the morning I broke the rules and spoke directly to the I.M. when he complained that my hands were shaking. I let him have it with a sharp, "Please sir, if you'd just let me sit down for five minutes I think I'd be all right," and he was so taken aback that I got my five minutes.

At half past seven I finished the alternate premium offer for the Mountain States area, and everybody shot out of the store to make way for the cleaners who had clustered around to sneer at the last few takes. I discovered myself suddenly alone with one of the technicians, who said, "I'm afraid all the official transport is gone, but I can take you down to the railroad station and you can take a commuter train into town."

I thanked him and shortly climbed aboard a car filled with the *bons bourgeois* of the Custom Cape Cod class, all of whom began to examine me with distaste. I realized with horror that I was still wearing a generous smearing of pink pancake, when a bridge player who joined his four-some at Old Greenwich murmured loud enough to be heard, "I suppose he got on at Westport."

I wanted to go into the razor spiel so they would realize the reason for my make-up, but at that moment I never wanted to hear it again, and neither, it transpired, did the razor people who inspected our twelve-hour minute and threw it away.

Since that occasion I have had happier experiences as an actor-salesman, but even as to that terrible night my only real regret is that the nation was not repeatedly belabored with my sweet-and-sour performance.

E. M. Forster wrote, "It is pleasant to be transferred from an office where one is afraid of a sergeant-major into an office where one can intimidate generals, and perhaps this is why History is so attractive to the more timid amongst us."

The same, of course, may be said of criticism, and I, who said "Please" to the Impatient Man when I should have barked an order for a cot, am not asking for a network to run if I criticize one aspect of TV which seems to me both as actor and viewer to be deplorable.

The cries about not enough good music and not enough high-level drama, I think, are partly false. There is so much of everything, with a multitude of channels pouring out stuff all the time that you can see and hear almost anything you want. As to having to wait up for it or get up early for it, that's not a very impressive argument either, since it should not be too much to ask someone who claims to be starved to make an effort to get to a feast. For goodness' sake, get up or stay up! When Edwin Booth was touring the country, people used to drive hours through the snow in springless wagons to sit in an unheated opera house. Today people don't mind standing in line for hours to get tickets to hit plays for dates so far in advance that they may have to leave the tickets to their children.

One difference is, I think, that the people who drove through the snow to see Booth did not do it for any cheerless "dose-of-culture" reasons. You don't beat your way through the drifts to get at an intellectual medicine bottle.

It seems to me that too much of the cultural programing on TV is consciously and proudly dull, a vapid tonic of vaguely defined purpose.

How too often are the high-level dramas the lives of impossibly worthy historical figures. They seem to be Elbert Hubbard's *Little Visits with Great Men* brought to the clock-work life of a department-store Christmas window. Even the not-so-great have scraped off them the warts that

Oliver Cromwell wanted left in his portrait. Majestically, jokelessly, somnolently, they set us an example that no one could follow, and even their doubts, if we are allowed to see them, add up to no more than elegant melancholy.

Beethoven listens wistfully for chords through his growing deafness, but he doesn't blackguard his friends, fight with his colleagues, or question his laundry bills. Wellington sees his way clear through Waterloo, and Shakespeare is never at a loss for words.

Each of these heroes is sustained rather than weighed down by his role. The statesman gets a big kick out of being prime minister, the scientist knows that he will find the boon to humanity just before the last commercial, and the painter brushes his way toward the Metropolitan, painting each time a slightly better picture than the last.

Sometimes we are taken on a guided tour through the work of the great artist. The guide—a celebrity who loves nice things—tells us, softly, as befits one in church, what a soothing uplifting experience it is to look at great art and shows us, with a little not-too-technical talk, the magnificent final self-portrait of Rembrandt without any reference to the awful look on Rembrandt's face.

Into each cultural life a carefully measured amount of rain must fall, however, and for the requisite gloom we have dear old Henrik Ibsen. It is hard to remember that he once made people angry. Now he just gives them the wholesome depression they might get from a suburban sermon.

I don't think you can lay the blame on any basic ills of the medium, because the same tubes which are squeezing out the pale paste of "cultural TV" are, at other hours, and under other names, giving us wonderful programs which, by avoiding uplift, are uplifting. News specials, "white papers," discussion programs, and, yes, comedy shows show the vitality that is supposed to make what we vaguely call "culture" an important part of our lives and not just something to keep the children out of mischief.

It is these shows which make me say there is something for everybody. Some of the stuff of which the networks always speak piously when they are chided seems to be not for people but for what someone thinks people ought to be.

Well, that's as long and as circular as a good average editorial, so let's take it as meant and look at a couple of examples.

Of all our rebels, the most "in" at the moment is Thoreau. He rebelled against a society so different from ours that we can take him safely to our hearts and show our own precious nonconformity by leafing through a few pages of *Walden* every night.

I appeared as an actor on one of the many TV programs that have honored the degerminated sage. I was a pompous fellow who did not understand why Henry wanted to go off to think and grow beans in the woods. There were several of us insensitives, and I remember how gently and persuasively the Thoreau character talked to us. It's a wonder we didn't all go with him, but then it wouldn't have been a rebellion and he wouldn't have been the leading man. When he said good-by to us and disappeared into the canvas woods he gave a last wave which reminded me suddenly of Ronald Colman's farewell in *The Prisoner of Zenda*. Well, that was a wonderful farewell, but Zenda wasn't real and Thoreau used to be.

Some years later I chaired a panel show where six living and practicing poets were to discuss the age in which they lived. Such anger there was! Such bad manners, such shouting all together, such irrational overstatement! But then, too, such caring there was, and such involvement both in themselves and in the world! They did not agree, they had no message for the age which could be reduced to any order, and a couple of them ripped out unpoetic oaths, which had to be excised from the tape.

I don't know that any of them is today's Thoreau, but Henry didn't know he was yesterday's Thoreau, in the sense of having an influence or a passport to fame. No one consciously spurns immortality, but none of these poets was making graceful gestures in its direction. Of course, they want recognition and its rewards and indeed, on the program, discussed with good, practical bitterness the smallness of the fees they were receiving for doing it, but the important thing was that they didn't think that culture was something to Beautify the Home, Clarify the Mind, or Make a Wider Circle of Friends, and I suspect that their confused and passionate cries came closer to the real meaning of that fuzzy word than all the homages to Thoreau as a cross between Wordsworth and Doctor Doolittle.

Certainly as I hopelessly banged a glass ash tray and endeavored to bring them to a halt for the commercial breaks, I sensed a vigor that I don't find often in the embalming business that seems to make up the larger part of our public cultural displays.

One of the dreams of the actor has always been the repertory company. In this best of theatrical worlds he will have both continuity of employment and variety of roles. Television in a strange way has given to some few actors the first half of this dream at the complete cost of the last. The regular performers in the series shows have not only continuity of employment but salaries considerably above those paid in any repertory company anywhere.

They have variety of lines, new ones every week or, in the case of soap operas, every day, but none of character. Theoretically they should not be as bored as the actors who perform exactly the same part every night onstage for many years, and for all I know they aren't, since I am not able to describe either experience at firsthand. I have been an occasional performer on serial shows, however, and I must say that many of the regular actors seemed to be more miserable than the five-year veterans of a single script.

For one thing, the continued and hurried writing gives them less than deathless lines to learn; for another, they are so continually involved in the mechanics of production, whether it be for film, tape, or the viewer of the moment, that they begin to feel the puppet strings emerging from their wrists and knees.

I remember asking a lady who had performed for several years on a daily show whether she found that there was still variety of experience in doing it.

"Everything good or bad that could happen," she said, "seems to have happened years ago, but I still get frightened every morning."

Sometimes, too, the second identity has more reality than one's own. All that recognition, all those letters congratulating one on fictional accomplishments as though they were real, wedding presents when the characters marry, congratulations for successful operations performed on unopened actors, give a terrible ring of doom to the day when the actor is taken aside and told, "I hate to tell you this, Joe, but the big boys upstairs have decided that your character if going to die next week." Your character indeed! From a psychological point of view it is you, not the character, who is getting the death kiss from the gray-flannel Mafia. From a practical point of view you are not likely soon to achieve any other theatrical identity because you are too closely linked in the public mind with the just-dead doctor, cowboy, detective, or simple resident of Happy Valley, a typical soap city.

Sometimes the whole show dies, and then, if you were beloved enough, you may have a half-life for a year or two opening supermarkets in your old costume, but like the feebler phantoms of Gothic romance, you find your aura growing less and less until one day, without fanfare or phone call from a market, it's gone.

It is remembered only by the casting people who say things like, "Joe baby, I love you, but I just can't give you a part until the public forgets Precinct Psychiatrist. Jeez, you were great on that show! Remember the episode where you made the junkie on the ledge remember about his mother and his uncle, and he came down and was cured? They don't make actors like you any more, baby."

You may, if you wish, tell him that you are forgotten, that you shopped that morning and nobody looked across the melons at you and said "Hi, Doc," the way they used to, that nobody at a party has asked you to analyze a dream in months, that your unemployment insurance has run out, and that you are broke. He won't believe that you have more than passing troubles because he knows that you have inner strength. He saw you talk that boy off that ledge.

Perhaps by this time you think you have only passing troubles because you've been taken in by the same delusion. After all why did they pick you for that role if you didn't have some of the quality of quiet strength that would get a hysterical boy off a ledge?

If you think it incredible that anybody on the inside should believe that all that mimeography is real, I call your attention to the fact that confidence men are among the easier victims of other confidence men and that even the policemen whose specialty is running down confidence men have been taken many times.

Identification with role didn't start with television, but for the actors who spend a year or so in the ever-static yet ever-changing fantasies of the aerial shows, it is a problem that makes the sword of Damocles look as menacing as the cannon on the courthouse lawn. Horsehair threads are much stronger than the tangle of spider web that runs from sponsor to agency to producer to actor.

Through the not very many years I have been an actor I have tried to set up little landmarks to give some semblance of organization to a havey-cavey life. I have stored in memory various "firsts" and high points and parade them before myself in moments of discouragement.

Among the ones I particularly wanted to save was the first line I spoke as a professional—professional only in the sense of getting paid—actor. I can remember the occasion and the look of the television studio and that it felt wonderful to say it, but the words escape me.

I can only hope that as the pictures and sounds of the glass screen continue to pour over us they will not become vague experiences, never perfectly remembered.

I hope, too, that we don't end up feeling about TV as Mr. Leach felt about the beach in the child's poem of which James Agate was fond:

> I went on the beach
> And I saw Mr. Leach
> He had a sun cap on his head
> I sed do you like the beach Mr. Leach
> It's better than nothing he sed.

IN THE CINEMA at present the camera has become a sort of god. You have a camera fixed on its tripod or crane, which is just like a heathen altar; about it are the high priests—the director, cameraman, assistants —who bring victims before the camera, like burnt offerings, and cast them into the flames."

Such words from an actor would smack of the whine, but they are from a more impressive source, a very high priest indeed, the distinguished director Jean Renoir, speaking in an interview with the late André Bazin.

Upon reading them I went right to my encyclopedia and found a pair of succinct scholars named Hubert and Mauss who described sacrifice as an act "which, by the consecration of a victim, modifies the moral state of the sacrificer or of certain material objects which he has in view . . . a procedure whereby communication is established between the sacred and profane spheres by a victim."

I must say that except for the bit about the moral state of the sacrificer, the definition sounds a lot like movie-making.

Elsewhere I quoted Hazlitt on the rapid rise and even more rapid fall of art forms. In the same interview Renoir adds a parallel.

"All the industrial arts (and after all, the cinema is simply an industrial art) have been great at the beginning and have been debased as they perfected themselves."

I guess the movies haven't perfected themselves yet, since there are still some awfully good ones mixed in with the ones which even mass, Inca-style immolation couldn't save, but I agree that the imperfect silent films I used to see at Bim's 82d Street Theater—Two Features Changed Daily—more consistently raised—or lowered—me to an ecstatic trance than today's more glossy, noisy fare. Sophisticates may not agree, and I am glad that I am old enough to have seen Lon Chaney in *The Hunchback of Notre Dame* before these artistic agnostics began laughing at it in the basement of the Museum of Modern Art.

There was no laughter at such matters in Bim's. The gray, crumbling chocolate bars, which we bought from machines on the seats in front of us, hung, untouched, before our lips. Fortunately, the bars never melted. Age had dried them to the consistency of the contents of a canopic jar, and a good thing too, because the heat of our hands almost equaled that of the molten lead which Lon was tipping onto the besiegers below.

Our suspension of disbelief, that vital theatrical ingredient, was perfect. Was it because the picture was crude, the early product of an industrial art? Was the picture simply childish? Is there something childish about suspension of disbelief that can only be evoked by a piece of theater which is immature? Was it because the crowd I went to the movies with averaged nine years old?

We had to spend agonizing minutes in the lobby waiting for an adult to take us in, knowing from the sound of the piano inside that impossibly exciting things were happening.

When my father was a boy his father took him to see William Gillette in *Secret Service*. There is a moment in the play when Gillette, a Union officer disguised as a Confederate, is tapping out a message to Lincoln or Grant, or somebody important. A real Confederate discovers him and fires through a window in the back of the set. Gillette staggered and clapped a hand to his arm. Red fluid oozed through his fingers, and my grandfather leaned over and whispered reassuringly, "That's red ink."

"I knew better," my father wrote years later. "It must be blood. The hero had just been wounded."

He went on to describe the subsequent moment when the villain, sneering at the wounded Gillette, says, "Do you know why you're not lying dead with a bullet through your head?"

The crafty Gillette took a good long stage wait while he wound a handkerchief around the wound, and then, looking up with a faint smile, replied, "Because you're such a damn bad shot."

"I thought it," wrote my father, "the finest line I ever heard in the theater."

Even after many years as a dramatic critic he would put it no further back than third to "I never saw a woman burned," from *St. Joan*, or "I choose the weaker," from *Candida*.

Secret Service, as the name and the plot fragment I gave you show, was a childish play—or a primitive play, undebased because imperfect?

Once, with the late Frank Conroy and a young actress member of the most puritanical of the naturalism sects, I was discussing antique melodrama. Frank told us of a great favorite of provincial rep companies in 1912, a play which concerned the downfall of Napoleon. At the climax of the play Waterloo is taking place in the wings, indicated by stagehands setting off flares and whacking pillows with canes to simulate gunfire. The set was the Emperor's tent, and there a tubby actor with his hand in the front of his tunic brooded, staring out over an audience of Manchester cotton factors at the face of destiny. As the pillow-beating reached a crescendo, and the bowls of Greek fire flared with unearthly light, he advanced to the front of the stage and growled, "Damn these British bulldogs. They never know they're beaten."

Frank told us that in an instant the cotton factors leaped up as if it were they who had been whacked with canes, and were yelling and cheering like madmen. British bulldogs all, they had just won a historic battle.

Then it was my turn and I held the table spellbound with the plot of the movie *King Kong*. When I got to the part where the great ape is dying beautifully, hanging onto the top of the Empire State Building with one hand while holding Fay Wray in the other, the young actress broke in excitedly.

"Oh, how I would have loved to have seen that play and that movie!" she cried.

"But, my dear," said Frank sadly, "you and your friends wouldn't want to act in them." The young playwright in Leonard Merrick's *The Position of Peggy Harper* is ashamed of the cheap melodrama he wrote at the outset of his career, and you can see that Merrick doesn't admire the provincial manager who commissions *London Inside Out*, but there is something rather sage about this man's advice

when he says to the young writer, "The audience don't
want to hear *why* he wasn't drowned. Show him, my boy;
it doesn't matter how he was saved, bring him on: 'That
I am here to prove!' Terrific round of applause. See what I
mean? You lose your grip if you explain things, Tatham.
He's there! They know damn well he has been saved, because there he is! That's what we want in drama."

Of course, the book being a romance, Tatham goes on
to write better plays, and if I could make a small amend-
ment here to Messrs. Renoir and Hazlitt, it would be that
though ripeness is not all, it is not nothing. There is something special about primal vigor, but it is perhaps at its
best in lyric poets, leading men, and outfielders. Playwrights, character actors, and pitchers are at their best in
that brief golden noon when, not yet reduced to anxious
allegories, grotesque make-ups, or slow curveballs, they
have a wonderful mixture of youth and guile. Their eyes
still sparkle, but they have picked up a few of what can
be called, according to how you feel about it, tricks of the
trade or refinements of their art.

I suppose the closest thing I've seen to Tatham's first
play was a silent-movie serial in which three generations of
firemen were all played by Thomas Meighan. Everything
about that show was exciting. To begin with it was in a
strange theater. The doorman at Bim's, tiring of the endless oriental-beggar-whine of "Mister, will you take me in?"
had chased us urchins away, and we had gone all the way
to 101st Street in search of our fantasy fix. There we
happened to catch chapter one, and for months Eighty-
second Street knew us not, while we gaped at thousands
of feet of pink film—the fires, silly—and held our breaths
at a hundred rescues and a hundred collapsing, spark-
wreathed roofs. We followed the history of fire-fighting from the manually pumped handcart (Grandfather

Meighan) to the wonderful white horses (Father Meighan);
and at last we left modern Meighan sitting at the wheel
of a La France pumper, sharing the front seat with a girl
and a Dalmatian. I suppose a more worldly writer would
have made one of the Meighans an arsonist in Oedipal
rebellion against his father's preoccupation with the hose.

Please do not think of all this as another of those defenses of the simple wisdom of the unlettered, the validity
of the comic strip as modern folklore, or the pop-art philosophy of the Swedish films in which the character who
went to college is always sterile and miserable, envious of
the happy servants, and given to rimless glasses and stiff
collars. It is not that I wish to hoot Ibsen and cheer for
Hoot Gibson, it is that I want either the candle flame of
romance or genuine lightning bolts, and don't care much
for the stuff in between, the cultural soyaburgers, the efforts to engrave *London Inside Out* on stone tablets, and
the apocalyptic allegories which are among the fringe
crimes of the Bomb.

The purpose of the fire-fighting serial was to make us
cry, "And then?" and it fulfilled its purpose with agonizing
efficacy. Greater works are supposed, I guess, to make us
cry, "Why?" or "Whither?" These seem to me about the
only cries worth hearing, and yet I think the commonest
cry of stage, screen, and printing press is an indistinct
sound rather like "Waffle?" or possibly "Wabble?"—an
all-purpose question to which there is no answer.

But you are as tired now of standing outside the movies
as I was when I realized that unless someone took me in
quickly I would have to sit through the whole of the "love"
picture before I could see the beginning of the adventure
picture which vaguely audible chords indicated to be quite
exciting. You are entitled to cry, "Mister, will you take
me in?" and I will hear and heed you and get on with a

revelation or two about how we burnt offerings feel about the sacrificial process.

Let me quote M. Renoir again. Of the camera he says, "When it does move it follows patterns ordained by the high priests, not by the victims."

Please note that the word victim is not chosen by me, the self-pitying actor, but by the director. You may say that in the theater the actor's moves are not ordained by himself but also by a director, but the stage play belongs far more to the actor than does the screenplay, and I think it is fair to say that movie acting is not really acting at all, at least in the sense that we have meant acting since the theater's dawn.

In the same interview Roberto Rossellini remarked, "There are, strictly speaking, hardly any really creative artists in the cinema: there has been a variety of artists who come together, pool their ideas, and then translate and record them on film. And the actual filming itself is very often secondary. The real creative artist of the cinema is someone who can get the most out of everything he sees —even if he sometimes does this by accident."

How often I have been one of a variety of artists coming together to pool, I think he said, our ideas for translating and recording. I always wondered why this seemed such a havey-cavey business to me, but Signor Rossellini made it plain when he said that the actual filming was secondary. I, after all, am not there except for the actual filming and usually only for a day or two at that. Sometimes they seem actually to be keeping me away from the pool.

I was for ten weeks part of the pool of creative artists which made the movie *All the Way Home.* I spent the first four days of that time in a Knoxville cemetery silently supervising the interment of a box purporting to contain Robert Preston, and in a funeral home where I was em-

barrassed—wordlessly, however—to discover that I had taken
the mortuary business away from Preston's brother-in-law,
Pat Hingle. For nine and a half weeks thereafter I never
left my metaphorical cabaña, except to call and ask when
they wanted me to translate and record on film. At the
end of this long stretch I went to a studio in New York
and played a brief scene with lines in which, rather con-
fusingly, I collected the clothes in which to lay out Robert Preston. The actual filming of this was so secondary
that the rest of the team decided it hadn't been worth the
trouble and eliminated it from the final version of the
picture.

This is not the story of a grievance. I have nothing but
the warmest feelings about *All the Way Home,* which for
two and a half months made me feel like a *rentier* and
gave me only one difficulty, that of deciding what to tell
people who asked me, during those weeks, if I was working. Still, I did not at any time really feel, nor was it
appropriate for me to feel, like a member of a team. I
never checked it over with the once and future Robert
Preston either, but I suspect that distinguished actor
though he be, he didn't feel much like a team member.
The actors never do, because the filming is incidental.
Movie making is done when the last reel has been developed, and—but let me quote the distinguished director
M. Renoir once more. I am, after all, not used to obtrud-
ing my opinions when directors are in the same room even
as smudgy portraits in an open magazine.

"The creator of a film isn't at all an organizer; he isn't
like a man who decides, for instance, how a funeral should
be conducted" (*That's me, maître*) "He is rather the man
who finds himself watching a funeral he never expected to
see, and sees the corpse, instead of lying in its coffin, getting up to dance, sees the relations, instead of weeping,

running about all over the place. It's for him and his colleagues, to capture this and then, in the cutting room, to make a work of art out of it."

We actors then, do not really even know enough to lie down in our coffins (no reflection is intended on Mr. Preston—it's just an image). Sometimes what we do is quite out of connection with what will later be made of it.

Consider that peculiar, uneven picture *Journey into Fear*, which was made many years ago by Orson Welles. Early in the picture we learn that Joseph Cotten, a British engineer, is threatened with assassination—only-he-knows-the-plans kind of thing. The Turkish chief of secret police, played by Welles on that dangerous knife edge between the colorful and the silly, puts Cotten aboard an obscure freight boat bound for England and assures him he will be safe.

We get a shot of Cotten leaning contentedly on the rail while the ship is still at its pier. While he is registering comfort, safety, and relaxation, we cut suddenly away from him to a shot taken directly into the harsh night lighting of the dock. Shadowily, at the end of the long wharf, we see a squat, dark figure moving like a self-propelled mortar toward the ship. We know who and what he is, despite the fuzzy lighting. The cutting has told us that he is Menace, and the long chiaroscuro pan shot which brings him closer to the gangplank makes him flicker oddly like the negative of a candle flame—we know he will be formidable both as killer and actor.

We are given a brief glimpse of him getting aboard, and we note with an agreeable shiver that his eyes are covered with immense, thick glasses which give him the terrible, impersonal concentration of a praying mantis deciding where to put the spike, or a doctor looking at your X rays. We see him next in his cabin and his acting consists of combing his sparse hair with meticulous care, and putting the needle back to the beginning of a just finished phonograph record, but what "acting" Welles makes of this with his cameras and mikes! The glittering spectacles flash at us from a mirror. The record is a tinny, sweet waltz. How grotesque that this stout killer should be fond of it! The care with which he arranges his hair has a macabre, devil's-beauty-parlor air, and more chilling still, the action of combing lets us see the thick, powerful pudginess of his hands. We know what he is going to do with them, and we cringe when the syrup stops flowing from the little windup phonograph and the great paw reaches down to engulf the playing head and restore it again to the first melting bars.

Away we go to poor Cotten sitting down to his dinner with the relish of a man delivered from death. He looks smug, but we, with the waltz still coiling through our ears, jump when a cross shot shows the villain being seated at the table directly across the dining salon from our smiling hero. The killer stares openly at Cotten and, when his soup comes, without shifting his gaze, fumbles up a large pilot biscuit. Cotten, feeling uneasy under the stare, looks, and their eyes—in two reverse close-ups—meet. Here is the camera's great moment. It fills the screen with the hand and the biscuit. Convulsively the hand closes into a great, lumpy, menacing fist full of crumbs. Heightened sound makes the crunch of the biscuit remind us of "I'll grind his bones to make my bread." We cut to Cotten, and we know he KNOWS. Back to the hand, which springs open and releases the flinty shards into the soup. Of course—a strangler. Up to the face. Was that a faint smile? I don't really know, and the glasses make it hard to tell, but I do know that at that point I was ready to give that actor an Oscar. It is twenty-odd years since I saw the picture, and

I have never forgotten his performance, although I have forgotten his name—but I must confess that all but the left little finger of that Oscar belongs to Orson Welles and the other creative artists in his pool.

When Hedy Lamarr makes her first entrance in *Algiers* we see in a long shot that she is a beautiful woman. We cut to a close-up of Charles Boyer, one of the most expressive of actors, and we know from his flow of expression that he is struck all of a heap. Is it the lady he is looking at? The next shot tells us with tremendous impact. It is a close-up of her mouth. It fills the whole screen, and the moist lips quiver into a smile over the tremendous, perfect teeth. It is a startling moment, but whose is it? Miss Lamarr's? The director's? Hedy's dentist's?

A few minutes later Boyer has crossed the floor of the Casbah cafe, has wangled an introduction, and is dancing with her. As he speaks, the music is soft and melancholy. As she answers, it becomes—mysteriously—the unbuttoned wail of an American jazz band. It almost, but not quite, drowns her words. We must strain to hear them, but the music convinces us that they are excitingly delivered.

Sometimes a simple directorial device affects almost every aspect of every actor's performance. I am indebted to Garson Kanin for an account of how John Ford turned his *Stagecoach* from a rambling outdoor causerie into one of the greatest of all Westerns by the addition of a single additional word of dialogue.

When the picture was originally finished it told the story of a colorfully mixed lot of people crossing the prairie in a stage. As they travel, we find out a great deal about their backgrounds and their hopes and see them embroiling themselves in a sub-plot or two. A big Indian attack at last sets in motion the series of events that brings about the resolutions. The pre-battle part of the picture had the leisurely, densely detailed quality of a nineteenth-century lending-library novel. The many airshots of the coach trundling across the endless prairie were beautiful but nothing more.

There was panic in the front office when the film was previewed. The director admitted that something hadn't worked, that the film seemed to sprawl, but shook off the panicky cries of no more money. He could fix the whole thing, he said, with a couple of actors, a two-walled set, a telegraph key, and an hour.

The actors are dressed as soldiers, and the set represents a military telegraph station. The camera opens on the soldier beside the key. He is quiet until suddenly the key begins to hop and chatter. As the message rattles along, a look of horror crosses the telegrapher's face. We cut to the other actor, no Morse reader he, looking quizzical. Back to the first actor.

"Geronimo!" he cries, and a second later we are looking down at our stagecoach—pitifully defenseless-looking as it crawls alone across a valley. We search the horizon for feathers, and we do it now every time the camera leaves the interior of the coach. We even curse the actors when they do not look out at the barren landscape. Don't they know? But of course they don't. Only an impotent outpost and an impotent audience are aware of what's over the next hill—or the one after that. How powerful now and how pitiful are the discussions within the coach about the new lives that are going to start at journey's end. How many will get past the Apaches? As they speak, our knowledge gives all that happens and all the performances a tremendous dynamism and excitement.

The important accident, the use of the dancing corpse as it were, occurred after all the actors had gone home. Of course, they are important. Of course, this particular cast numbered some very distinguished actors, and it is fair to say that others in the same circumstances might have been bad despite any directorial aids and would have looked good only in close-ups of their departing backs. Still, there is no burking the fact that a good deal of movie acting is—from the actor's point of view—like playing roulette. It is wonderful to have the winning number, but it is foolish to pretend that percipience picked it. One owes those chips to the croupier's wrist, the turn of the wheel, and the fall of the little white ivory ball, even to the age and density of the elephant tusk which produced it and so on.

Let me give a perfect example of a winning number. It is the great moment, or one of the great moments, in *Casablanca*. In the splendid schmaltz-on-schmaltz scene where the German officers offend the crowd in Rick's cafe by singing "Die Wacht Am Rein," Paul Henreid, his mouth working like a sound wave, goes to the leader of the orchestra and demands that he play "the Marseillaise." The leader looks across the crowd to the balcony where stands Humphrey Bogart in lonely splendor and a white dinner jacket. The camera arrows along the line of his inquiring gaze. "Rick" Bogart has heard the request. Will this worldly cynic okay the patriotic gesture? Will he defy the Nazi might, which has the power to turn his thriving cafe into a forest of empty, upended tables? Is Rick chicken? The crowd looks up—Henreid looks up—I'm not sure but I think Ingrid Bergman led all the supporting players in looking up while Conrad Veidt and his cruel cronies went on singing and banging their steins on the table.

Rick answered the questions with a nod, a magnificent nod full of proud affirmation of the right of freedom to sing, the right of mankind to seek his destiny among the stars, the right of Rick to stand proud and tall and say what will happen in the place that bears his name.

You remember what happened then. The orchestra played and the motley crowd sang and the Germans sang back and the French whore jumped off the German officer's lap and—but thereafter—I don't really know because I was crying harder than the French whore.

Back to Bogart's moment. What actually happened when that great nod was filmed? Bogart arrived on the set that morning and was told what a lucky fellow he was. "A soft day for you, my boy," said the director. "All I need from you is a silent shot, medium close, standing behind that railing over there. Put on your white dinner jacket for it, and when I say 'action,' nod your head." Information as to the why of the nod was neither solicited nor given, but when you see it on the screen you know that Bogart broke the bank with that nod.

Do not, I beg you, think that I am implying that he couldn't act if he wanted to. I am old enough to have seen the 3-D or Broadway Bogart and when acting was needed he was there with overflowing measures of it, but he told the nod story on himself to someone who wanted to praise him.

There are some others in movies who cannot act but who have mastered a wonderful precision which means more than acting in the highly technical field of the film.

A famous Hollywood star, who has lasted many years on two expressions, a worried smile and a placid frown, once told a group of New York actors, "I know you people think yourselves superior, but let me tell you something. I can get on a horse, ride it over the edge of a cliff, slide down the gravelly slope, make the horse rear at the bottom, and bring him down with his feet in the marks which have been made for his hoofs. That, friends, is movie acting."

We are pretty far along in this chapter, and you haven't had any intimate glimpses of little-known sides of the stars. I wish I could help, but if you have plowed through all the philosophy in the hope that you were at last going to get the Real Garbo, the Cary Grant I Know, or the Doris Day Nobody Knows, you'd better ask for your money back. The stars I know and the kind of movie making I know best come from the earnest world of the educational film.

"People have nowadays got the strange opinion that everything should be taught by lectures," said Samuel Johnson. I don't remember that the Chautauquateers of his day taught much to many, but the strange opinion today is that everything can be taught by movies.

To me and to other toilers in the educational-film field you owe—should you have seen our efforts—your knowledge of—to name a few—how to use your telephone correctly, how to run a business conference, how to keep from cracking up when given added responsibility, how *not* to collect money for the Girl Scouts (I frequently play the role of the Bad Example), how a neighborhood should handle the problems of a new housing development, and what are the requirements for the proper fulfillment of the office of coroner. A medical group made that one, and I was the non-doctor coroner. I made a terrible hash of the case. I must say, after looking at the slides of necrotic tissue which were the climax of the film and the undoing of myself, the pantaloon-coroner, I don't know why anyone would want the job.

Our world has its own stars, its own Oscar-type awards, and its own sort of fame. Long after the big films have had their last runs in the triple-feature drive-ins, our earnest efforts are being shown again and again to little groups of sleepy executive-trainees, in the basements of churches as a rainy-day substitute for the Sunday School gymkhana, and to high school students who might be interested in running business conferences or winning the office of coroner.

College classmates have told me that they owe a good deal of their eminence in the business world to the "how to run a conference" film in which I was, for once, the Good Example.

I am pleased that they liked the picture, although a little surprised. Perhaps because its purpose was to point out common mistakes, it seemed to me to have an anti-business bias worthy of Frank Norris or the early Upton Sinclair, and the certainty of a terrible review in *Fortune*.

My classmates, however, and I guess all the other businessmen, since this is one of the really big pictures in the genre, don't identify with any of the Goops at the conference. They identify with me. They take great pleasure in recognizing their associates among the Goops, and some have told me that our cast exactly paralleled the group in their shop.

Well, who were we around that sample conference table? First there was the discussion leader, a colorless, spineless gentleman like one of Galsworthy's lesser Forsytes or a betrayed husband by Balzac. At his left hand sat a monomaniacal golfer who actually brought his clubs into the conference room with him and kept looking at his watch to remind us that the tee-off time of his foursome was more important to him than the solution of our grave production problem. On the other side of the leader was a coarse bully like a figure out of Brecht who shouted and chewed cigars. He had nothing constructive to say but simply demanded action in a witless way. Filling out the table was a collection of toadies and familiars who would not have been out of place in the night-club sequences of *Die Blaue Engel*. Down near the end of the table was a frayed, stooped, and silent man, yours truly, from the firm's laboratory of standards. In an earlier scene worthy of Ingmar Bergman, we saw him sitting in his shabby little windowless office being bullied by his wife's photograph, which hurled contempt at him from a leather frame on his desk. The director worked with me for hours to get the proper look of neurotic gratification-cum-pain on my withdrawn face in this searing sequence.

As the conference ground to a halt in a babble made ugly by terror, the group leader remembered a maxim from some executive-education course, a maxim which was to be the motif of the picture. ASK THE MAN WHO NEVER SAYS ANYTHING.

"How about you, Jim?"—or Bill, or Manfred, or whatever my name was—"Don't you have anything to contribute?"

Something about his kindly tone emboldened me, wiped away the memory of the sneering photograph, and brought me to my feet for a five-minute talk which had been an agony to memorize.

My suggestion, highly and incomprehensibly technical, was something to the effect that if we loosened the tolerances on the camshaft drop-forged castings, we could use simple cold-rolling to braze the interruptor armatures, which would reduce our unit costs on a FIFO inventory basis to the square of the hypotenuse, and the best things in life are free—well, I think that was the gist of it. If you want the whole thing, ask your in-plant training exec to screen the film for you.

The rest of the conference actors simulated delighted understanding for which every one deserved a Golden Reel

Acting Award—and crowded around me, all tension gone, to carry me off for some gaiety in the coffee shop. Later—although it wasn't in the film—I suppose my wife spoiled the whole thing with cruel mockery.

I imagine that since the release of that picture, innumerable bemused executives have been poked out of their reveries on the grounds that their silence must indicate knowledge, but we must have genuinely stimulated someone, because the company which sponsored the film has since split its stock twice, and that certainly looks as if we helped, doesn't it? I never found out, though, whether they adopted my idea about the cold-rolling.

My reception from that group of businessmen was certainly very different from the reaction of the foreman who, in another film, was cracking up under responsibility, when I told him how to avoid muddy feet in the parking lot by shifting the space assignments for maintenance and production. He was so busy trying to remember the endless shopping list his wife had given him, regretting his rage at his daughter when she jammed a doll bottle in his mouth at breakfast, and wondering what he was going to say to the Bull of the Woods about retooling building C, that he didn't pay any attention to me, which, of course, is bad for Employee Morale. Later, after some truly well-written inner turmoil sequences, he straightened out, and the picture was a deserving prize winner in its year.

I mention this prize because it taught me about the elaborate class structure which exists even in the sturdy no-nonsense world of the training film.

The director of this prize winner was to direct the business-conference picture, and he had me in to meet the sponsor's representative. The rep was giving me uninterested tolerance and waiting for a look at the next candidate when the director said portentously, "Mr. Broun was in *The Inner Man.*"

The bored executive snapped to. Here before him was no longer a tweedy nobody with a deplorable mustache. Here was a member of a Winning Team. Winners Can Help You Win. Get the Victory Habit. It Spells Sit-Up-and-Take-Notice, Growth Prospects. Winners Give You the Aggressive, Hard-Hitting Campaign Which Means Maximum Penetration.

"Of course," he said, "you are the fellow who wanted to change the parking lot. Certainly I remember you. Damn fine job. Yes, Bob (to the director), I see your thinking on this, and I'll buy it. The office here will go over the grubby details with you, Mr. Broun. Glad to have you aboard."

When this second film won a prize, I became, for a time, the Donald Meek of the industrial-film world. Of course, as in Hollywood, there are struggles for power, savage in-fightings, and sudden changes in fortune, and for the last few years I have felt more like the Norman Mayne of the industrial-film world ("Norman Mayne is the most fin-ished actor in pictures"—"You can say that again, buddy" —*A Star Is Born*, remember?).

We don't whimper in our world, however, and there are some things I'll always be proud of. For example, when you go to the telephone, and somebody wants to give you figures, you always get a pencil immediately, right? That way you save the person at the other end from doing a lot of reading before you say, "Let me go and get a pencil," after which he has to read the same dull numbers all over again. This is a simple thing, but you might very well not do it if AT&T and I had not made a little film which showed how mad I got when I had to read figures twice to thickheads in my office. By the end of the film they carried pencils even to the washroom, and a lot of time was saved.

I forget how a neighborhood should handle a new housing development. I know we actors had a very pleasant day outdoors, spoiled only by the fact that half the landscape looked like Flanders at the height of Haig's offensive. Like the unhappy Tommies we had to stay on the duckboard paths or sink out of sight. I don't, as I say, remember the answer the picture gave, nor do I know what answer the people in that development found for what was obviously a nasty flooding problem.

There were lots of other films. Some taught through humor, some through fear—"This could be your car, your Loved Ones! Now Let's See It in Slow Motion!"—some through charts—"The row of little men shows the proportion of high school graduates among the skilled operatives," and some—using the technique of which Johnson spoke, just gave you a lecturer—"Oh, hello there. My name is Harris, and I'm a dentist. You don't have to be afraid of me today (warm chuckle), because I'm going to drill into your memory, not your teeth, and talk to you about a few simple rules of oral hygiene which will keep you out of my office and leave me more time for fishin'" (engaging grin and widening of angle to include mounted trout behind the speaker).

There is even a kind of educational film which makes you do your own educating. The Methodist Film Board in Nashville, Tennessee, makes pictures which present moral problems in play form, and the words "The End" appear on the screen before the trapped characters have arrived at any solution. It is then up to the audience to thrash out what should be the real end.

These are very stimulating films to work in, because between takes the actors and crew debate the issues they are shooting. In one script I was so sure of the answer that I begged the director to tack it onto the end of the picture and film it, but—now mind you I'm not saying they were immoral, just wrong—they didn't agree at all, and you'll have to work it out yourself.

Sometimes the issues were so balanced that there wasn't any satisfactory answer. When the English critic James Agate was unable to sleep he used to call up a friend and debate the Wallace case, that most mysterious of classic murders. Sometimes when I can't sleep, I run through my head the film about the machinist who cost his friend the fingers of one hand.

At the beginning of the picture we see the machinist and his wife sending their daughter off to college. It will be difficult for them to afford this, but the machinist is confident that it can be managed. He has invented a device to speed up a metal-cutting machine and he knows it will earn him promotion. Without telling anyone, he installs it, and it runs wild, injuring his best friend. The device is surreptitiously removed in the subsequent brouhaha. No one knows what happened. Insurance takes care of the friend—an office job is found for him—nothing practical can be accomplished by telling the truth. It will only result in disgrace and the end of his daughter's chance for a college education. But what of the man's feelings? What of the guilt that gnaws him, sours him, breathes a fog of wretchedness over every relationship and drives him to lonely pointless walks through weedy vacant lots? As he starts out on one of these, his wife (played by my wife) says desperately, "I know there's something wrong, but since you won't tell me, I guess I'll just have to trust you."

Unable to accept even this generosity he growls a denial and slams out, and—oh, not yet!—we see "The End."

The best I've been able to do in a large number of sleepless nights is a miserable call to the deus ex machina. I have the machinist win first prize in the Irish Sweepstakes and send the money anonymously to his injured friend. This clears his conscience, and he comes back to life. Please don't tell me the logical, moral, and probability flaws in this solution. I know them, and I haven't stopped working on it. This is just an interim solution, just something I use when I want to doze off.

The aims of educational films are usually precise, and even the ethical agonies of the religious films are aimed at a particular decision, but what of art? and art films? and the statement of M. Renoir that they are the result of the blending of accidental elements?

At one point in his argument he seems to say that handicaps are essential. "The Bayeux Tapestry is more beautiful than the modern Gobelins tapestry. Why? Because Queen Mathilda had to say to herself: 'I haven't any red, I'll have to use brown; I haven't any blue, I must use some colour like blue' . . . Obliged to make use of crude contrasts, constantly struggling against imperfections, her technical difficulties helped her to create great art."

The idea that improvisation helps the artist to achieve that purpose so often unclear to him, which started him on his odyssey, his treadmill, his downfall, or whatever it turns out to be, is an interesting one and seems to have worked well for the Queen and the director, as their work attests. My own first connection with an attempt to make a movie on these principles did not completely convince me that the idea was as unchanging as a law. The producer-director-author of the film had no green, or money, and was trying to use something like green, persuasion. Instead of building sets he convinced jailers, school principals, hospital superintendents, and house agents that their locales were just right for a movie and would be all the better for its presence.

I did my work in the hospital lobby where, as an unsympathetic reception clerk, I dampened the hero's hopes of a fancy operation for his mother.

One of my lines in the script was, "Your mother will get adequate care," to be delivered in a manner to cast doubt on even this modest promise. A real-life hospital official, overhearing my rasping snub at a rehearsal, flew into a rage.

"Isn't it enough that you filled the lobby with machinery," he cried. "Now you want to make us look like a bunch of monsters. Make him say, 'Your mother will get very good care,' and make him say it nicely."

The harried director, called away from adjusting his lights—he filled more cabinet posts than a South American colonel—took me aside for a conference.

"Listen, Woodie," he said, "when I say, 'This is just a rehearsal,' say it our way and I'll secretly film it. When he squawks, hit your hand against your head and say how stupid you are and you forgot and all, and I'll say, 'It's okay, this one coming up is the take,' and you'll say his crummy line and make it as smarmy as you want. We won't roll the cameras."

The picture turned out something short of Bayeux but a little ahead of Gobelins, and it must be said that without a great deal of wool-color substitution it wouldn't have been made at all.

My first meeting with an improvisatory situation in a major picture resulted from an opposite problem, too much money. The scene in which I played involved some cooperation from the pigeons of New York's Central Park. The star of the film, Judy Holliday, was to throw peanuts over the shoulder of a seedy grasscomber who is curled around a portable radio. The advance of the hungry birds annoyed him (me), and there was an altercation with Miss Holliday which brought her to the attention of Jack Lemmon and Cupid.

This film had an army of stagehands, and every one of them had been given a wad of money to buy pigeon food and spread it. The grass was a tacky mass of Melba Toast, Zwieback, Holland Rusk and even—it was a big-budget film—pounds of preliminary peanuts. The pigeons had, by the time we arrived, breakfasted like Roman senators and were reeling around, stopping to put claw to beak and looking for soda-mint tablets among the nuts.

When the cameras began to roll and Miss Holliday threw the peanuts that were in the script, the pigeons moaned and stood still, looking like Dylan Thomas' uncles after Christmas dinner.

Now improvisation was unwisely cast aside, and artifice was summoned in the persons of a troupe of fifty trained pigeons said to be as well disciplined as the Swiss Guard. Their trainer briefed them, Miss Holliday again threw the nuts and the professional birds, advancing in an eerily perfect column of fours, spread themselves over me as if I were a dove dancer.

We moved on to the dialogue, and a couple of days later, after the stars and director had returned to Hollywood, improvisation became fashionable again. Somebody had looked at the pigeon pictures and decided that the feathered army looked too much like just that, and I was summoned back to Central Park with a cameraman and a stagehand with a small bag of parched corn.

The tremendous heat of the original day in the park, a baking agony that would make Fort Zinderneuf look like the balcony of Loew's Murmansk, was gone. A cold rain pattered down on the deserted sheep meadow, a cold, bracing rain, which made it very disagreeable for me to resume the sprawling position in which the cameras had first found me. The rain had livened up the pigeons, however, and the parched corn was greeted by a lively, high-stepping crowd (I guess the cold ground was disagreeable to their naked feet), which, demonstrating a simple naturalism, earned that highest theatrical accolade, "Why, they didn't seem to be acting at all!"

As they whirled through a greed pattern, I rubbed pools of water off the top of the portable radio and tried to pretend that I was soaking up sunshine. A few minutes produced the requisite shots, and the artists of the laboratory, faced with this saturated tapestry thread, rose to the occasion with a masterful overexposure job so that now, when I see the film late at night on television, I can't remember when I was hot, when I was cold, and if I ever looked that young.

However loose and free the creative talents at the top may feel, however, the average actor feels more like the shuttle than like the tapestry weaver. The precision with which the sacrifice—to go way back to the original image —is carried out makes for a neat ceremony: the high priest's weapon is a tape measure.

Filled with creative fire or whatever, the actor stands ready to give life, dimension, and the certain magic something to his character, while people measure the distance from the lens to his nose, and hold light meters against his cheek. Reading the meters, they cry, "Put a piece of gauze in front of that light—no, wait, it's bouncing off the desk top. Props—wax the desk top, please. Now try the gauze in front of the light behind his head. Now bring it down a point"—the magic something gets the least little bit round-shouldered, the actor shifts his weight a little, and a drop of sweat runs down his cheek. An alert make-up man runs out of the shadows and pats at the drop with a powder puff still damp from the previous drops—"making movies," said Fred Allen, "is like being beaten to death with wheatcakes."

A lot of other light jargon has been said and implemented, and the actor has begun to concentrate on a foot cramp when the cameraman announces that he is satisfied with the artificial sunshine. The actor straightens up and kicks the magic something into a position of attention. The director cries, "Roll 'em," a functionary looking at a dial I've never quite understood, says, "Speed," the camera says, "Sticks," an assistant holds up that familiar black-and-white clapper, says, "Scene 27, take 8," and snaps the clapper, the director calls, "Action!" the actor says, "Mr. President, the rocket is over—" and the sound man says, "There's a hum in one of those lights," and everything stops.

Imagine that through a good deal of turning on and off the hum is located and stopped. Imagine that the discovery leads to a shift in the light plot and that everything is then the same except that the clapper man says, "Take 9," and the actor says, "Mr. President, the rocket is—" and someone says "Airplane!" Everything stops. You see if you have an airplane sound in this long-establishing shot and not in the close-ups—well, I mean, I understand and all, but if I don't get to tell the President pretty soon I'm just going to burst, and maybe the rocket will too.

Precision is the watchword, the byword, and the last word in the making of movies. We spoke earlier of the hoof-mark hitter and his address to the eastern actors. They, filled with the burning desire to preserve "integrity," which everybody knows is consumed in Hollywood like peanuts at a ball game, determine that their horses will always be allowed to act like real horses.

They will maintain spontaneity, freshness, and the spirit of Queen Mathilda, but the atmosphere at last defeats them, as it seems to defeat even people in the higher echelons.

I remember once when I was trampling on the intentions of the author and director of a movie through some misunderstanding which now escapes me, and the director called a halt and left his chair to come and talk it over. Before he could reach me he was engulfed in a crowd of men carrying lamps, lamp hoods, gauze circles of varying thickness, and a rainbow of gelatin sheets for coloring the lights. His words were lost in a babble of a up-a-point and down-a-point, until at last, in despair, he gave a high shriek that brought a moment of stillness.

"Please," he said, "give me just a moment to speak to the actor."

Holding their burdens, the men stood patiently, but indicated by occasional shiftings of feet that we could not expect too long a reprieve. Hastily, and with many glances over his shoulder, he tried to explain to me what was wrong and what might make it right. He got most of it out before the martial clangor revealed that the real battle had begun again. The subsequent film revealed that he needed more time.

Of course, all that stuff with the tape measure is very important, but I can't help thinking of the words of John McGraw as Tom Meany reported them in his book *There've Been Some Changes.*

McGraw was lecturing a young outfielder named Al Moore, who had made a magnificent on-the-fly throw to the plate.

" 'I thought I explained,' " Meany reports McGraw as saying, " 'that I always want throws from the outfield to take one hop in case a cutoff is necessary. You probably think you made a fine throw. You heard the fans cheering. Let me tell you something, young man. If I were to announce that tomorrow afternoon there'd be a throwing exhibition by Al Moore, how many fans do you think would show up? They come here to see the Giants win, not to see Al Moore exercise his arm.'"

I don't doubt that all these details are helpful but I do wonder how many people go to a picture because of its high print quality.

Neither do I wish my words construed as another of those high-level things about our mechanistic culture. Everyone ought to try to do his job the best way he knows how, and it is foolish to natter at the technicians for not goofing off. They are in the "variety of artists" of whom Rossellini spoke. They are among the tapestry weavers of Renoir's image. They, with us, are among the cast of the sacrificial rite. It's just that they, the directors, the writers, the producers, and the bankers have got the obsidian knives, and we actors have got the bared breasts.

The end result is wonderful. I think Movies are Better Than Ever and that Movies Are Your Best Entertainment. I know that most of the time my discomfort doesn't show or matter—except to me.

An eighteenth-century physician invented a system of medicine called Brunonia, which argued that all diseases arose from too much or too little excitement. From an audience point of view, movies get a very good Brunonian health report. Looking at my own chart, I'd say that some kind of powerful tonic is indicated, possibly a change of scene to, say, the stage.

THAT MOST WONDERFUL THEATER of chance, the race track, is a highly disciplined form of anti-organization, a calculated confusion, a drama with as many different protagonists as there are names on the card and, according to your luck, skill, or information, a triumph— "I won!" a tragedy, "I lost!"—or a realistic drama of everyday life (cashed a couple of tickets, lost the big one on a photo, met a friend who paid for lunch, met another one who borrowed five).

No avant-garde play can start such an argument about relative values as a simple sprint race for cheap horses. To you the hero is Helen's Dandy, 2–1, jockey J. Billings, while to me Helen's Dandy and several other early-speed horses are villains over whom I trust to triumph with a stretch finish and Tiger's Tail, 5–1, urged on by H. Smith. Others in the crowd regard you and me and our choices as enemies of the good, the true, and the beautiful, on all of which they hold mutuel tickets.

The drama is never completely resolved, for no sooner has one group in the audience been vindicated by the flashing of the results and the official sign, which is more binding but less permanent than the judgment of a whole academy of critics, than we begin lining up at the windows for the next act and the possible reversal of not only fortune but the philosophy of fortune. When the favorite wins and long queues await a return of $3.60 for a two-dollar ticket, much is heard of the essential orderliness of the world and the scientific method by which all the workings of the universe may be understood. It is a triumph for the Age of Reason, for Pope, for Johnson, and for Isaac Newton, the man who devised a system for handicapping the stars.

A half an hour later, when a crippled eight-year-old gelding feels a glorious and mysterious flash of youth and beats his betters to the tune (a far-off tune heard but by a lucky and sensitive few) of 50–1, the classicists are routed, and Swinburne rides down Pope, while the long lines of scientists at the payoff windows are replaced by short lines of alchemists and soothsayers.

Sometimes the outcome suggests Wordsworth. Romance, yes, but the comfortable, genteel romance of tea among the flowers, or the victory of a well-bred second choice.

Sometimes, as in most modern comedies of protest, it appears that there is going to be a terrific upset, until a favorite rushes up to take the photo in the last few yards and assure the perpetuation of the things which had seemed in such jeopardy at the half-mile pole.

My father first took me to the race track when I was eleven years old. It was the old, luxurious Agua Caliente in Mexico, a fantastic haven of agreeable idleness, where the horseplayers sat at wrought-iron tables, sipping tropical drinks and glancing over the form, while beautiful, uni-formed girls hovered at the elbow waiting to purchase the indicated tickets. After the race they cashed the tickets with a smile of admiration or tendered a smile of sympathy while they waited for you to try again.

I was admitted to the track without any cavil about cor-ruption of youth, but the management of the hotel drew the line at my entry into the roulette casino, and so my father, in order that I should not be without occupation while he was at the tables, taught me the first principles of horse handicapping and provided me with the elaborate past performance charts which are the foundation stones of the horseplayer's castle of dreams.

Every evening I pored over the figures with fierce con-centration, since, at eleven, science appears far more credi-ble and exact than it does many years, and exceptions, and reversals later.

I learned that one fifth of a second equals one length in difference between two horses and that five pounds dif-ference in the weights they carry means a half length. Using such simple tools and the pad of laundry blanks provided for hotel guests, I arranged the orders of finish of all the next day's races. With youthful arrogance I did not stop with the first three horses but worked out the putative positions of whole fields down to the group which the pro-fessional handicapper dismisses under some crushing re-mark like "better off in barn."

I find it hard to believe that the successful debut day at the track is a matter of chance. I have listened to too many long, dull stories of the triumphant innocent to believe it. It is always the same story. The teller, fresh from convent school, or the farm, or a strict home, goes to the race track with a lot of shrewd pool-players and sharpies. The sharpies talk a great game but are shut out, while the tyro, using hunches, or an oyster fork, or the pricking of the thumbs, has a wonderful day.

To tell you the truth, I was once the innocent and have many times been the sharpie. The terrible thing is that all those stories, however uninteresting, are true. The belief of the ancients in a bunch of mischief-making gods or immortal Tom Sawyers must have been based on their experience at the chariot races. The powers of these sprites extends no further than the placing of a banana peel or the finish of a few horses, but they do seem to enjoy giving you that wonderfully deceptive first day which you never quite forget, even a thousand losers later.

So Napoleon was thinking only about the first part of the Moscow expedition when he left his comfortable island and bought a win ticket on Waterloo.

I don't think the mosquito gods stick around to see that you or I or Napoleon loses. They just get you off to a good start and then leave you to the mercy of the Percentages, that group of Furies whose priests are called the Accountants.

Since I have already condemned first-day stories as dull, I cannot in good conscience, tell mine, except to say because of my extreme youth and innocence the track trolls let me win for six days running.

I brought from the hotel one of those little bags that slip over your hand to polish shoes, and as the days passed, the Caliente patrons became familiar with the piping child who pounded a shoe bag full of silver dollars on the table top as the field wheeled into the stretch. If you listened to his soprano cries, more often than not you heard the name of the winner.

I made my retreat from Moscow in high school, and to tell the truth I have never felt like having a try at Waterloo, contenting myself with occasional two-dollar bets, stepping up to five for such events as the Triple Crown, keeping track of the whole business in a little notebook like one of the postulants of the Percentages.

This seems to me a powerful argument for admitting children to race tracks. Nowadays they are barred in many states and are not allowed to learn valuable lessons while they have limited funds. Instead they are kept from knowledge as Eskimos were once kept from the flu, until, all unprepared, they are exposed and destroyed.

When I found out that that five-pounds-half-a-length business fails to take into account such things as the cyclical nature of neurosis in horses as well as men, I did not find it out at the cost of money belonging to my employer. I didn't have any. I found out at the cost of a schoolboy's allowance, and missed a lot of movies that I now see for nothing on television anyway.

When I discovered that the knowledgeable man in the tweed suit with the big 7×50 racing glasses was not a trainer but a tout, it cost me forty chocolate bars and probably saved a tooth or two. Later I made the further discovery that even when he *is* a trainer he is as likely to be wrong as the tout, and I had to stop betting until I got the next week's allowance.

Mixed in with all this were moments of triumph that I am willing to go on paying for through an infinity of little notebooks.

When I was a senior in high school I was spottier than some, shyer than most, and less self-confident than any of my classmates. In the presence of girls I brooded in a corner and tried to behave as if something rather terrible but very interesting had happened to keep me from dancing with them or charming them, or doing any of the other things I hoped they thought I could if only I would.

Later I found out what they thought, which was that I was shy and lacking in self-confidence.

All this changed when science or inspiration or a kindly return of the trolls caused me to bet five dollars win, five dollars show on Bold Venture in the 1936 Kentucky Derby. Since you didn't have the winner—few of us did—you don't remember the race any too well. I will spare you the pole-by-pole description, which I run behind my eyes when I am depressed, and just tell you that Bold Venture won by a nose, survived a foul claim, and paid $43 for a two-dollar ticket. Counting my show bet, this left me with a net of $112 and a reputation as the most glamorous boy in school. I emerged from the corner with a sophisticated smile and made the money and my confidence last all the way to college.

It took a while to get the betting arrangements worked out at a small Quaker college in Pennsylvania, but they were completed in time for the second fragrant memory, the twelve straight winners in the spring of freshman year, which gave me for a stretch of days a feeling of omniscience and enough money for a shawl-collared white dinner jacket and the gay life that it was made for. My dancing never got beyond a parallelogrammatic box step, and I don't know that the girls were really all that interested in my pole-by-pole accounts of my triumphs, but I "strolled along the Bois de Boulogne with an independent air," sure that everyone would "stop and stare." Twelve straight winners is right up there with breaking the bank at Monte Carlo, although the modest size of my bets kept my bookmaker from feeling more than a kindly pleasure in the good fortune of one of his younger customers.

I used to call him from the college drugstore, using the New York number which led, I was told, by subterranean cable to Jersey City and headquarters. He was kind enough to let me call collect, and since my own financial action didn't always justify the toll charges, I took to collecting a few bets from classmates to flesh out the volume of business.

This led to the formation of an informal turf club which bespoke a dinner on Saturdays, listened to the broadcast of the feature race in the bar of the country inn we favored, and then with appetites made keen by the greed of victory —sometimes fulfilled, sometimes not, but always good for the appetite—fell to. It was all extremely innocent, and although the club was coeducational, we stayed on the ground floor of the inn. Still I guess it speaks well for Quaker tolerance that I was never summoned by the dean.

Right after the war, while on leave in Paris, I attended some of the French tracks and found the racing conducted there to be as icily passionate and as sloppy in detail as the French classic theater, where the world's best acting is done in a maze of missed light cues.

Only the French would think of something like a race for maiden jockeys, that is, boys who had never ridden a winner. To give the event further panache, the race was scheduled over a difficult jumping course, which is like having a competition for maiden tightrope walkers without a net.

The juvenile cavalry charged at the fences with the endearing mixture of daring and ineptitude that has kept the memory of the Light Brigade alive. Their numbers were thinned as rapidly as if they were under the Russian guns, some leaving the saddle and some the course, but two of them managed to draw out from the field as they came to the last jump.

As they approached the takeoff one horse crossed sharply in front of the other, whether through the boy's design or the horse's, I don't know, and caused the horse behind to pull up sharply. The crosser got over the fence and maintained a margin of a length or so to the wire. I was detached about the mishap since my maiden had got lost in the woods on the far side of the Auteuil course. (He never emerged, and for all I know is now seen only on the eve of the Grand Prix, galloping soundlessly over the fields, glowing in the dark, as he endlessly seeks a finish line.) I did notice, however, that the crowd was strangely and ominously silent. There was none of the usual cheering or happy display of winning tickets.

As the boys came to the weigh-in, a crowd gathered which alternated in pelting the white-faced, defiant winner with clods, and shouting sympathy to the white-faced, sobbing loser, who caught a clod or two along with the good will.

As the crowd grew and there seemed a movement on foot to pull the winner from his mount and give him the treatment accorded the Princesse de Lamballe by another French mob (I spent a lot of time in high school trying to find out what was the plight of the Princesse de Lamballe "whose fate was too horrible to discuss here" —that is, in my mealy-mouthed history book. My other big project at that time was to discover what were the misdeeds of that earlier Pope John "which were too revolting to discuss here"—same book. I found out, but if you don't know, it probably wouldn't be fair for me to tell you. Research can be fun).

At that moment the results board lit up with a sign which said "*Intervention.*" I asked one of the potential rioters, who had stopped to read the board, whether this was the same thing which we call in America "a claim of foul."

The man looked at me with the scorn of an older civilization for a younger and said, "In a foul claim one admits of debate. In an intervention the honor of the track itself is at stake. The numbers will of course be reversed and, unimportantly, the boy's life will be saved."

Indeed I noticed that the crowd had at once stopped the pelting and shouting now that the track had pledged its honor. Indeed, it seemed to be a matter of honor with everyone, since both finishers were long shots which could not have had more than a handful of backers.

Many years earlier I had stood in the infield at Auteuil for the aforementioned Grand Prix, the great race of the year. From my spot against the rail I could see only one fence, but at a French track the cries of the crowd are as informative as a Euripidean chorus and as full of bad news. There is a kind of vast minor sob which goes with bad landings, and if the landing is the final one for that horse, his name rises to the skies in a ululating scream, as, "*Qua-si-m-o-do-est-tombé-é-é!*"

Sometimes you will hear a name murmured by a thousand throats, and you know that something is making a move. If the voices grow louder and more numerous, you know the horse is still gaining. The name will grow more frequent like the last go-round of letters in a locomotive cheer, but let the horse shorten stride, and in a perfectly descending diminuendo his name will be spoken softer and slower until it is dropped and the next excited murmur begins. These choruses involved everyone, and include people whose horses are out of it and sandwich and soft-drink sellers who don't bet.

When the final move is made in the stretch one name grows until it is chanted like a Kyrie, and back over the heads will come the exact state of affairs, as, "*Agitato—Agitato—par deux—par trois longeurs. Agitato gagnera par quatre longeurs.*"

If, like me, you had a ten-franc bet on Agitato at 6–1,

this wonderful chorale by a bunch of people who held tickets on Quasimodo, is both inspiriting and touching.

In America, where most of the noisemakers appear to be ladies in rimless glasses and runover white shoes, who yell, "Come on, number seven," the sound of the crowd, like the laughter of fools, is "as the crackling of thorns under a pot"—in stereo.

When I was a junior in college, a young newspaperman and I got hold of two passes to the clubhouse at Churchill Downs and, unaware that the clubhouse is a mint julep-peddling area shut off from the race track, decided to take a twenty-nine-hour bus trip and see the Kentucky Derby. We presented our passes and were ushered into a stockade lined with trestle tables containing trays of glasses which appeared to contain pond samples taken as part of a study in diseases of cattle. Thousands of others, victims of the same dodge, nay more—they had *paid* to be shut into this open-air barrel house—milled about helplessly. Some even purchased the glasses and attempted to squeeze the alcohol out of the mashed green detritus which gives the drink its name.

My friend and I had not spent twenty-nine hours sitting behind two matrons discussing the horrors of breached birth just to buy bourbon schav, however, and, wrapping our hands in pieces torn from our undershirts, we dragged ourselves up the chicken wire fence of our jail. When we got about ten feet up, we had a fine view of the track, and, hanging there, we described, with cries, groans, and ululating screams, the victory of Johnstown to our fellow prisoners below.

Lafayette, we were there.

I still have my ticket on Challedon and a small crease in the middle finger of my right hand.

Later, that young newspaperman became city editor of

the Louisville *Times* and invited me down to see the Derby in style. It would make a better story if I had gone, but in fact I listened on a pocket radio while rehearsing some now forgotten comedy. These are the sacrifices an artist makes for his muse. I do remember, though, that I didn't have the winner that year either.

I was not to have a winner again until 1946, when my horse ruined the day for Louisville's Brown Hotel. The Brown announced that it would name its new cocktail lounge after the '46 winner. They expected that this would be Lord Boswell and liked the patrician sound of the Lord Boswell Room, but when the gallant Assault raced home in front, they sighed and called their lounge the Kentucky Derby Room.

There is a peculiar similarity in atmosphere between a race track and a theater where a play is being rehearsed. I find it hard to explain, but I know that I feel it. Perhaps it is the air of controlled hysteria, the intense concentration on a rather specific and urgent problem which seems at the moment to be overpowering and answerable only by an inspired guess.

Finding an exit line and finding a winner both seem to be jobs for experts, and yet how often the experts are up the track with their answers.

Sometimes, of course, things turn out more perfectly than anybody dreams, and at the track as at the theater, this is most likely to happen as a result of boldness than of caution. Boldness can lead to triumph or disaster, but a series of show bets never brought anybody home a winner. Even in caution there will be some mistakes, and the rewards of caution, the $2.10 show ticket on the favorite, the familiar chuckle from the sure-fire seduction joke, are usually too meager to make up for the mistakes.

Many years ago the distinguished pair of American

horsemen John A. Drake and "Bet a Million" Gates, took a horse to England. They took a horse and a lot of money. They bet all the money, believed by many old-timers to be a million dollars, on the one horse in one race. They did not take their bank roll out for any preliminary exercise, they did not run their horse for any purses just to pay hotel bills.

Gates, who handled the financial details, and left the training and picking of horses and races to Drake, went to Tattersall's betting ring day after day and placed whatever sum he could, always on the one race, and achieved an over-all price of 4–1. Everything on one circuit of the turf, but they had done their best, and anything less than a complete commitment was not their best in courage.

They won the race, collected their five million, and sailed for home without trying for one more quick one.

Gates died soon after, not of the poverty which is always comfortably predicted for gamblers but of excitement from still another of their coups.

One day at Saratoga in the 1930s before the pari-mutuel machines replaced bookmakers, I was chatting with a fatherly bookie who took time out from his serious business to write down my two-dollar bets, when a perfectly-turned-out breath of the past strolled past us swinging a light bamboo cane. He was a slight man dressed in McKinley Sporting—white linen suit, bamboo-colored silk shirt with starched white collar, black silk four-in-hand with subdued but expensive stickpin, and a wide, stiff straw hat. A careful waxing had put needle points on his silver mustache.

Mr. Rogan came to attention and grasped my arm.

"Do you know who that is, young Broun?" he said. "Take a good look at a legend. That's John A. Drake."

I took a good look at the spry nonagenarian walking,

with springy step, on a carpet of his own courage, and asked the inevitable question.

"Does he still bet?"

Mr. Rogan smiled wistfully. "Just a few hundred dollars a race for laughs," he said. Reverent, we watched Drake climb into his limousine and hurry off to spend his beggarly profits on a champagne and pheasant dinner.

I wish John A. Drake, or someone like him, produced plays.

There are, as a matter of fact, a great many people around the race track whose singleness of purpose and invulnerability to panic would make them invaluable as theater producers. There are lots of jobs around the race track for some of our theater producers, if it comes to that. When a horse comes in from a race, perspiring and tense, someone must walk him round in a circle for a couple of hours, all the while murmuring soothing and encouraging things. It's not so different from talking to possible theater investors.

You thought I was going to say cleaning out stalls, didn't you? Don't confuse discontent and bitterness. I don't even want to hand the pitchfork to any newspaper editors, but perhaps that's just because my newspaper career wasn't very long.

The race horse and the actor have in common a terrible purity of intention and the fact that the major rewards go to the exploiter. The thoroughbred horse will run till he drops, even though he receives the same rather dull dinner whether he wins or loses. The joy is in the racing as it is in the acting. When the gate opens, when the curtain goes up, the world is ours, though the prize is yours.

Of course, horses are none too brainy (cries of "There's another parallel!"), and it might be that if the situation could be explained to them, they might hold out for a share of the purse. It's true that actors have on occasion performed for nothing, but one can go too far about the nobleness of the performer. Ask any company manager. Still, you can often chop something off an actor's salary by increasing his billing. You can, depending on your viewpoint, call this childish vanity on the actor's part, or a touching dream of glory.

Perfection has a special kind of magic that often makes us cry. A psychiatrist may be able to tell you the reason, but I can only tell you that I cried when I saw the great Sun Beau run and when I saw Sir Ralph Richardson being wondrously comic in *The School for Scandal*. Here was the terrible purity of intention, the leap beyond what seemed possible, the effortlessness achieved only by overwhelming effort ("Your easy reading is damned hard writing," said Sheridan, the author of *Scandal*), and the feeling that you, the watcher, must concentrate completely so that no part of what you see will ever be forgotten.

On second thought, don't ask the psychiatrist. I think I have the reason. There is a kind of innocence, a belief in one's own power, which produces such perfect performances and thereby gives the rest of us, who considered such innocence Eden-lost, a wistful envy under our joy.

Once you have achieved perfection, the memory of it will follow you like a small sun. So George Borrow in *Lavengro* describes seeing an old, one-eyed horse at a fair.

"But stay! there *is* something remarkable about that horse, there is something in his action in which he differs from all the rest; as he advances the clamour is hushed! all eyes are turned upon him—what looks of interest—of respect—and what is this? people are taking off their hats —surely not to that steed! Yes, verily! Men, especially old men, are taking off their hats to that one-eyed steed, and I hear more than one deep-drawn ah!"

An old man tells him, "If you should chance to reach my years, you may boast to thy great grandboys thou has seen Marshland Shales.

"Again I did for the horse what I would neither do for earl or baron, doffed my hat; yes! I doffed my hat to the wondrous horse, the fast trotter, the best in Mother England."

Baron Hill said of the actor Thomas Betterton, "The blind might have seen him in his voice, and the deaf have heard him in his visage."

Stable owners and theatrical producers are by and large respectable men, but I doubt they hear many "deep-drawn ahs" or see much spontaneous baring of heads.

Both sets of men have, however, achieved a social acceptance which is out of reach of their employees. Despite the fact that in working hours they associate with a group ranking just below gypsies and just above tinkers, theatrical producers are often seen hobnobbing with socialites on terms of easy familiarity.

The rising businessman who wants to put his wife on charity committees ("Seen lunching at the St. Regis for the benefit of the Hypertension Gala"), and make his daughter a debutante ("Country Club becomes Old Tiflis as debs make bow at St. Griselda Cotillion"), can take a giant step by purchasing a few horses. His employees in many states will have to be fingerprinted, are assumed by most people to be generically dishonest, and will have as much trouble getting insurance as actors do. He, like the producer, floats on the dark waters in a gilded barge.

It must be said for our fluid modern society that there is a way open to the top, to respectability, to a seat in the boat. Become a proprietor.

When an actor gets together enough money to interest an accountant and has himself turned into something

called Erewhon Productions Ltd., he ceases to be a root-
less and suspect vagabond. He has an office and Goes
Downtown with Daddy, like the other grownups. When
Erewhon puts on a show, he will move up, and if the show
is a success, he can be knighted if he is English, given a
theater of his own if he is French, or an honorary Doctor-
ate of Humane Letters if he is American.

The public's attitude about all this is a little hard to
understand. We are supposed to be a society which has
exalted work and accomplishment to a point where no one
can really enjoy a weekend unless he had made something
out of plywood or spent Saturday afternoon grubbing for
crab grass. Our Sunday mornings, by the way, seem to me
more taxing and somber than the Puritan sabbaths of the
seventeenth century. You can, after all, doze off in church,
but when you start into the Sunday *Times,* your eyes are
open and, when you emerge from it hours later, they are
sometimes red-rimmed, sometimes brimming with tears.
All those rotogravured columns of marching men in steel
helmets—"Iran, Tinder Box of the Middle East?"—all that
historical raw material—"Full Text of the President's Address to the Foreign Policy Association"—all those vague
but important-sounding samplings—"Changing Trends in
Consumer Acceptance"—"Psychiatrist Sees Women in
New Role"—"Carloadings Reflect Shipping Decline"—
"Broadway At the Halfway Mark"—"Suburbia in Transi-
tion"—as we go whithering on.

For relief there are the humorous bits—"I Married an
Ad Man"—"We Bought an Old Barn"—"A Little League
Father Tells All"—"The Day the 8:17 Never Left Westport," all with whimsical line drawings. They take the
place of the rector's waggish announcements.

Please do not think I am singling out the *Times* with
any malice. It is simply the Cathedral of Newspapers. In

other cities there are other thick bundles of worthiness to give the feeling of Sunday rectitude that used to be provided by hellfire and hymns. All of them reflect the fact that the hard-work cult of the nineteenth century has changed but not loosened its grip.

Why then the social acceptance for the man who just holds out a hand for the trophy or the box-office statement? Why the faint distaste for the doers?

Perhaps it is really just a fair compensation for men who get so close to the fun without having any of it, who have heard no deep-drawn ahs, who have looked into the heavens but not been there.

The distaste for the doers is fair enough too. We are breaking the rules by living in a world of chance, and to make it worse, the rewards of this world are not doled out according to any discernible system (ask any actor or horseplayer) and are not even measurable in terms which sensible people can understand.

There is one thing which ought to be made clear to moralists, however. Money you win on the races is not "money for nothing." It is exactly the opposite. It is money given you for being intellectually superior to all those about you, for being bold (if it's a long shot) when others with similar information were fainthearted, for being sound (if it's a favorite) when others with similar information were feather-witted and greedy. It is given you for being especially good at mathematics, logic, and the psychology of both man and animal. It is given to you to make up for past injustices, and because you are Especially Deserving.

If the winner is wise, he will spend his winnings on real, permanent objects, which, suitably marked, can be fondled in pleasant reverie. My small winnings go into books which read on the flyleaf: "This book bought by Jerry B., $6.20 in the 7th at Delaware Park, May 9th, 1938."

I can't tell you how I came out for that day at Delaware Park, although I used to do well there, but it doesn't matter now. I have the book and the memory of victory, and I enjoy both.

For larger killings, larger objects, or as I did in college days, a course of gaiety that couldn't be justified or afforded out of "real" money.

I take particular pleasure in a splendid John Held, Jr., woodcut, which portrays a heartless bookmaker counting the last of a fool's money while the fool drinks copiously from a bottle marked "poison," and the field for the next race canters by unheeding. On the back of the frame I have pasted a card which gives the names of three winners I put together in the spring of 1958 for the express purpose of winning this picture. For the record they were Cavan in the Belmont, Nadir in the Monmouth Select, and Judge in the Shevlin. Did you have any of them? You should have. They were all standouts to the discerning eye, although I admit that Cavan would not have won if the favorite had not broken his ankle in the homestretch.

One thing popularity does to any public art or entertainment is to rob it of intimacy. I am not now talking of the "in" feeling which comes from being one of thirty-five people seeing an Esthonian film at an Obscurity Festival. I am talking of the casual gaiety of a free-moving, uncrowded group, close to what is happening, and with minds unclouded by thoughts of what hell it will be to get home through the crush. It is awe-inspiring to be part of a record-size World Series crowd, but it was perhaps more fun to be one of the two or three thousand fans who spread themselves across the fifty thousand-odd seats in the old Polo Grounds on a summer afternoon and sunned themselves and gave constructive criticism to the Giants. True, you never heard the blood-tingling roar of the packed stands, but you heard all the other small, pleasant sounds of the sport which are drowned by the pre- and post-roar drone of the packed stands. Fifty thousand people saying "How about another beer, Charlie?" can keep you from hearing the pleasant chunk of the ball hitting the center of a well-oiled glove, the singsong chatter of the infielders encouraging the pitcher—a peculiar sound somewhere between a Chinese market place and a chicken house—the minatory shouts of the base-line coaches, employing their James Bondian lingo, where only every fifth sentence means anything, and then only if the hand is touching the belt buckle, and the mournful, insistent cries of the vendors, who believe with Buddhist priests that if you chant something often enough, be it "Om Mane Padme Hum," or "Hey, Getcha Redhots," you will find salvation.

Present-day vendors, by the way, seem all to be graduate students ashamed of their temporary calling, avoiding your eye as they think about higher mathematics, and unable, because of the vastness of their numerical concepts, to make proper change. To be fair, it may be okay when it leaves their hands, but somewhat short after passing through the hands of the twenty-five Little Leaguers who seem always now to be sitting between you and the hot-dog man. Twenty years ago the vendor would have thrown you the coins with a careless brio which you shared as you plucked the glittering stuff out of the air, feeling momentarily like Mel Ott going back into the right-field corner for a long fly.

The noises that we made ourselves were very satisfactory too, since they could be heard not as noise but as words. It did not matter that Travis Jackson did not play closer to second base when you told him to. You knew, at least, that he had heard you, and that if the batter hit one up the middle, he would know that you had been right.

There were always a few hundred Dodger fans scattered among the Faithful, but we showed them the tolerance that Moslems display to the mad, and we listened to their shouted abuse with the detached connoisseurship of dinner-jacketed opera lovers hearing Mimi's death cries in *Bohème.*

This intimacy extends to more than sport. Think how pleasant it would have been to be one of those sixteenth-century Romans who, meeting a friend, heard, "Say, Niccolò, drop in at St. Peter's on your way home. Buonarroti has done a really charming thing in white marble. I think he calls it 'The Pietà,' and it's over near the place where Uncle Cesare always lights a candle. Plan to spend a lot of time. It's worth it."

Recently the amount of time any of us could spend with it was measured by the speed of a moving walkway at the New York World's Fair. This was in fact eminently sensible, for without it many would have starved or fainted while waiting for a look, and the flashbulb-proof screen didn't really interfere with one's view; it's just that one cannot but feel wistful in thinking about Niccolò's afternoon.

Of course, someone will point out that future ages may envy me my chance to have seen the wonderful non-objective scrap-iron "Pietà" made in the late 1970s by the legendary "Master of the Blowtorch," which by 2300 will be visible for two seconds at a time to groups of 10,000 citizens holding art-priority cards of grade A-8 or above.

That is entirely possible, but some, at least, of the future citizens will envy me more that I was able, in New York City to go to a country racecourse with three little green-and-yellow wooden towers for a grandstand and a track so close to the patrons that you could, from the outdoor restaurant, have dropped butter pats on the post parade. This wonderful place was Empire City, the off-Broadway of New York tracks. Crowds of fewer than a thousand were quite common and cozy on weekdays, and even on Saturday we drew smaller crowds than have been drawn in the last couple of years by the last working cow on Long Island, which I am told is good for several thousand ranch wagonloads of viewers every weekend.

We Empire City fans looked on Belmont Park as the last word in soulless modernity. The stands were too far from the horses, the track itself was too big, with its vast mile-and-a-half oval, the giant grandstand was of cold and soulless metal and stone, and you had to walk miles to find your bookmaker.

Only a part of a short lifetime has passed since those days, and yet any Sunday sports section today is good for a nostalgic evocation of the graciousness which was "Beautiful Belmont." The wrecker's ball had barely finished with the fifty-dollar window before the wailing began, and curiously enough, I was taking part in it. If they will give it back to us, I will promise never to complain again about the steps, or the claustrophobic restaurant under the stands, or the hundred ways to get lost on the way to the paddock. Intimate it wasn't, but it was beautiful, and beauty will soothe a loser only a little less than will intimacy.

Long after Empire City had disappeared I was sent to Phoenix, Arizona, to cover the spring doings of the Giants for my newspaper, and there I found a little structural steel shadow of my old off-Broadway track. Outside of Phoenix, under a mountain, someone with a Meccano set and a lot of time had built a little grandstand, in front of a sharp-cornered half-mile track where your butter pats could hit the horses even on the backstretch. Fields were limited to eight because of the narrowness of the track, and there was no nonsense about registered owners' colors. The number one jockey wore red, the number two jockey blue, and so forth. A certain amount of pageantry is lost, but at least you never had to turn to your neighbor and say, "Is that 'ash rose with turquoise hoops' running third, or is it 'cerise with aqua sash'?" only to have him reply, "It's 'salmon with azure belt,' and it's moving into the lead."

There was no doubt where you stood on Phoenix's little living carousel, although where you stood might change very suddenly. When the ancient thoroughbreds who made up the fields stumbled, their jockeys would pull them up sharply and go to the outside. At that age the horse might not just be stumbling. He might be having the first symptoms of a stroke, so that the leader at the eighth pole might at last canter home at a speed suitable for an old gentleman taking restorative exercise. Thoroughbreds may not race in America past the age of twelve, and a great many of them come to Arizona for that last twelve months ("I'm as good as I ever was. Did you see the figures on my workout the other day? It's just that they're making the tracks harder these days, and the boys seem to be a bit heavier. Bet on me Saturday. I can still beat this bunch") before the final post parade.

It is ironic that Arizona, the haven of old race horses, is full of those retirement villages for old people. When the retired horseplayer goes home to Sunset Cottage, the retired horse more often than not goes off to Petfood Hall.

One of the standard rainy-day newspaper stories is the one about how a whole, rich life can be lived in Grand Central Station or Kennedy Air Terminal. The reporter has an assortment of meals, sends out some laundry, sleeps on a bench, buys shirts and paper-back books, and, if in Grand Central, goes to the newsreel theater and learns new things about Ecuador—"These panama-hat makers practice their ancient art under three inches of water"—for as long as it takes him to work up an acceptable feature.

This reporter got to Ascot in England recently, and I want to say that you can live a finer, fuller life on that noble course than you could if they gave you all the depots in the world for your very own.

You can see the Queen, listen to music, walk through splendid gardens, eat a variety of foods (What's a variety of English foods? you say. Well, different sandwich fillings and beers), get your fortune told, watch Punch and Judy shows and music-hall turns, and see some of the most colorful touts in the world. Most of this goes on in the infield at some distance from the Queen and the gray-top-hat crowd, but even the infield touts seem to have their royal connections. Colin Keith-Johnston tells of going racing on a routine day when King George VI and the Aga Khan had runners in one of the lesser races. An elderly tout caught Colin in an iron grip and husked "the word" in his ear.

"I'm just going to tell yer one thing. The King is 'ere and the Ayger ain't. Take it as meant."

Colin also reported on Lashbrooke, the passionate tout whose performance was worthy of the Old Vic. Lashbrooke deplored the tipsters who disappeared after selling information, unwilling to face the customers after the race.

"Lashbrooke ain't afeared to face yer at any time," he would cry in the regal third person. "'E scorns to 'ide. He don't need to. 'E'll show yer 'ow you'll know that 'e'll be right 'ere after the race." So saying, he would detach his artificial leg and hurl it from him, calling in a sky-cracking voice, "You see. Lashbrooke is powerless! Lashbrooke is powerless!"

I cannot see Lashbrooke at the Big A. Aqueduct is a

truly American institution. Like the supermarket which it resembles, right down to the pastel-paneled walls, it is a marvel of engineering and efficiency. You cannot quarrel with it because it does the job of putting on nine races for fifty thousand-odd people with the snap and dispatch of Brigham Young moving the Mormons across the country. It doesn't think much more of touts, fortunetellers, Punch and Judys, and itinerant clog dancers than Brigham Young would.

Odds are instantly calculated by electronic machinery, and the machine deducts 17 per cent of every betting pool and returns the rest every twenty-five minutes with no more than a blink of its memory bank.

Aqueduct scorns the bookmaker and his tick-tack man, who, standing on a high stool, does a wonderful Balinese hand dance in white gloves to tell all the other bookmakers how the money is flowing, and on occasion, to ask some of them to absorb some overflow. On a busy day at a British track the forest of gloves is a sarabande of snow-flakes, a moving arabesque, and probably 7 per cent less efficient than the squat machine clicking away in its hut in the Aqueduct infield.

In the old days in New York, my father had an ambition to win with a 100–1 shot, and in pursuit of this ambition bet on every such outsider who showed on the bookmaker's slate of offered odds. When my father finally saw one of his crocks come home on top, the admiring bookmaker, in honor of my father's courage, and in consideration of all the ones that hadn't come home, threw in a silver rosary with the payoff.

No machine will do that, nor is there a computer eccentric enough to give a small boy 2–1 on an 8–5 shot as the Rogan brothers used to do for my dollar bets. No machine will take a bet from a small boy at all. It will not deal with anyone who isn't at least eighteen and in possession of at least two dollars. Then it will give you the cold comfort of mathematical justice. I think of the Scot grumbling over his change in the old joke.

"Aye, it's richt. But it's only just richt."

It must be said in fairness to Aqueduct that Ascot gets off only six races a day and that it takes more than twenty-five minutes to complete the cycle of calculation-commitment-resolution-reckoning. Still, who minds the delay? It gives you time to get your fortune told or to see the Queen. I missed out on the fortune—who can tell an actor's fortune?—but I did see the Queen, who showed up in the paddock to inspect a runner she had in the day's last race. Her Majesty was attired in a two-piece lime-green silk suit with what the magazines call "matching accessories," which means she had sense enough not to carry a red purse, and looked as cautiously hopeful as any other owner, while the horse moved springily and inscrutably up and down on the sward before her. Her trainer, who was so faultlessly turned out that he appeared to be a nude with tweed skin, murmured confident instructions to the jockey, while all around him other trainers murmured equally confident advice to their riders—if all did exactly as they were told, would there be a multiple dead heat for first? How simply Sir Charles Bunbury put it more than a century ago when he whispered to jockey T. Goodis, "Here is your horse, Tom; he will do *his* duty, if you will do yours!" How lucky was Sir Charles. The horse, Smolensko, won the Epsom Derby.

As the Queen left the paddock two lines formed on either side of her path, and the gentlemen removed their hats. My thirteen-year-old son and Colin Keith-Johnston's nine-year-old got rather carried away and scurried very close to Her Majesty. I was just thinking how unguarded she was and what havoc the boys could wreak if they were midget anarchists instead of excited kids, when a man whom I had marked as a dotty earl out of Wodehouse put a finger on the left shoulder of each boy. What followed could best be described as kindly karate. They told me later that they felt no pain. It was simply that they moved twenty-five feet without knowing how. The Queen proceeded without noticing, the "earl" straightened his bowler, and the boys laughed with the excitement of those who, for a moment, have been in Zenda.

With no malice toward the Queen, but because, like many of Scottish descent, I am loyal to the Stuarts—did they have to call the heir Charles? Considering that they are Hanoverians, Otto or Herman would have been more suitable—I bet against the royal entry. To tell the truth I wouldn't back Bonnie Prince Charlie's horses at less than even money, and the Queen's horse was a very hot favorite. Colin made a good figure for an outsider, and we backed it.

I can't tell much about the race because my wife took my binoculars to watch the reactions of the Queen. My wife is an actress and quite properly wanted to use this chance to study royal emotion.

I do know that our horse came into the final straight with a good lead and that then the Queen's horse came on with a great rush and that the stands roared in loyalty to their sovereign and the principle that odds-on horses must win. I know that I cried out in a despair going back to Culloden, "We're beaten!" and that Colin, watching through his glasses, suddenly shouted, "No, by God, we're not!" and that then the Queen and I and all the crowd except my wife, who was watching the Queen, saw that her boy had made his move a bit too soon, as the royal standard bearer shortened stride and fell back.

What my wife saw, she later used with brilliant effect when she played Lady Macbeth. What I saw was a triumph for the Old Virtues, the Old Kings, and Me.

Since that day, the British have spent some millions on Ascot, none of it, I hope, for the plastic turquoise and orange oblongs that make so many American public places look like suburban linoleum stores, so that perhaps some of what I saw is lost. I doubt it, though. The Windsors aren't my dynasty but they are racing people and they wouldn't let Aqueduct happen to Ascot.

Whatever they charge there is one thing that doesn't change much anywhere. In *Right Royal*, John Masefield called it

> A tide of horses in fury flowing,
> Beauty of speed in glory going.

Through the little round windows of the binoculars this is what you see, whether behind you is Longchamps in Paris, the racecourse so beautiful even the Nazis left it untouched, the utilitarian vastness of Aqueduct, or the sleazy, jolly, tart-on-a-holiday look of the now gone Oriental Park in Havana, a track where the horses were entered in claiming races with price tags marked as low as $200, and where the roulette wheels in the clubhouse casino stopped turning only for the seventy-six or so seconds it took these decayed gentlefolk of the horse world to go three quarters of a mile.

It was while I was in Havana with the Brooklyn Dodgers that the managing editor of my paper, who always felt that going to baseball games and race tracks wasn't really work, sent me a wire suggesting that I improve the shining hour of my stay by dropping in at the dungeons of Morro Castle and interviewing the late Lucky Luciano, then held there by Cuba on representations from the United States Government that Luciano was operating an American crime empire from Cuba.

A real newspaperman would have jumped at this and would have bribed guards, gotten himself smuggled into the prison disguised as some prisoner's father—covering the language difficulty with a feigned cold—or palmed himself off as a State Department man. He would have used any of the ingenious devices by which we of the Press keep alight the searchlight of truth, or the flickering torch of distortion, or the steady-glowing lamp of reason, or whatever it is we're doing.

I went directly to the Ministry of Justice, stated my business, and asked for a pass to the dungeon. The functionary to whom I spoke explained that a press ban was in effect and then said in a tone which curled round my lapel and tugged at it, that he might arrange an interview with a superior who might be able to arrange a talk with someone, and so forth. With sturdy honesty I ignored the proffered quo and kept my quids in my pocket. I thanked him and said I quite understood the ban. I was turning to leave, when, in desperation, he seized me and dragged me to the superior. This man, across a much larger desk, expressed keen regrets because of a long-standing admiration for the American press. Because of that admiration he might be able to get me in to see a man quite close to the top. It would, of course take a good deal of valuable time and—I thanked him and assured him that his word of prohibition was quite enough. With a philosophic shrug he picked up the phone and gave another colleague a sporting chance at me. This man had an office with two exposures and discussed the difficulties of the matter with me on an international diplomatic level. Of course, he pointed out, elasticity was the essence of diplomacy and—

I reviewed Cuba's position with the tact so necessary in

the representative of a larger nation. Succinctly I sketched
the highlights of our policy changes since the Monroe Doc-
trine and took my stand with Franklin Roosevelt and Cor-
dell Hull foursquare behind the belief that Latin America
had a right to work out its own destiny. Despite all this, he
wouldn't let me go but took me down the hall to an office
almost as big as the lobby where I had started the whole
business. The man here was in diplomatic morning dress,
and our conversation was on such a level that even at this
late date I fear that I can do no more than say that no
guarantees were exchanged but that our talk was exploratory, that a good deal of misunderstanding was cleared up
and a good start made toward removing some of the stumbling blocks in the path of a general détente, and that I
never saw Luciano.

It was always one of my faults as a newspaperman, and
perhaps one of my strengths as an actor, that I was able
to put myself in the other person's place. When I put
myself in Luciano's place—and a cold, uncomfortable place
I felt it to be—the last thing I wanted was to talk to an
American baseball writer. Putting myself in the managing
editor's place, I had grudgingly to admit that Broun had
done his duty, all right, and the wire hadn't authorized any
bribes, and putting myself in the shoes of the Cuban of-
ficials, I deplored the young American's denseness on the
subject of arrangements, but I was genuinely pleased by
his lack of Yankee arrogance and by his real feeling for my
country.

With a clear conscience and a singing heart, I went off to
the track to get some material for a column. I should add
in my defense that none of the real hotshots with dis-
guises got in to see Luciano either. So again, Goneril and
Regan ended up as dead as Cordelia.

At Oriental Park, however, I did discover something

which made our official belief that Lucky was a big spider twanging a web in all directions look a bit overdrawn. I mentioned Luciano to a couple of trainers I knew, and they told me that before his arrest he was notorious around the track for his large losses and for the many close finishes that his selections lost. A great big spider who can't arrange to reverse close finishes at a track where a whole horse costs $200 strikes me as having a pretty tattered web.

It's just possible, of course, that Luciano had a special feeling about horses and voluntarily kept this side of his life pure. Perhaps he was one with Masefield and me (There's an unlikely parlay!). Perhaps the laureate put it for all of us when he said of *The Racer:*

> Would we might see the end to which we stride,
> And feel, not strain in struggle, only thrill,
> And laugh like him and know in all our nerves
> Beauty, the spirit, scattering dust and turves.

AMONG THE FIRST dramatic presentations in the western world were choral celebrations of victorious performances in the Olympic games. The Greeks linked sport and theater as contests to please the gods, and saw nothing grotesque in commissioning a major poet to commemorate a discus victory with an ode and getting together a bunch of performers to put on the ode at a victory banquet. Indeed, last year's sprint winner might turn up to do the script or take a part in the ode for this year's fastest Hellene.

Victory, which showed the fullest use of the whole man, was prized by the Greeks whether in a playwriting contest or in a pentathlon.

The notion of the inarticulate, muscular hero who has trouble gasping thanks is a later development, as is the idea that the poet and the playwright are merely observers of the world's movers and shakers, talented voyeurs somewhere between social secretaries and street singers.

Pericles was a great general, but when he stood before the Athenians and told them the world would never forget how they behaved in their war with Sparta—a war involving about as many people and as much territory as a war between Greenwich and Westport—he said it so poetically that the world never has forgotten. Eventually, Stamford and Cos Cob joined Greenwich, and Westport was crushed, but even in the brutality of battle there remained a feeling that the arts were something more than a diary of the world's doings. The Spartans—to abandon our suburban metaphor—determined in victory on the destruction of Athens, but on the eve of the demolition an Athenian poet read his work at a banquet of Spartan generals, and they agreed that a city which could produce such a performer could not be destroyed.

As one who has been ode writer to the Dodgers, Yankees, and Giants as well as a member of a number of Thespian teams, I am pleased with the linkage of sport and theater, although I don't know that the gods are all that pleased with some of the games we play for them these days.

My own career as an active athlete was hardly a subject for odes. I won my only letter as manager of the college football teams, and heard the cry of "*Nike!*" only as a member of the school's informal badminton squad, but I remember how I felt when we drove the birds past Haverford, the traditional rival, and I know that the actor and the athlete have in common the fierce concentration which reduces the whole world to a single goal, and that at the moment of striving, the whole world seems well lost if one can achieve one's will with a line or a ball.

Pindar wrote of an athletic victory:

> He who wins, of a sudden, some noble prize
> In the rich years of youth
> Is raised high with hope; his manhood takes wings;

He has in his heart what is better than wealth.
But brief is the season of man's delight.
Soon it falls to the ground; some dire decision
    uproots it.
Think of a day! such is man; a shadow in a dream.
Yet when god-given splendor visits him
A bright radiance plays over him, and how sweet
    is life!

This seems to me to describe the evanescence and the compensations of actors' lives as well as those of wrestlers, one of whom was Pindar's inspiration.

In Greece both sports and theater had a rhythm which was governed by feast days and seasons, and actors and athletes could bloom and sleep as regularly as the trees in the sacred grove. In the intervening millennia the theater's rhythms have become staccato and uncertain, but baseball, at least, keeps sport on a wonderfully soothing and predictable course.

It is one of the most elaborately structured enterprises in our society, which probably explains why so many unstructured people devote a large part of their waking hours to identifying with it and consuming the miles of small-type trivia which measure its every aspect.

Everything about it has a statistic, from attendance to accomplishment, and what I suppose sociologists would call "negative accomplishment"—"His seven errors at 2d base gave Thornton Bascomb a new record in this department and his four errors on one play ties a record held by many." Well, cheer up, Bascomb. There is more than one way of achieving immortality, and at least you know exactly how bad you were. In the wider world some people feel that they are setting a new record for errors every day, but there is no way of making sure.

There are big records in baseball, like Babe Ruth's 60

home runs and Roger Maris' 61 home runs (marked with an asterisk to show they were accomplished in a 162-game season as opposed to Ruth's 154), and there are tiny records like highest percentage of successful base thefts (Gus Triandos tried it once in a long career and made it—average 1.000). There are records covering a lifetime—511 pitching victories for Cy Young, and records for a day—most hits, one game, seven, held by Wilbert Robinson. There are even records for doing nothing. The other day, while listening to the ninth inning of a Yankee game on the radio, I heard the announcer say with real regret, "There goes a bouncer to Kubek at short. That spoils his chance to join the list of men who have played a whole game at short without accepting a chance." One would hardly have blamed Kubek if he had flung himself on the grass to avoid the play, but true to a strong tradition of victory, he seized the ball and erased himself from the record book.

Whatever is first or most in baseball will be written down somewhere. The faraway flavor of failure is preserved in the note that the first professional player to be fired was Richard Hurley of Cincinnati in 1870. I wonder if Hurley would have felt any better with the knowledge that his inadequacy would get him into the June 1963 issue of *Baseball Digest?* To tell the truth, I don't know anything about any of the other boys who were active in 1870, so here's to Dick Hurley, a toast across the years from Woodie Broun, who was the first actor to be fired in the season of 1961–62.

One great advantage that Dick and Babe and Roger and all the other record holders in baseball have over those other players to the gods, the actors, is that the very precision of the game lets them know exactly how successful or unsuccessful they are.

Scott Fitzgerald wrote that baseball players were the

luckiest of people because they never had any doubts about where they stood. An artist is never quite sure whether his last time at bat was a strikeout or a home run, but a ballplayer can tell what happened, and the box score will preserve it, whether it be good or bad.

I know players who demur at this comforting notion. I remember a Brooklyn utility infielder who was good enough to ask me to accompany him to a movie one night during a road trip. I was fond of him and suggested that the flickering screen was not the best cure for a protracted batting slump. "Remember Stanley," I said, "Ty Cobb used to spend every evening in his room thinking over what had happened that day."

"Do you want me to sit in my room saying to myself, 'four times up—no hits, four times up—no hits,' all night?" said Stanley. "Let's go to a movie."

The statistics are bread and butter to the players, and however we may philosophize about the arithmetical comforts of the structure, a batting average down around .200 means you are going to get what poor old Hurley got, and then there will be no more statistics, at least not in the big leagues, and once you have been in them, that little bush-league park no longer looks like a cozy way station on the way to big things. It looks like a staging area for oblivion.

"Brief is the season of man's delight."

For the fan there is none of this briefness. The only thing that can really hurt him is some dire decision that uproots his team and takes it elsewhere. Short of that, he has a ready-made dream life. His working hours may be spent rising and falling in a freight elevator that will eventually deposit him at the Social Security office, but he has a very nice winter, talking over trades with his friends, reading the statistics which are compiled in October and doled out like soothing syrup over the sparse months before the winter meetings and another batch of trades. Then there is spring training, and the elevator leaps like a young colt at the thought of all those strong-armed, fleet-footed new players who are going to put us—note that "us"— right at the top. This year we will be champions. Some of us will do our part with base hits, some of us will do it by listening to portable radios and rooting very hard. As spring training progresses there are games, the first box scores of the season, the secondary statistics of the Grape-fruit League—"Lefty Pringle's three doubles were a high in the extra-base-hit department for the Florida training grind. No other pitcher has as yet gone five innings this spring. The club's six homers yesterday, a March high, au-gurs power in the months to come."

Soon there's the regular season, all 162 games of it, fol-lowed by the World Series, and then it's time to start dreaming of the changes which will make the club a cham-pion next year.

There are, during the regular season, between fifty and a hundred happy stories to read, depending on whether your team is in first place or last, and as for the games you lose, you can avoid the larger pain by checking on your favorites, one of whom may have had a good day.

In any case, you are identified with a cause, and you can see exactly how it stands in every morning's paper, which is better than generals can manage in wartime or than artists can manage at any time.

It's wonderful to be a ballplayer—"It's great to be young and a Giant"—cried Ross Youngs one bright morning long ago, and it's soothing and agreeable to be a baseball fan. The one thing that seems to me not much fun is to be a baseball writer.

The writer is enlisted under no banner. Vaguely he wishes victory to the team to which he is assigned, but there are many occasions when defeat will make a better story, and a better story is really what he is there for. He is also expected to be relatively objective and cannot take the satisfaction of calling umpires names—"The crowd seemed to this writer to have some justification for the dissatisfaction which led to the pelting of ump Ed Krundle"—is very daring stuff indeed. After all, you will see Ed Krundle on the train, and he, like you, is a part of the baseball Establishment. The thing is that you are a part of the Establishment but not really part of the gang. The players treat you civilly most of the time, but it is the bored civility which aristocratic children are taught to use to servants—"Remember dear, they don't have our advantages." A very few of them break through to a genuine friendship with newspapermen, unconnected with self-interest, but sadly enough such players are usually the utility men and fringe pitchers, who feel almost as detached from the battle as the reporters. Just about the day you look forward to chatting with them about something other than yesterday's game, you look down the bench and discover that they have gone to Montreal, giving way to hard-eyed young men on the way up who are ready for you with the usual bag of prepared pap.

"My only interest is in helping the club," one will say. "I'll play anywhere they put me, and any time. Yes, I've always wanted to play in this town, which has the most wonderful fans in the league. Sure, I've got a lot to learn but a great manager like Shorty Morton can teach you a lot just talking to you on the bench."

All this with an engaging grin and the naïve, eager eyes of an old corporation lawyer.

In a way I don't blame the players for speaking to us in words they have picked up from our own stories, thus making an endless Quaker Oats box image out interviewing (a Quaker holding a box with on it a picture of a Quaker holding a box with etc.).

The occasional player who speaks the truth is as shocking as the young businessman who drops the ritual of team-talk and confesses that he wants to beat everybody to the presidency of the company.

I remember a first baseman who came up with the Boston Braves right after the war. With the breezy cockiness which is admired in victors he told the reporters that he intended to make the baseball world forget Lou Gehrig. From the shocked reaction of my colleagues you would have thought the young man had been responsible for Gehrig's tragic death. They wrote of him as one who had smeared a monument, rather than as a kid with the arrogance an athlete needs, who was willing to challenge the best.

I saw the young man again some years later when he had neither made us forget Lou Gehrig nor mellowed into an acceptance of his own lesser stature. A newspaperman was given an estimate of a pitcher which he had heard from an old manager.

"Listen," said the ballplayer, "when that old man or any of the rest of you have hit against that guy, I'll be glad to hear your opinion. In the meantime keep it to yourself."

It was rude, but there was something basic to all the players in that statement. They are the ones who play the game, and no matter how expert we may become up in our press box, we will not know how it feels inside, or what it costs inside, to do what must be done.

One of the things required of the athlete is an arrogance which defies reality, an espousal of the implausible to which modern psychology has given the dreary name of rigidity.

There has been a lot of sophisticated laughter about the Merriwell slogans by which athletes are aroused. "The team that won't be beaten, can't be beaten," and all that sort of hopeful purple plummery. An old prize-fight manager put it to me somewhat less elegantly but with considerable earnestness.

"You sportswriters are always putting in the paper about how both guys in a fight is as brave as lions. That's a lot of ———. One guy is always braver than the other. That's why he wins. You write about how some guy gets off the floor four times and how he should get a medal or something. What I noticed was that he was afraid of getting hit in the stomach and carried his hands too low, which is how he got knocked down all four times."

This, of course, is not to claim that a spunky child can take on a heavyweight fighter of uncertain nerve and thrash him by the use of moral superiority, nor is it to claim that every loser is a coward. It is to claim, however, that in most contests which were arranged as reasonably even affairs, and even in some where the eventual winner was considered hopelessly overmatched, the margin of victory is not skill, but simply a stronger desire to win. Nothing strengthens this like the aforementioned arrogance, which does not really take into account the possibility of loss.

The thing that wars against this feeling is common sense, is reality, is what we sometimes call "maturity," or acceptance of things as they are.

When Pete Reiser, playing center field for the Brooklyn Dodgers, went into the concrete wall rather than give up on a flyball, he was committing an act of madness or of panache, or of both, if you consider them indivisible.

I recall a night game at Ebbets Field when Pete and the ball converged on the wall with a terrible inevitability. The crowd paid his concentration the tribute of terrified silence, and the only sound in the park was the high despairing voice of right fielder Dixie Walker, warning Pete of the wall. For Pete the wall did not exist any more than did

Walker. There was only himself, the ball, and an out-fielder's job, to catch the ball.

At the last moment, as the ball seemed about to pass over him, Reiser leaped up at the face of the wall with extended hand. For a fraction ball and glove were one, and then they disappeared as the flying body crushed them against the stone. Slowly the protagonists, ball and player, slid into a heap on the grass. As the runner tore around second, Eddie Stanky, the second baseman, reached the fallen player and, coming up with the ball, threw it in to hold the runner at third. No one will ever know whether he took it from the ground or from Reiser's glove. Only when he had performed this duty to the ball did he turn to the fallen player to see how badly he was hurt. He waved for the stretcher, and the unconscious Reiser was carried in toward the infield. We in the press box were notified that two priests were making their way to the dressing room in case last rites were required. As the stretcher passed second base, all eyes in the park turned to the um-pire who covers that bag and things that happen in center field. There had been no ruling on the play. He looked at the still form going by and gave the proper answer to the defiance of reality. He ruled that the ball had been caught, and the runner unprotestingly took himself back to the dugout.

Pete recovered to do it again, but eventually his career was cut short by the damage which his intransigence did to his body. You may, if you wish, call his actions foolish and see tragedy in the tremendous effort for no better purpose than that of winning one of the season's 154 games. If you are going by results, that's a tenable notion, I guess, but in the long run Pete Reiser, George Washington, Julius Caesar, and Michelangelo will be forgotten.

If Arnold Winkelried, when about to cast himself on the

spears, had thought, "The only result of what I'm doing is going to be the creation of Switzerland," he might have tipped his hat and gone home, but he would have been wrong. Things become important by our wanting to do them, and Pete and Arnold were very clear about what they wanted to do, and existed for a few glorious moments unhobbled by doubt.

I can hear the soft rustling of philosophy students moving in on me from every side with arguments about wider implications, but let's skip the wider implications and stay in the ball park for a while.

The ballplayer's awareness of the crowd is slight, unlike the actor's. Where an actor woos an audience and begs it for approval, the athlete woos victory and is aware of the crowd as something that makes noise at the wrong time and often interferes with the outcome by grabbing at baseballs still in play or pushing men trying to make catches near the railing. To the extent that he thinks about the audience at all, the athlete lessens his concentration on the game.

I remember a player who never lived up to his springtime promise because, when at bat, he watched himself like a spectator.

"I stand up there," he told me, "and I think—fifty thousand people are watching me. They are thinking how terrible it would be if I struck out. I start thinking it too. I see myself at the plate, and while I'm looking at myself and thinking about all this, I see the pitch coming and try to look just at it, but it's too late. Strike three!"

Pitchers, too, have been destroyed by becoming aware of their own motions while delivering the ball, an awareness which robs them of the instinctive, unthinking grace which is essential to their art. Stop for a moment and consider your own breathing. If you think of it for more than a few seconds you will find that even this simple act becomes gulpy and unnatural. If breathing correctly meant the difference between winning and losing, success or failure, you would be lucky not to choke on the spot.

When absolute concentration is in control, all of these things are done right—good actors never cough or sneeze onstage, good ballplayers don't blink as the ball approaches them.

Baseball writers, however, cough, sneeze, yawn, and sometimes, if the players and the readers are to be believed, fall asleep. I deny that I ever fell asleep, but I must admit that sometimes in warm August doubleheaders involving a sixth-place team against a seventh-place team I have felt a certain heaviness of the lids and a drowsy humming in the ears.

On such occasions the players are driven on by that professional pride which failure cannot quench, and the fans are there in hopes of a memorable day in an unmemorable season, but I am only there to watch and report. My position gives me a detachment which tells me that it really doesn't matter, and to think that a ball game doesn't matter is a sad state of affairs.

It is a tradition of the press box that we do not root, that we be above the battle, and it's pretty dull up there.

I did find a certain excitement in my first baseball trip, because it was unexpected and undeserved. Two people in our office were taken ill on the eve of the Yankee trip to Washington to open the 1941 season. My job at this time was opening press releases and extracting from them usable facts, a job about as rewarding as panning for gold in the Hudson, and I was frankly delighted when my paper knife was taken away and I was given a ticket to Washington.

On the train I felt a little nervous, since everybody seemed to know everybody but me. I received a few speculative glances, and as someone said to me later, "You looked too old to be hunting autographs and too young to be a process server." While I was beginning to wonder about such fundamental things as how you write a baseball story, a brisk, elderly man came up and said, "You're young Broun, aren't you?" When I admitted this he said cheerily, "Well, I broke in your father in 1915, and if you need any help, just call me. My name is Sid Mercer."

Poor Mr. Mercer! I never had to call him because for three days I never left him. I don't know if he came to regret that kindly offer, an offer which afflicted him with a talking mustard plaster, but I doubt it. Sid Mercer, after all those years, still had a fresh delight in baseball. It seemed to me then, and seems to me now, impossible to stay happy very long in the press box, but Sid managed it very well, and a man with such a nature cannot have been too put out with a tiresome tyro.

I was delighted with the big hotel room all for me, with the fun of signing for my big steak with "New York Yankees" under my name, little realizing that only a few steaks later I would be annoyed about having an inside room or a slightly off-perfect steak, even though they were steaks and rooms that would be far above my touch as an actor.

I discovered how players felt about the press when I was sent over to Ebbets Field for my first game as a National League writer. After the game, which the Dodgers won 9–2, I essayed to interview the winning pitcher, a moody man who I thought would be cheered by his four-hitter, marred only by two home runs.

The clubhouse attendant seemed to feel that there was a ring of credentials counterfeiters at work and gave my baseball writer's card every attention short of laboratory equipment. When I approached the hero I struggled for an intelligent question and, unable to think of one, asked

"Were you tiring when they hit those two homers in the eighth?"

He turned on me with a snarl of hate. "You writers are always after me about home runs," he cried. "Why don't you write about something else? All I hear is home runs. I ought to make an example of you. I ought to beat you to a jelly."

The muscles that rippled over his towel-clad body made this seem an easy job, but I tried to explain that I had never written anything, was unaware of the persecution, and was full of good will. I was saved by the clubhouse man, who arrived growling, "I knew you was a fake," and hustled me out of the dressing room.

A couple of weeks later in Chicago the pitcher gave me a handsome apology, but the clubhouse man always regarded me with suspicion, sure that I was some kind of fraud. The years proved him right. I always wanted to root or to play. My colleagues stopped me from rooting, and boyhood experience taught me that you can neither hit nor catch a ball when you are ducking away from it. As a writer I was aware that the enthusiasm a good baseball story should always have was getting harder and harder for me to command, and that in another couple of years I would take refuge in that overstatement which is a substitute for excitement, as with an actor large gestures and a loud voice are often used to cover lack of inner feeling. I knew that some day soon I would begin to write stories which would describe athletic contests in terms of Thermopylae, Dunkirk, and the siege of Mafeking, and that I would not even know how bad these stories were. In my pages the horn of Roland would summon the Harvard football team to the second half of the Yale game, and a September slump of the Yankees would be likened to the retreat from Moscow.

Before I got round to leading off with, "Tell them in

Lacadaemon that the Yanks fell in the tenth after a battle that will live whenever brave men's deeds" etc., my newspaper beat my integrity to the graveyard.

Looking back from my seat in the spectators' stand, I realize, however, that the trouble with that kind of exaggeration is that it obscures and cheapens a genuine romance which has nothing to do with the greed, stupidity, chicanery, and coarse puffery that goes on around the boundaries of the playing field.

No matter how often baseball owners shift their franchises like snake-oil merchants plundering the prairie towns —no matter how often college presidents call stadium building character building—no matter what financial rabbit punches boxing managers may deliver to their hapless fighters—there is on the field, in the ring, and on the track a wonderful, uncomplicated dedication. The sound and sight of television "personalities" insisting that the games exist simply as their material, obscure it. The rows and rows of empty boxes with corporate names on them may keep us far away from it, but when the pitcher stares down at the batter as he goes into the windup, the vulgarities, inanities, and tax dodges are where they belong, on the other side of the foul line.

Among the players there has always been a delicacy in matters of honor which seems, according to how you feel about it, either childish and artificial, or admirable and sensitive.

I remember a World Series game in 1947 when Pete Reiser of the Dodgers had a terrible time playing center field in Yankee Stadium. He misjudged a couple of balls and—final humiliation—stumbled and fell down while maneuvering under one. As he lay on the ground, the crowd of status-seeking, seat-stub-saving, once-a-year fans who attend Series games in New York gave him a hearty jeering.

After the game, which the Yankees won, Joe DiMaggio was anxious to see the members of the press, and, composing humorous variations on Reiser and the goat theme from our stories of the game, we hurried over, surprised that the quiet Yankee center fielder was asking to be interviewed. Joe wanted to give us a lecture on the peculiar difficulties of center field in Yankee Stadium. He told us how hard it was to get used to the thick haze that winds and smoke created in late September and early October over the Stadium outfield. He told us of tricky gusts off the Harlem River, of the importance of knowing instinctively where were the depressions in the ground caused by drainage pipes. The whole purpose of his talk was to defend a man whose humiliation he understood, and yet an hour before Joe would have gone into the wall to keep Reiser from getting a hit.

Consider the words of Jim Corbett, describing his victory over John L. Sullivan for the heavyweight championship of the world.

"So the roar of the crowd went on. I should have felt proud and dazed, but the only thing I could think of, right after the knockout, was Sullivan lying there on the floor. I was actually disgusted with the crowd, and it left a lasting impression on me. It struck me as sad to see all those thousands who had given him such a wonderful ovation when he entered the ring turning it to me now that he was down and out. . . . I got him when he was slipping and that goes for all the champions down the line."

In the last game of the 1948 World Series the Cleveland Indians were running up an easy victory over the Boston Braves, and as the game drew to a close I went down to the Cleveland dressing room to beat the crowd and be ready to get the winners' words. I was the first reporter to arrive and found the dressing room empty save for Bob

Lemon, who had pitched the early innings for the Indians, and Frank McCormick, who had pinch hit for the Braves. They were chatting amiably about incidents in the Series, which we all believed to be concluded, and listening to the final moments on a small radio above the rubbing table on which they sat.

Then the radio told us that the Braves were coming to life. There was a hit and then another, and then a run scored, and the crowd—we were at Braves Field—came to life and began to scent victory. Our conversation stopped, and we hung on the announcer's words. Suddenly I noticed that McCormick had slipped away. It is one thing to talk about the battle when the fight is over, but while there is a chance of change such talk is treason in war, tactless and uncomfortable in sport. Quietly and without fuss he had returned to his own lines even though he could take no further part.

I do not find this kind of punctilio in such of our business and political life as I have had a chance to see, and the arts tend to shun codes as smacking of restriction on creative freedom. I don't know that any of these phases of our society would work any better with a little more chivalry. I only know that I like it and respect it and feel glad that someone is keeping it alive against a day of need, even if that someone be instinctive in his approach and unaware of his guardianship.

Joe Louis' famous wartime remark, "We are on God's side," which reversed the usual order of things, came out of that instinctive code and means more than all the flannelly editorials about sports which suggest that our superiority to those around us is based on extensive Little League activity. This is, of course, nonsense, because the values of sport are not nearly that pragmatic.

When Joe DiMaggio turned down a hundred-thousand-dollar contract for one more year of baseball on the grounds that he couldn't give the owners their money's worth and did not want to play at less than his best, he was talking the language of another age.

When middleweight champion Tony Zale complained about the stopping of a fight to save him further punishment with the words, "A champion has a right to be killed," he was—what do you want to call it?—magnificent in his pride? or dangerously and harshly out of touch with the realities and showing overtones of masochistic hysteria? In any case it is not a common attitude in our society and has nothing to do with the anxious pettiness of suburban infant competition.

I do not suggest, as football coaches do in talking to possible scholarship athletes, that there is something in sport that will mysteriously turn a second-rate person into a first-rate one. Sport, both amateur and professional, is full of people who are very good at games but whose presence anywhere else is a signal for the sewing up of pockets and the placing of backs to the wall.

The claim that team sport is a testing ground for mature consideration of one's fellows is as specious as the scientists' claim that a year of making stinks in a high school chemistry lab will teach you something called the "scientific method," which will keep you from ever again being prejudiced, will make you stop generalizing from the particular, and will sweep your mind free of every kind of superstition and cant.

After all, look at some of our teams. Look at some of our scientists.

What sport does do is provide for the idealist, for the person with absolute values, and for the romantic, about the only milieu in our society where he is not continually being made to feel like a psychological misfit. Running

your head into the wall will earn you respect in sport, but
running your head into a vice president will get you known
as a troublemaker in business.

When the 1933 baseball Giants sent to the minor leagues
in midseason for a utility infielder of modest accomplishments, he heralded his arrival with a telegram reading:

THEY CANNOT BEAT US. ON MY WAY.

J. RYAN.

As if the whole thing had happened in the pages of a
bad boys' book, Blondie Ryan made it all come true by
scrambling earnestly and awkwardly around the infield and
producing, out of a very small number of hits, an amazing
percentage of critically important ones.

A young executive in the field who sent such a wire to
a summons from the home office would be turned right
over to the testing boys or sent out to Alaska to watch
over a warehouse. Of course, running a company isn't at
all like playing baseball, says a sensible person somewhere,
but might not some of Blondie's cockiness be as useful in
the board room as one more depth study of packaging pref-
erences among college graduates?

Of course, we don't much care for arrogance any more,
except on the part of besieged generals, but I must admit
I was refreshed by the attitude of Kirby Higbe, a Dodger
pitcher of twenty-odd years ago when I attempted to discuss with him the greatness of Cleveland's Bob Feller.
When I asked Kirby what he thought of Feller's fast ball,
he replied with magnificent irrelevance, "Feller wouldn't
get a foul off me."

To look down at the whole world from a pitcher's
mound with a strong arm and a good assortment of pitches
may be a narrow view, but it is a commanding one. Indeed,
when you are young, the strong arm is enough. I once

asked the late Hugh Casey, then in his twenties, whether he had any trick deliveries. He looked at me with scorn. "That —— is for old men," he said. "I just throw the ball."

I was to see him later as an old man pitching relief for the Dodgers in a World Series when he came in with men on base, studied his infield, moved a couple of men a foot or two this way or that like a fashion photographer arranging models, and then throw a soft, drooping pitch which could have been caught with a bare hand except that the batter sent it on one hop to one of the shifted fielders for double play. The look on Casey's face as he stuffed his glove in his pocket and started for the dugout was no longer the expression of moon-reaching Hotspur, but it would have done quite well for Henry V.

Television dilutes baseball so that to many who consider themselves fans, ballplayers are little gray men who run around on glass. To try to see the panorama of what nine of them are doing as they shift their defenses would be like looking at raisins in a rice pudding. The moments of drama are selected for you by a director, and since he is an able and knowledgeable man, you won't miss any of the orthodox moments, the strikeout, the close play at first, the home run falling among the outstretched hands of the bleacherites, some reaching for the ball and some for the camera and the immortality of registering on sixty million eyeballs for a glorious second.

You probably would not have seen how Hughie Casey looked savoring his power, because that double play ended the inning and you would have been treated to a chorus of humanoid beer bottles singing in thirds, or a smartly drilled platoon of cigarettes with filter busbies.

It is pointless, however, to natter on about televised baseball in the same way that it is pointless to complain about frozen orange juice and powdered coffee. All three are convenient, all three are "almost as," and all three are here to stay. For those who don't like them there are available oranges, bean coffee, and seats at the ball park. I brought it up as a preliminary to a wonder as to what happened to Heroes. When I was a boy every team had two or three Heroes, men who were not just good ballplayers but gods. Some were admittedly only local lares but quite a few were so Olympian that they elicited worship all around the league. Who would boo Christie Mathewson or Walter Johnson? Who would not feel elevated and rather special just from having watched them pitch or even walk across the grass to the dugout with the special stride which does not quite touch the turf but has somehow still the portentous weight of majesty on the move.

Perhaps it is television, perhaps it is one of the hundreds of other sociological factors which are always being hashed over by professors in those frightening paperbacks called *Robotia, Our Dissolving Society* or *Prosperity without Hope,* but whatever it is there don't seem to be many Heroes any more. I thought I was perhaps a little jaded, but I have checked with my son and his friends, and they all seem to be interested only in teams. They have favorites, of course, but the big thing is the team.

I told my son that when the Yankees gave Babe Ruth's number to the rookie outfielder George Selkirk, I tore up my roots at Yankee Stadium and became a Giant fan. He thinks I was hysteric, that the assignment of numbers is not the business of boys, and he's still for the Yankees.

I thought perhaps television had reduced the hero to the same size as all the other little flat men on the tube, but perhaps the reason goes back to the need for identification with an understandable structure which was discussed earlier. Certainly the need for understandable structures is much greater now than it was twenty-five years ago. There are now so many that aren't understandable.

Whatever the reasons, and I haven't the advanced degrees which would entitle me to speculate on them, we are woefully short of Heroes. They're somewhere, however, and when we need them enough they will come back again with all their grandeur and all their flaws. The Heroes of baseball, like those of Aristotle, were never perfect. Some drank too much, some had terrible tempers, some were what used mysteriously to be called "womanizers," and some had professional faults like not being able to hit a curve ball or, in the case of Walter Johnson, an inability to throw one. Mathewson seems to be the exception. He was both flawless and loved. Even such an immortal as Lou Gehrig did not really become a Hero until the tragic end of his career, when the fans honored him with especial warmth to make up for the relative neglect with which they had treated him in the days of his greatness, days when they had been much more fascinated with the Babe, his bat, and his bellyaches.

Emerson said "Every hero becomes a bore at last," but he was thinking of those impossible people on whom history jams halos—Aristides the Just, Joan of Arc, Patrick Henry, and the rest who smile blandly at us from the pages of improving books.

Our Heroes admittedly occupied a smaller stage, but they never bored us. Their fierceness delighted us even when it led them to disaster.

Babe Ruth had a bad World Series against the Giants in the twenties but came to bat at last with the bases loaded and a chance to atone. The count crept up to three and two, and McGraw of the Giants trotted out to the pitcher and said briskly, "Throw it in the dirt."

The pitcher demurred respectfully, pointing out that a

pitch in the dirt would be ball four and would force in a run.

"Don't worry," said McGraw. "That big S.O.B. is so anxious to hit he'll swing at anything, and if you put it anywhere but in the dirt he'll probably hit it out of the park."

The pitcher obeyed, and the great man struck out on a ball that hit the ground before it reached him. To fail dramatically as well as to succeed magnificently is an earnest of immortality.

After all, we remember Mighty Casey, but who remembers the names of those who singled before he came to bat?

Merkle, Snodgrass, Mickey Owen—excellent players every one, they are remembered for things they might like forgotten, but they are remembered. Their errors at critical moments in baseball history gave them an eminence which, however uneasy, is better than having people say, "A ballplayer, eh. Were you in the big leagues?"

Here, of course, is the rub for the athlete. We may talk all the wistful wool we want about his wonderful world with its clear goals and satisfying rewards, but what a short time he is allowed to spend on it! Without even having done anything wrong, he is ousted from Eden somewhere between thirty and forty years of age. His statistics, never to grow again, are removed from the filing cabinets in the great nerve center which tells every ballplayer where he stands against his fellows and against the past. If he is lucky he leaves behind some records, but records or no, he enters the outside world only a step too low for the double play but many steps behind his contemporaries who have spent the last ten or twenty years wearing a different kind of flannel.

It makes one see the point of Solon's remarks to Croesus,

when that wealthy king, in hopes of a "Who but you?"
asked the Greek philosopher who was the happiest of men.
Solon first named Tellus, a soldier who died heroically in
battle while still one of the most respected of men and
warriors. Next he named a pair of athletic brothers,
Cleobis and Biton, who I would guess to be field-event
men from their final exploit. It appeared that it was
essential for their mother to be driven to the temple in
her oxcart, and the oxen being slow in getting home, as
is the way of oxen, the boys hitched themselves to the
cart and pulled it six miles to the ceremonies. They spent
the afternoon accepting congratulations on their strength,
and their mother prayed to Hera, the goddess in residence,
that they should receive some special mark of favor. They
received it that day. Still aglow from universal admiration,
they fell asleep in the temple and never woke up.

Croesus was very sulky about all this at the time, but
after he had been sent to the minor leagues by Cyrus the
Persian, he had second thoughts.

In this respect, at least, the actor is more fortunate than
his show-business colleague, the athlete. Where the thirty-
year-old ballplayer broods over a creak in the knee, or a
newspaper reference to himself as "the wily veteran," the
actor moves gracefully from Pierrot to Pantaloon or from
Hamlet to Claudius to Polonius. Indeed, I read recently
of a Polish actor who was still a full-time member of a
Warsaw repertory company at the age of 99. Charles
Macklin essayed Shylock at the same age, 57 years after
he had first electrified London audiences with his playing
of the part, but he isn't such a good argument for me,
since he broke down after two or three speeches. Still he
lived on to the age of 107, which seems, if you'll accept one
more generalization from the particular, to argue for the
salubrious nature of our work. Even the shuffleboard play-

ers of St. Petersburg, Florida, the oldest athletes I know, usually hang up their jewel-tipped pushers at 90 and go over to the checker tables.

As a character man I accept the signs of advancing age with equanimity. At the moment I am too bald to get the girl, not bald enough to play her uncle, but the hairbrush tells me that uncles are just over the horizon. A few more wattles and I can play bankers, psychiatrists, and tax men, favored butts of playwrights, who seem to have trouble with all of them, and rich material for mature comedians.

Some few ballplayers stay in uniform as managers and coaches but these jobs lack the wonderful competitive simplicity of active play. A manager's records are made for him by others, and no matter how blazing his competitive fire he cannot set all his players to the same temperature often enough to escape the inevitable end of dismissal.

"It's the only job in the world," said Birdie Tebbetts, several times a manager, "where you know on the day you're hired that the only thing sure is that you'll be fired."

Even Connie Mack, who owned the team he managed, was eventually pushed aside by the impatient princelings of his own family.

The manager, like the theater director, must give his vision into the hands of others and, too often, watch them drop it, step on it, and leave it looking like Venetian glass after a hailstorm. Direct a rock 'n' roll singer as Shaw's Marchbanks for the tent trade, or manage the Mets, and you must sometimes pray for the merciful hemlock of the pink slip.

The old fight manager whose dictum I gave at the beginning of this chapter was such a man. Heavy glasses and advancing years have forced him to the job of instilling his knowledge and spirit into others, and it is a terrible task.

"Sometimes," he told me, "they pick up everything very quick in the gym, they're very stylish with the punching bag and the old guys you send in to spar with them, and they nod their heads like they get it when you tell how they got to move inside punches and not try to pull away, and then one night you send them up the steps into the ring for a fight and the other guy fires a real one and they start to go toward it, inside it, and then something they can't control grabs them by the neck and they pull back, and maybe the first time they get away with it, but you know all that nodding didn't mean nothing. You can't get mad about it because it takes a lot to go towards something that's going to hurt like hell if it hits you, but you get the smelling-salts bottle ready and start sizing up the other guy. Maybe you can buy a piece of him."

"Once, long ago," he said, "I had the perfect guy. Intelligent, but he had no imagination. He was afraid of nothing and he didn't worry about the other guy's reputation as a hitter, he just wanted to look at where he carried his hands. One night we had a big Italian dinner and I took him to a movie and left him there. I went back to the hotel and a guy calls and asks if I can bring my guy over to Newark in a hurry. Some guy broke his hand and Newark needs a substitute. I go to the movie and I find my man sitting there full of pasta and belching a little olive oil and I whisper, 'Come on, we got a fight tonight.' You know something? We got all the way to Newark before he says, 'By the way, who am I gonna fight?' "

Science reinforces my manager's notion with something called Krause's Hypothesis or the CCCC principle ("Complete competitors cannot coexist"). Howard Ensign Evans in *Wasp Farm* explains it this way: "The theory behind this is that if two species do in fact do everything alike—live in the same place, feed on the same food, and so forth—one of them is bound to do something very slightly better than the other and will, over a period of time, completely eliminate the other."

Here you'd better open your notebooks, because Mr. Evans goes on with a piece of advice to beleaguered species, and if you're having a little trouble you may wish to note it down: "But if in fact they impinge on their environment just a little differently in some respect, they can coexist indefinitely."

There is a world of useful advice for us all in that sentence. If, for example, you are a welterweight fighter who is being completely eliminated, you might think about taking on lightweights. If you are an actor who finds too many living in the same place and feeding on the same food, you might try directing or producing or becoming, as one actor did, governor of Connecticut.

The temptation to go back to the old feeding ground is very strong, of course. I know a distinguished but seldom employed actor who opened an antique shop during a long stretch when the other species were pushing him toward extinction. Still, occasionally he acted, and once, when he was again in a play, I met him on his way to a matinee. He had spent the morning accumulating stuff for his store, and after accepting my congratulations on his job he looked at me glumly over the armload of dusty attic trove in his arms and said, "What a terrible business the theater is. For twenty-five years I've been trying to get into it—or out of it, and I failed at both."

When I was a baseball writer I felt something like him. I wanted to be in baseball or out of it. I wanted to care very much about winning or not see the scores at all.

It was not that I wanted, like Pete Reiser, to go into the

wall, it was that, living in an atmosphere which accepted this as a possible act and not be a part of it as either rooter or performer was too hard. It was as if one were company clerk to the Musketeers or veterinarian to the Light Brigade.

Now that I am a fan again, however, I am glad of the time I spent backstage at ball parks, race tracks, stadia, gyms, et al. It made me feel that I need not abandon all the baggage of rah-rah romanticism that I picked up as a boy, that somewhere among all the trunks of tosh was a satchelful of the real stuff. Sometimes I have a little trouble finding it, but it's nice to know it's there. Occasionally it helps to take it with you to the theater.

WHEN CHILDREN PLAY pretending games they organize a theatrical enterprise quickly, joyously, and with an efficiency that is sometimes lacking when grown-ups play pretending games with real money.

"Let's play cowboys and Indians!" cries one, becoming the producer.

"I'm gonna be the Indian chief!" shouts another, showing the quickness and firmness which marks the star, and soon a casting agent has been appointed to divide the other roles among the remaining players in the best traditions of repertory theater—"You were an Indian twice yesterday. Today you got to be a cowboy,"—and a couple of property men have gathered enough branches and broom handles to supplement the supply of plastic weapons and assure everyone the right to say, "I got you, you're dead!"

Every pistol-packing cowboy and bow-bending Indian has this right, because in these games writing and directing are group enterprises, and no child may sit out front on a rock with a mackinaw draped over his shoulders, making life miserable for the other children.

The group manages its spectacle sensibly so that there shall be that well-balanced conflict which is vital to good theater—a massacre, after all, would bring down the curtain too quickly—and the direction is of a straightforward and graphic sort—"Fall down! I shot you," although it is sometimes a bit more complex and emotional in that first and most enduring of soap operas called "Playing House." The dying here is more protracted and may require some finely shaded suffering both before and after the arrival of the doctor.

The beginnings of adult theater are much closer to this vacant-lot drama than to a mélange of metaphysics and confidence tricks which have encrusted it through the centuries.

My own favorite theory is that which links us to the Dionysian revels of the Greeks. It appears that whole towns used to proceed to the temple on the feast day of the god, and those who felt like playing cowboys and Indians dressed themselves in goatskins and capered around the marchers.

On arrival at the sacred grove the first rite was that of sacrifice, human at first, goats in a later and softer age. From the Greek *tragos*, goat, is supposed to have come our modern word tragedy, certainly an apt derivation from the goat's point of view, if not from ours. (Today we have substituted investors for goats, but the permutations of the tax laws make tragedy too strong a word for their sacrifice.)

The priest then began to tell the story of Dionysus to the assembled townspeople, and here is where theater began, for the goatskin group cried out comments and glosses on the story and acted out bits of it in pantomime, much to the delight of the watchers. Perhaps the priests found this stimulating, perhaps they felt it to be distracting, but one historic day a priest assembled the revelers the week before the festival and said something like this:

"Boys and girls we've got a lovely show right as it stands, but we're all of us artists, and if there's one thing an artist loves it is to refine his art and make things just a *leetle* bit better. If you'll get out your tablets and *styli*, I've got a wonderful idea. We're going to write down in advance everything we're going to do, and then we're going to do it over and over again. The first thing you can write down is the word for that. The word is 'rehearsal.' I have derived it from the harrow with which we prepare our fields for the harvest. I think you'll see a wonderful harvest next week if you'll all pay attention.

"Now first off—some cuts. You may have noticed a lot of coughing when we've been telling the story of how the blinded Lycurgus, angry with our wine god, hews down his own son, thinking him to be a vine. Well, to begin with, I don't think it's believable, and for a second thing it's ugly, and the last thing people want after walking five miles over these dusty roads is a lot of ugliness, so that whole scene is out. We are going to make a lot more on the other hand out of the scene where Dionysus turns the Tyrrhene pirates into dolphins. It's a good chance for some graceful dancing, and I think there are some laughs in the comic surprise of the pirates. Oh, and before I go any further I want to say that I want a more serious attitude this year. I want you to get inside these characters and really know them. When you turn into a dolphin, you must really turn into a dolphin," etc. etc.

On that day direction was born, and before you could say "right, chief," trained choruses were dancing and singing the Dithyramb, and soon after that somebody said,

"*Dionysus, Dionysus*—really, I'm so sick of that stale story. Why don't we do a whole new show this year?" On that day playwriting was born, and before you could say "option money," everybody was turning out scripts for the annual Greek playwriting contests. The first that we know of was won in 534 B.C. by a man named Thespis. His immortality rests in having given his name to actors. Any writer could tell you what happened to that prize-winning script. It got lost.

I am not scholar enough to try to give the history of theater from Dionysus to David Merrick, but I would like to examine here a crotchet that all actors, including myself, seem to cling to in the teeth of the evidence.

This is the notion that all previous ages in the theater were golden and that only today—whether today be mid-twentieth-century Broadway, or mid-thirteenth-century Provence, did things turn lousy for actors.

For myself, I suspect that actors began brooding way back when that first priest turned our spontaneous game into a discipline. Not, mind you, that discipline is a bad thing, although almost as many crimes have been committed in its name as in the name of that other troublemaker, liberty.

In the spontaneous dawn, you got the part because you began performing it. Somebody could always use another cowboy or another Indian. When the whole thing was put on an organized basis, it turned out there were more actors than there were parts for actors, and it's been that way ever since.

Still, most actors will tell you that just behind them, in an immediate past which they were so unlucky as just to miss, the theater was a vital place with an abundance of jobs in an abundance of good plays.

Partly this misconception is born of the lies of old actors

who, looking back from nowhere, find it unbearable to think that the past is equally empty.

"There were actors in those days, laddie," they cry, "and plays for them to act in. None of your psychological rot, but good, clean Shakespeare, beautifully spoken. Forty weeks a season, regular as clockwork, doing full weeks at all the best houses. One year with Beerbohm Tree I alternated Laertes, Hotspur, Edmund, and Mercutio . . . When I finished 'Good night, sweet prince' and the soldiers lifted Mantell to their shoulders, the applause began, and it grew until it could be heard for blocks around. Twenty curtain calls and the stage covered with flowers . . . We all waited after the curtain for Her Majesty, and she spoke individually to every member of the company. Later we received medals struck off for the occasion. It meant a knighthood for our star, but what the Queen said to me was as good as any title . . . The stage manager kept making faces at me through the door, and I could hear the rhythmic clapping of the impatient audience, but how does one tell a Sultan that it's time for the second act and he'll have to buzz off back to his box? . . . Champagne . . . The Duke was kind enough . . . Shaw clapped me on the back and said . . . Struggling through the great blizzard to fill the house and warm it with their cheers . . . Matched pearl studs to every member of the company . . . He wrote in it, 'from one Prince of Denmark to another' . . . Applause . . . laughter . . . caviar . . . Immortality."

When you hear this sort of thing while sitting on a bench waiting to see if you are right for the Second Pickpocket and understudy to the Pimp, it does turn you around a bit.

Of course, it is beyond cavil that the theater has a sawtoothed historical chart, and that it was demonstrably

better to be an English actor at the turn of the seventeenth
century when one could play Shakespeare fresh and new
before audiences that really wondered whether Othello
would do something silly and fondly hoped that all could
be made easy between the Capulets and Montagues, than
it was forty years later when by statute a performer was
whipped the first time he was caught acting and declared
an incorrigible rogue and vagabond the second time. Even
audiences did not then escape the proscription and were
fined five shillings a person for witnessing plays.

So also one would probably rather be an actor in the
great eighteenth-century days of David Garrick than to be
around at the beginning of the nineteenth, when all that
could save the famous Drury Lane Theater was a dreadful
play called *The Cataract of the Ganges* with a real onstage
waterfall in the title role. For forty years thereafter actors
were frequently obscured behind clouds of smoke and fire,
torrents of water, and other mechanical rivals, until in 1849
not even spectaculars could keep the great theater in business. An American circus moved into the Drury Lane that
year and cleaned up with animal acts and acrobats, while
the actors took to the road and told each other how wonderful the theater used to be, no matter how wet from
waterfalls.

To me the low point would seem to be the early eigh-
teenth century when the English stage, although reasonably vigorous, appears to have been more a meeting place
than a home of drama. It was at a London performance
of *Macbeth* in 1721 that a nobleman rose from his seat
on the stage and wandered across to greet a friend on the
other side. The actor, John Rich, caught in mid-pentame-
ter, rebuked the nobleman and drew a blow in the face.
At this point Shakespeare ceased and the fighting started.
Rich and another actor whipped out their stage swords and,

aided by the rest of the troupe, drove the fashionable audience from the house. The angry crowd refreshed itself with alcohol and reinforcement and returned to wreck the theater. Troops restored order sometime the next day. I don't know when they finished *Macbeth*.

The writer Tate Wilkinson gives this picture of the theater of that time:

"On crowded nights an amphitheater of seats was raised upon the stage, where there would be groups of ill-dressed lads and persons sitting on the stage in front three or four feet deep; so that in fact a performer on a popular night could not step with safety, lest he should thereby hurt or offend, or be thrown down amid scores of idle or tipsy apprentices. But it was the beaux who usually affected that part of the house . . . They sported their own figures to gratify self-consequence and impede and interfere with the performers who had to come on and go off the stage."

In an age in which actors throw frowns at latecomers and coughers, such a state of affairs seems as unreal and frightening as the dreams which oppress the sensitive after a summer-stock dress rehearsal—"Then they said, 'No, no, it's not *King Lear*, it's *Ten Nights in a Barroom*. Well, there isn't time to learn the part now, you have to make your entrance—wait a minute, you can't go on like that. You're naked.'"

In all the march, or treadmill, or whatever it is, of Western civilization, the one age that everybody agrees to be nostalgic about is the Golden Age of Classic Greece. Actors, poets, athletes, architects, schoolteachers, and many more, seem agreed that long ago on the edge of the Mediterranean, things were done better in their lines of work than has ever been the case since.

"The Greek world that lives in the Western mind," says the historian Herbert Muller, "is the kind of world pictured by the aging Goethe: a world of beautiful form and order, perfect in harmony and proportion, controlled in emotion and balanced in thought, altogether 'classical' in its simplicity, restraint, poise, serenity." Muller regretfully points out that "there was always considerable hell in Hellas" and that despite the real accomplishments of that remarkable age, the general atmosphere was as simple, poised, and restrained as a Times Square Saturday night.

"The Emperor Cyrus of Persia described a Greek market as 'a place set apart for people to go and cheat others on oath.'"

What of the Greek theater? Certainly no other body of plays has achieved the awesome standard of the canon left to us by the great Greek playwrights, and we can only groan to think of all the hits that were burned up in the Alexandria library fire, but what was it like to be an actor then?

We don't have much information about it, but some of what we have is a little depressing. Owing to the large size of the amphitheaters it was necessary for the actors to be amplified by megaphonic masks and built up to heroic size on wooden clogs. Granting that the words are immortal, the talents required of the performers seem closer to those of the train announcer than to those of the actor.

Those rough stone stages are no fun when you're on stilts, and when I think of my Athenian confrere stumbling around on a blazing hot day such as only Athens can produce, shouting into a claustrophobic leather hat pulled down to his shoulders and trying to back away from the drops of sweat between cheek and soggy cowhide, I must admit that air conditioning can mean almost as much as Aristophanes. It was not only the discomfort, however. There was also the impersonal stylization which left so little creative function to the actor that he must have felt about as much of an artist as the music maker who pumps the pedals on a mechanical piano.

Perhaps you'd like to move ahead into the Roman theater? You would lose your mask, but also most of your civil rights. *Scenici* as the Romans called actors, were branded with *infamia*. Even if your Latin is poor I think you get the idea of where we *scenici* stood, and it is not much consolation that the emperor who gave us back some of our rights and lightened the burden of our *infamia* was Nero.

The reputations of the theater's friends have often been a handicap. Sponsor of one of the first two "protected" companies in England was the Duke of Gloucester, later Richard III. I am among those who believe his reputation is undeserved (it is sad that the theater, for which he did so much, was the medium of his monsterization), but undeserved or no, it is his reputation, and—in modern terms—it is not an image that will help you to get a bank loan.

Christian Rome was no improvement and in 200 A.D. Tertullian rubbed his hands over the notion of the last spectaculum—to be seen in hell.

"Then," he purred, "will come the time to listen to the tragedians whose lamentations will be the more poignant for their proper pain. Then will the comedians turn and twist, rendered nimbler than ever by the sting of fire that is not quenched."

This kind of thing makes Oliver Cromwell look like Show Business Statesman of the Year.

As Christianity spread, various fourth-century councils discussed the problem of the actors, and although it was decided that no Christian could be one or marry one, a tolerant group of churchmen decreed that any of us who would forswear the stage forever might receive baptism and forgiveness for the sin of acting.

I suppose there were some lodge shows and smokers in the Dark Ages but it doesn't seem to have been a good time for a more organized theater or a more organized anything above the level of an Arthurian rumble. Those good people who had time to think about theater didn't think about it very warmly, and from Chrysostom in the east and St. Jerome in the west came the word that actors, among others, were probably responsible for the Dark Ages.

Let's skip ahead to the next dream world, the Middle Ages.

Say "Middle Ages" nowadays, and nobody thinks of plague, plowing with a burnt stick, or what it must have been like to have a toothache when the dentist was primarily an astrologer. What one does think about are pennons, tournaments, cathedrals, chanting monks, and those wonderful religious plays which grew up as the church forgave the theater and began to use it for the glory of God.

The other medieval theatrical phenomena that make everyone go all warm and cozy are the guild plays. Think of all those wonderful old craftsmen lovingly carving wood, molding leather, weaving cloth, beating gold, and several times a year getting together in simple reverence to perform their colorful religious dramas! What high purpose! What dedication! No cheap commercialism for these lucky folk—no fabrikoid fantasy, no plastic Plautus, no pinchbeck passion—but the Real Thing, from the Heart!

This is, of course, partly true. No one doubts the dedication or the high purpose, but did you ever see a carpenter or a weaver who was much of an actor? What we are really dealing with here is large-scale Little Theater. In many cases, according to contemporary writers, the prompter did

most of the talking, and all the actors got to strut around
the stage before plunging into their parts. When Hamlet
in the advice to the players talks about sawing the air and
splitting the ear, he is referring to these actors. The remark about out-Heroding Herod refers to the fact that the
goldsmiths and tanners who played Herod, Pilate, and
other shady royalty were allowed and encouraged to shout
and stamp in a manner which Hamlet and his professional
friends quite properly found revolting.

Of course, it is wonderful that the theater somehow
manages to stay alive, and it is charming to think of the
whole bourgeois community playing theater instead of golf
or canasta, but a golden age for professional actors it wasn't.

The guildsmen did receive pay, but the prompter appears, deservedly, to have got more for "beryng the boke"
than the actors for echoing him.

At this distance some of the wages paid to these semi-
professionals seem a little mysterious. According to E. K.
Chambers, the wage in Coventry was the same for "savyd"
souls and "dampnyd" souls, twenty pence. In recent years
"dampnyd" souls have had better parts, but the Middle
Ages had not the benefit of modern psychological thinking.
Demons apparently weren't as interesting as the disturbed
are. The part that seemed most interesting to me, "The
worme of conscyence" only got eight pence, but was better
off than God, who got only sixpence at Hull. I know that
money went further in those days but sixpence just doesn't
seem enough for that part when wormes of conscyence are
getting eight and just plain souls twenty.

I am not going to labor my point through all of history,
but I cannot leave this stretch of good old days without
some mention of what the Little Theater crowd was doing
in the churches. The words were set down by the Abbess
Herrad of Landsberg in 1150:

"The old fathers of the church, in order to strengthen the belief of the faithful and to attract the unbeliever by this manner of religious service, rightly instituted at the Feast of the Epiphany or the Octave religious performances of such a kind as the Star guiding the Magi to the newborn Christ, the cruelty of Herod, the dispatch of the soldiers, the lying-in of the Blessed Virgin, the angel warning the Magi not to return to Herod, and other events of the birth of Christ. But what nowadays happens in many churches? Not a customary ritual, not an act of reverence, but one of irreligion and extravagance conducted with all the license of youth . . . The church is desecrated by feasting and drinking, buffoonery, unbecoming jokes, play, the clang of weapons, the presence of shameless wenches, the vanities of the world, and all sorts of disorder. Rarely does such a gathering break up without quarreling."

Here we can see that as early as the twelfth century the "good old days" business was well launched. Somewhere in the immediate past the abbess felt there had been a pure theater behind the altar. The coarse jokes had slipped in while her back was turned, and what a shame. So also today's actors look at those rotogravure-brown programs so recent that they feature ads for recognizable automobiles, and feel that the actors listed therein—funny that so many of their names are unfamiliar—had a wonderful time. Who turned his back to let happen the present state of affairs? Men with more title than I discuss this endlessly in the sterner weeklies and the Sunday papers. The only thing on which they seem unanimous is that *someone* turned his back and that the results have been disastrous.

Shallowly and unfairly I have skipped about in a couple of thousand years of theater history in support of my notion that the back has always been turned. I don't make any pretense of scholarship—well, that's not quite right either—I make one, but it doesn't fool scholars. I started my investigations, however, in the way I believe most scientific observers employ; that is, I began with a theory and sought a mass of reasoned and objective evidence to support it. I have a lot more of it but I am sure you will take my word for its existence even if you have a mass of reasoned and objective evidence tending to prove something else.

To sum up, as we used to say when we got lost in high school debates, I think that the theater has always been, for the professional actor, a coil of dreadful difficulty. In his striving toward the realization of a daydream of impossible glory the actor has sustained himself with the notion that the daydream must be possible because it was recently true. This despite the fact that demonstrably it never has been a fact, which, accepted, suggests that it never will be, an impossible stone to add to the load already being carried.

Of course, for some few the dream has come true and stayed true, but even these few fortunates can see the hungry hound of chance grinning at them from the corner.

In 1863, for example, the famous actor Samuel Phelps starred in Byron's *Comus* at the Drury Lane. He made a great hit in the piece and was adjudged by all to have equaled the performance given by Denvil some years before. Where was Denvil when this judgment was rendered, when this performance was given? He was taking tickets at the Drury Lane and not even orchestra tickets. He was collecting stubs in the gallery.

Consider William Henry West Betty, known as "The Infant Roscius." He made his stage debut in Belfast in 1803 at the age of eleven, and two years later, after taking Dublin, Glasgow, and Edinburgh by storm, he made his London debut at Covent Garden before a record crowd. The crush in the theater was so great that fainting members of both sexes were dragged out of it every few minutes and propped up in lobby corners among a milling throng who could not see but counted themselves luckier than those in the street being pushed about by soldiery.

For all that season Betty was London's idol, and reputable critics seriously and favorably compared him to Garrick. Duchesses fought for the privilege of driving him in their carriages, Mr. Pitt adjourned Parliament one afternoon so that all the MPs might see Betty at a matinee, and when he was ill, hourly bulletins were issued, as if he were an astronaut or a Beatle. His fees ran from fifty to seventy-five pounds a performance. John Opie painted him as Young Norval in Douglas, so that forever young and successful, he waves from the wall of the Garrick Club at an audience that forgot him the following season.

His money was wisely invested, and for sixty-five more years he lacked for nothing except the sound of that applause which had brightened his youth and was to echo in the dreams of his son, Henry, who jostled along among "average" actors until almost a hundred years after the date of his father's triumph.

Perhaps poor Betty wasn't a very good actor, but even those famous ones like the Kembles and Mrs. Jordan, who played to empty houses while he was piping out, "On the Grampian hills I tend my flocks," must have felt for him after his fall. After all, they could be next.

Of course, critics became testy with Beethoven when he began to write the last quartets, and painting fanciers found the later Rembrandt rather warty, but nobody just walked out and forgot them. True, Betty was no Beethoven, but on the night it took a regiment to clear a path into Covent Garden it would have been hard to prove that the boy wasn't at the gates of immortality.

Remember also that the neglected geniuses whom posterity pulls out of corners and dusts off for the delight of later ages were never stopped from practicing their arts. Beethoven scorned covered as much stave paper every day as Beethoven chic, and Rembrandt, balked of sitters, painted portraits of himself, but when Betty as a middle-aged man was recognized by a critic at an inn, he could only mutter, "That's all over now," and hurry away.

You may, from your position in the "real" world, think that we make a great deal of fuss about a rather trifling profession and that our ladder is really a rather shabby ferris wheel, ending always where it began and meaning little.

Oliver Wendell Holmes said that misery was caused by a tinge of genius which spoils a man as water is spoiled by being poured into a glass containing wine dregs.

Commenting on this, Arthur Machen said, "I would not limit the maxim to genius. The true tragedy is the juxtaposition of desire and impotence. It must be horrible to long to write film scenarios—and to long in vain.

"Most of us have always found the career of the *raté*, the artist who misses fire, distinctly comic. The poet who can hardly get into the corner column of his country paper, the novelist whose novels are simply 'rot,' the painter whose pictures are a joke; we laugh heartily at them all. But, on the other hand, we are not in the least inclined to laugh at the small grocer who goes bankrupt, or at the widow with children who fails lamentably in the stationery shop—tobacco, sweets, newspapers and fancy goods included—in the new suburb."

The actor has the knowledge, bitter in some ways, comforting in others, that the damping of his fire may not be his own doing. The widow mismanages her tobacco shop, the small grocer is too sanguine about the flow of perishables, the country paper poet writes demonstrably bad verse, but what of Denvil taking tickets in the gallery? Was he a bad actor? If so, why all the cheering when he played his *Comus?* Well, perhaps he was, as perhaps Betty was. Years later, the poet Thomas Campbell wrote frostily of the infant Roscius, "The popularity of that baby-faced boy who possessed not even the elements of a good actor, was an hallucination in the public mind and a disgrace to our theatrical profession."

But if they were bad actors and if they were hailed, how valid are the cheers of today? Should I enjoy my applause or brood on human folly? Well, of course, I'm going to enjoy the applause—why else am I acting, but the nagging worry about human folly is in the back of my mind and there is no "scientifically" critical way to remove it. Musicians and poets produce an enduring product which can be run through the test of centuries, but actors, as thrilling as fireworks, are as short-lived and as hard to recall correctly and objectively—"No, it was blue stars and then white— white stars first, silly, anyway, it wasn't a patch on last year's, when they had the shower of gold—The shower of gold was two years ago and I thought it was dull—Well, it doesn't matter much now, although I get excited every year when they start."

An old actor I knew spent years of his youth talking to people who had seen Edwin Booth, in the hopes of hearing something which would explain the great reputation.

"They all said he was great," the actor told me. "But when I asked why, they could only shrug and say that he seemed very natural."

Well, let's take it on faith that he was great. We have to start somewhere and believe in somebody, and the "natural" Edwin Booth is the theater's Babe Ruth. Faith is what we must have, however, for there are no Ruthian statistics, no volumes, canvases, or manuscripts, only some mementos preserved at the Players Club, which, were they not known to be his, would not arouse interest in a warehouse browser. We have the world's verdict on Shakespeare, but only Hamlet's memory speaks for Yorick.

The standards which govern our lives are, then, admittedly terrifyingly imprecise and subject to change without notice. I remember hearing a bridge player's nightmare in which a man holding the perfect no-trump hand bids a grand slam and is doubled, redoubles, is redoubled, etc. As the play begins, a little man across the table leads a green ace, and when the terrified bidder asks what it is, the little man replies, "Why, the ace of hippogriffs, of course," and produces twelve more of them to sweep the hand.

Actors are always running into the ace of hippogriffs just when they think a slam is budding, and if, by some delightful freak, they are dealt honors in hippogriffs, it turns out that the game is now Parcheesi.

The good side, of course, is that we can blame our troubles on others and carry a warmly glowing ego under our cloaks along the darkest of roads.

"Hard beside each other run the roads of night and day," and as we trudge through the gloom the inner glow convinces us that the next turning will take us to bright Broadway and that we only got onto this path through improper direction.

There are exceptions, usually depressing ones, to almost any rule you can think of, and I know one actor who, while trying to puff his ego-glow to a bonfire, blew it out.

"I had always dreamed," he told me, "that I would be the ideal Richard III. I *knew* that if I ever got the chance to play it, all previous Richards would be forgotten. I sustained myself with this dream through a hundred movies and plays. I had some success, got together some money, and realized my dream. I financed and put on my own production with myself as Richard, directed by myself, and with just the cast I wanted around me, and—Oh, God, I was awful!"

Not Enoch Soames creeping back from posterity's rejection to his bad bargain with the Devil could have felt any worse. I have not seen my friend in years, and I can only hope and trust that he now believes that his conviction of mediocrity—even fortified by critical agreement—was only undue modesty, reinforced by the thoughtless scribbling of hacks.

So, with recognition uncertain and often of limited duration, with more back-to-the-beginning penalties than are found in the most brutal of children's board games ("You have stepped in the radiated swamp. Return to the rocket for decontamination which will make you miss your next two turns. Take a mutant card."), with the continual "juxtaposition of desire and impotence," it is not surprising that actors turn their eyes backward in contemplation of supposed Arcadias rather than forward into the teeth of the storm. We in the mid-twentieth century tend to look longingly at the bright lights, big hats, and long runs of the days of Good King Edward and jolly T.R.

Wonderful days, you say? Here is a note from *The Stage as a Career*, written by Philip G. Hubert, Jr., in 1899.

"In a mercantile community such as that of New York or of any of our large cities no one is likely to deny that the shoe dealer, for instance, is held in infinitely higher esteem than the actor."

I find this particularly hard to take, since I was fantasizing about good King Edward's time long before I became an actor. I just happen to *know* it was the best of times. Through the years I have seen myself in a hundred Edwardian roles, and now, if Mr. Hubert's cold common sense is going to balk my theatrical dreams, perhaps I could shift my reveries. I could see myself in faultless morning clothes presiding over an exquisitely appointed salon. Before me, crouched, shoeless, in a chair, sits a noble duke who looks at me pleadingly.

"Has Your Grace considered," I say magisterially, "the possibility that a box-cloth vamp might relieve the tenderness of which you complain?"

With a hoarse cry of gratitude the sore-footed nobleman seizes my hand, but with a condescending smile I indicate that it is nothing and break away to greet a Royal Personage whose pinched mouth indicates a need for our Special Fitting Service.

Later, as I sit by a fire in my library, sipping a sample from a dozen of ducal sherry just sent up from his estate, I watch the flames flicker over a signet ring that a monarch slipped into my hand as her foot slipped into a specially modified seven EEE.

But then, what if, like Nicholas Nickleby, I "have genteel comedy in my walk and manner, juvenile tragedy in my eye, and touch-and-go farce in my laugh"? Would I really be happy running a shoe store? After all, Mr. Hubert wouldn't have written the book if the stage were an impossibility, and when you're willing to take a chance—well, before you know it, I've closed the store, pawned the ring— and set out to see if there's any concert party work in Brighton.

If that doesn't work I'll travel a good deal further, some hundreds of years, in fact, to a theater about which I don't know much—but know enough to feel that it must have seen some marvelous shows. On January 6, 1575, a man named John Carow presented a bill to the Court Performers for the following list of supplies:

"Monsters; Mountains; Forests; Beasts, Serpents; Weapons for war, as guns, Dags, Bows, Arrows, Bills, Halberds, Boarspears, Fawchions, Daggers, Targets, Pollaxes, Clubs; Heads and Headpieces; Armour counterfeit; Moss, Holly, Ivy, Bays, Flowers, Quarters; Glue, paste, paper and such like; with Nails, Hooks, Horsetails, Dishes for Devils' Eyes, Heaven, Hell, and the Devil and all: The Devil, I should say, but not all. £12, 14s, 4d."

None of your dreary suburban comedies in that theater! What did they do to the Devil that he had had to have a dish to hold his eyes? What marvelous things did they make with the glue, paste, paper, and such like?

Historically, of course, the theater in England was just piddling around waiting for Shakespeare to stop holding horses and get going on the Complete Works, but the Court Performers seem to have been a splendid oasis in the cultural desert. It is these oases which make everything worth while, which make the actor keep on going whether he be looking backward, forward, or down at his feet to see if they are bleeding.

In the worst of times, in the bleakest of theatrical eras, there are the snug hideaways where, at least for a while—and what actor asks more than a reasonable while—everything is humming and ticking and turning in the happiest imaginable manner.

One such was Sir Barry Jackson's Birmingham Repertory Theater, which flourished for several years right after World War I. Colin Keith-Johnston, who was a member of this happy band, told me that nothing that happened afterward ever equaled the perfect happiness of the Birmingham Rep.

"We got five pounds a week," said Colin, "which would do you very comfortably in the early twenties, and we worked forty-eight weeks a year. We used to take walking trips during the four-week vacation and the management used to hold back a week's salary so that when we came back to work, relaxed and gay and stony broke, there was five pounds waiting along with a new script."

Among the new scripts they did was Shaw's *Back to Methuselah*, which had been produced in New York without success and was having its first English showing at Birmingham. The five segments of *Back to Methuselah* were done over a four-day stretch from the ninth to the twelfth of October, 1923, and at the end the audience gave, not the terrible, prolonged, and even applause with which we now pay weary homage to culture, but what the critic of *The Times* called "a shout very different from the ordinary gallery cheer—a short sudden involuntary outbreak of long-held emotion, such as we have never before heard in a theatre."

The actors, who must have been exalted by their reception, were sent even higher when the author, never one to give credit away, said in a curtain speech, "I know my place as an author, and the place of the author is not on the stage. That belongs really to the artists who give life to the creations of the author and are the real life of the play. I have had the luxury of seeing my own play, which only existed until they took it and made it live."

Colin took his copy of the play around among his colleagues and had them all sign it. Each wrote: "I played," then the name of the character, and his own name. Among the names in that provincial repertory company in addition to Colin Keith-Johnston were Edith Evans, Cedric Hardwicke, and Melville Cooper.

Others wrote that they had designed the costumes or the sets or done the lights, and on the last page in red ink in a large, bold handwriting were the words: "I wrote the lines, Bernard Shaw, and you forgot to put 'I paid the bills,' Barry Jackson."

This ideal company finally produced a new script, *The Farmer's Wife* by Eden Phillpotts, which was so successful that they took it to London, where it ran for three years. The company never returned to Birmingham, and so the great days were over, but what a time it must have been! First an exciting string of plays and parts, and then the comfort and prestige of a long-running London success.

Birmingham Rep companies or something like may exist again, but they are admittedly rare. Long-running plays are rare too, though not so rare as perfect reps. They are, for most of us, however, almost as productive of happiness.

Somewhere in the background of most actors is a need for acceptance on a large scale. It's not enough to see smiles on the faces of your friends—the real tonic is the massive laughter of strangers, lots of them, the breathless attention of mobs, big ones.

A melancholy poet I knew in the Army wrote to me after the workings of the personnel system had sent us to opposite ends of the earth, and in discussing loneliness said, "What do any of us really want? Hello from a stranger, a smile from a dope." I'm afraid he is right, and that after all the high-flown talk about identity and dignity has died away most of us are mightily cheered if the silence is broken by hello from a stranger, if the outlook is brightened by a smile from a dope. Actors differ from the poet in needing large numbers of strangers and dopes. Smiles aren't enough either. You can't hear them on the stage.

A long-running play is a special treat because of the several kinds of security it provides. Not only does it provide the rare phenomenon of a regular income, it also piles up the weeks toward the collection of unemployment insurance when the final curtain falls. In New York—for those of you in the real world who think only about pensions and fringe benefits—it is necessary to have been gainfully employed in

twenty of the previous fifty-two weeks in order to collect
unemployment insurance. This is irrespective of rank and
station. An understudy with twenty weeks of humble
Wednesday and Saturday morning rehearsals is eligible,
where a star whose name has gleamed over the marquee for
nineteen weeks is not. A hit therefore piles up future treasures even as it gives one a delicious feeling of belonging,
of steadiness, of respectability.

Most of all, however, it provides us with a regular, predictable diet of attention. An actor in a hit can wake up
six mornings a week knowing that some hundreds of people must remain silent that day while he speaks.

Logan Pearsall Smith wrote: "Every author, however
modest, keeps a most outrageous vanity chained like a mad-
man in the padded cell of his breast."

Employing the tranquilizer of attention, the actor can
turn his vanity loose for an agreeable outpatient life.
Soothed and cosseted, the vanity appears to be no more
than colorful high spirits.

When the pills run out, however, it must be admitted
that no padded cell can contain the cries of the deprived
fellow within. The longer an actor goes without work, the
more outrageous become the stories he tells. The following
patchwork is made up of scraps from my nonwork basket.
Every piece is an authentic, yarn-dyed sample of desperation.

They differ from the elegiac fantasies earlier in this
chapter in that they are all aggressive, loudly colored scraps
recounting the actor's triumph over chicanery, indifference,
or powerful figures who fail—temporarily—to reckon with
the actor's importance.

"So I said to him, 'I'll be frank with you. I haven't got
the money to pay the rent, and I've run up so many tabs
I can't go into my club, but I'm a proud man and I've

spent twenty years getting my salary up to $500, and I'm
not coming down to $475 for you or anyone else.' Then
he said, 'I appreciate your feelings, boy, but I've got a
budget. How would it be, if for bookkeeping's sake you
signed a contract for $475 and I gave you the other money
on the Q.T.?' Well, God help me, I weakened, but believe
me, I didn't weaken when he tried to renege on payday. I
guess he thought I'd leave well enough alone. He knew better when I picked up my hat and cane and told him he
could reach me at my hotel when he had something more
for me than his lousy direction. He caught me in the alley
with the money and we didn't have any trouble after that
. . . When he showed me the poster I said, 'I think you
forgot something, pal. My name is supposed to be in
larger letters than anybody else's except the star's,' and he
said, 'Oh, you're not going to make a fuss about a little
thing like that, are you?' and I said, 'I guess you don't
know me, pal. I got where I am today because I never let
anything be a little thing.' . . . So I said to him, 'Gadge,
you're not talking to one of your disciples now. I don't
take that kind of stuff from anybody.' And you know something? He respected me for it. He told me later he was
sick of people fawning over him all the time. They don't
mess with me, pal, more than once, anyway, no matter how
big they are."

There is never any explanation of why the actor is not
now in the exalted position he describes. The vicissitudes
of the profession are supposed to explain that. Neither does
anyone ever question the probabilities. After all, after you
close, you may need a listener.

In all fairness it must be said that this characteristic,
marked in actors because of the nature of the calling, is not
exclusive to them. In the Army, which gathered in the
members of every profession, it was notable that the scruff-

iest-looking soldiers always returned from a weekend leave
with long stories about the girl in the convertible who had
a bottle of scotch and an inexplicable eye for a pot-bellied
Pfc. with a missing front tooth and the social graces of a
Goth. The contented-looking men always said they'd been
to the USO for bowling. Their smiles never looked like
bowlers' smiles, however.

Let's turn away now from the cold-turkey world to the
blissful realm of eight performances a week. A successful
play is more than all the things I've called it up to now.
For the actor it is also a club which he is paid to join. As
exclusive as any fortress in St. James's Street, it offers the
same clubland virtues, that is, a ready-made circle of com-
patible people whose social life you share but whose cares
and everyday problems are, by common consent, left outside the door.

Like their brother clubs, hit casts enjoy the accretion of
small rituals and traditions. I joined the company of *Bells
Are Ringing* when the show was six months old, but it was
obvious that a much longer life than that stretched ahead
of it, and my arrival, not of great import to the show, was
of large importance to the social life of the third floor of
the Shubert Theater. I was quietly examined by an informal
committee, actors in the company who had worked with me
before were asked for a character sketch, and then one day
a smiling deputation told me that I was to bring the dough-
nuts for next Wednesday's matinee and that I was invited
for cookies baked every two weeks by the wife of a character man—on Saturday afternoon. Our tea hour was during the longest "love" part of the show when the comics
were, naturally, not required onstage.

As time went on I was inducted into the payday poker
games—very sensibly there were two, one large, one small,
conducted concurrently. When you got thin in the big

game you could move over to the little game until you recouped or gave up, and if the luck seemed to be running well with the nickels, you might want to move over and see how it went with half dollars. These games rotated among several apartments, and everyone supplied food and drink except the person who supplied the place and the ash trays.

In addition to the poker games there were many other competitions, and it sometimes seemed ironic that a group which was called on for team play on the stage was so often engaged in leagues, round robins, and tournaments in the dressing rooms. I was involved in a chess league, darts league—had the show run much longer the darts players would have chipped their way into the Broadhurst Theater next door—and a complicated racing game which called for my dressing roommate, Frank Aletter, and myself to go through vast calculations of paper profit and loss based on a full card of selections, and end with the exchange every evening of a dollar in cash.

The people who were next in the dressing room would be forgiven if they imagined that something rather high-level and atomic had preceded them, for we had covered the walls with penciled figures.

We celebrated each other's birthdays, collected funds to buy presents for the departing and the marrying, and at Christmas we had an elaborate grab bag in which we all received presents from unknown donors, while giving anonymously to the person whose name we had drawn from a hat.

Our gossip was largely based on happenings within the theater, since, except on poker nights, we saw no more of each other outside than club members usually do, but the intensely intramural nature of the talk disturbed no one. Every small mishap was a matter of intense amusement, and we had also, as every close group does, a company leper. This person was supposed to be responsible through selfishness and ineptitude for almost everything that went wrong in the show. Endless stories were told about the leper's dressing-room behavior, failure to sing on key, blurring of others' jokes through awkward movement, et al. In fact, of course, the leper was simply a social polarizer and when he or she left the show we did not improve, but immediately picked another person, heretofore considered harmless, to be the new leper.

I don't think I was the leper, although goodness knows the whole thing was so discreet that I might have been and on at least two occasions was responsible for large things going wrong with the show.

The first of these was innocent enough but devastating in effect. I had taken to bringing in the chess problems from the *Manchester Guardian* for the third-floor chess-league members to try to solve. Now when we played games, two people were involved and the rest were kibitzing and listening with half an ear to the P.A. box, which told us what was going on down on the stage.

It turned out that the puzzles involved everyone, and there came an afternoon when four people were bending over a chessboard, and suddenly someone said, "My God, that's the music that comes after our scene." I never will know now how white was to mate in two moves, but I remember that we were all downstairs in one move and pell-melling onto the stage. One man tried to hang back while he tied his tie, but a fire-breathing stage manager put him on like a sixteen-pound shot, and I was held back from entering by my fellow detective, who, not a chess player, had been downstairs all the time.

"There was no one for us to discover," he whispered, "so I didn't go on. No one knows you missed the entrance."

I forget how we managed to straighten out the plot, and

I don't think the solution was very satisfactory. On behalf of the *Manchester Guardian* and myself I confess to that matinee audience, should they be reading this, that we owe each of them about a quarter.

The second occasion was more spectacular and was a mixture of triumph, tragedy, and farce, a little moment of Anton Chekhov in a Broadway musical.

Every actor in a long run knows uneasily that the day may come when he forgets a vital prop no matter how many notes to himself he writes on the mirror, no matter how many times he pats himself, murmuring the list of things that ought to be in his hands or pockets.

It was my duty on my first entrance to carry on a miniature wire recorder, which we are to use to record what my police supervisor believes to be dark doings at Susanswerphone, an answering service run by our star, Judy Holliday. During the course of the first scene the Inspector takes the little machine from me and affects to turn it on, and the audience hears a recording from an offstage tape machine.

I must have been in the show for about six months when it happened. The Inspector and I were about to enter, and, full of good actor's energy, I was running my hands together, when it occurred to me that I couldn't rub my hands together if the machine were in one of them. I wasted half a second thinking of such subterfuges as telling the Inspector that the recorder was under my coat or concealed in some book that I might snatch up, then gasped out, "The Machine. Right Back!" and set out for the third floor, leaving the Inspector to enter alone. I bowled over Miss Holliday's dresser both coming and going, but I think I got up the two flights of iron stairs, grabbed the machine, and got back, all in a very creditable thirty or so seconds. When I went onstage the Inspector had just turned for his first line to me and, delighted to see me, gave me a big smile with the line, "'Francis, the minute she gets on the phone, turn on that tape recorder.'"

I smiled back and triumphantly gripped the recorder. My heart was fairly bursting with pride. Or was it pride? Certainly it was fairly bursting, and I found out why when in the fullness of my pride I tried to answer. I sounded like an octogenarian reporting a mugging, or a long-distance call between two coffee cans joined with rosined string.

"Are you sure about this, Inspector Barnes?" was what I tried to say, and in fairness to myself I can say that I articulated the words with extra care. It's just that the dreadful wheeze in which they came out reduced everyone onstage to amazement followed inevitably by laughter, so that for a terrible minute or so we looked like a dress-rehearsal mishap at the Junior League *Pirates of Penzance*. ("When half of Jim's mustache fell off, I thought I'd split a panty button.")

At intermission, when I had my breath back, I apologized to everyone and was, we being a happy company, forgiven. Sometimes, though, I wonder whether I achieved leperhood that day.

A great many of our experiences are pleasant only in retrospect, but I must say of *Bells* and of the two other successes which agreeably punctuated my series of failures, or to be grammatically accurate and fair to myself, the series of failures with which I was associated, that I knew myself to be fortunate every day and most fortunate of all just before my entrances.

When I was in hits and when, God willing, I am in one again, the theater was and will be a predictable, repeatable, three-dimensional daydream.

Of course, the theater is always in trouble. I'm sure you don't want any more monody from me on that score, but there is always hope. The London city authorities once denied a license to a theater company on the cold grounds that "To play in plague time increases the plague by infection: To play out of plague time calls down the plague from God," yet we're still going, and if bad theater caused plague, earth's final curtain would long since have fallen. If the theater's final curtain seems to fall, be of good cheer and keep your eye on the tomb of Dionysus. I don't say it's probable, but it's just possible that a group in goatskins will show up and start the whole thing going all over again.